JIM BLINN'S CORNER
A TRIP DOWN THE GRAPHICS PIPELINE

# The Morgan Kaufmann Series in Computer Graphics and Geometric Modeling

SERIES EDITOR, BRIAN A. BARSKY

*Jim Blinn's Corner: A Trip Down the Graphics Pipeline*
Jim Blinn

*Interactive Curves and Surfaces: A Multimedia Tutorial on CAGD*
Alyn Rockwood and Peter Chambers

*Wavelets for Computer Graphics: Theory and Applications*
Eric J. Stollnitz, Tony D. DeRose, and David H. Salesin

*Principles of Digital Image Synthesis*
Andrew S. Glassner

*Radiosity & Global Illumination*
François X. Sillion and Claude Puech

*Knotty: A B-Spline Visualization Program*
Jonathan Yen

*User Interface Management Systems: Models and Algorithms*
Dan R. Olsen, Jr.

*Making Them Move: Mechanics, Control, and Animation of Articulated Figures*
Edited by Norman I. Badler, Brian A. Barsky, and David Zeltzer

*Geometric and Solid Modeling: An Introduction*
Christoph M. Hoffmann

*An Introduction to Splines for Use in Computer Graphics and Geometric Modeling*
Richard H. Bartels, John C. Beatty, and Brian A. Barsky

# Jim Blinn's Corner

## A TRIP DOWN
## THE GRAPHICS PIPELINE

Jim Blinn
Microsoft Research

MORGAN KAUFMANN PUBLISHERS, INC.
San Francisco, California

Sponsoring Editor *Michael B. Morgan*
Production Manager *Yonie Overton*
Production Editor *Julie Pabst*
Cover Design *Ross Carron Design*
Cover Photograph *Christine Alicino*
Text/Color Insert Design & Composition *Studio Arno*
Illustration (Chapter Openers 5, 7, 12, 20) *Timothy Ingham*
Indexer *Steve Rath*
Printer *Courier Corporation*

Morgan Kaufmann Publishers, Inc.
Editorial and Sales Office
340 Pine Street, Sixth Floor
San Francisco, CA 94104-3205
USA
Telephone 415/392-2665
Facsimile 415/982-2665
Email mkp@mkp.com
WWW http://www.mkp.com
Order toll free 800/745-7323

Library of Congress Cataloging-in-Publication Data
Blinn, Jim.
      Jim Blinn's corner : a trip down the graphics pipeline.
            p.    cm.
      Includes index.
      ISBN 1-55860-387-5 (pbk.)
      1. Computer graphics.    I. Title.
T385.B585          1996
006.6'6--dc20                                                  96-23163

# Contents

*Noted: 14 June '04*

*Good research project. Generating icosahedron-dodecahedron pair from 3-D pt. symmetry groups operating kaleidoscopically on a seed shape . . . . . 90*

*} How to do a Tensegrity presentation for SNEC? Not quite. I have physical demos, not just slides.*

# Contents

# Preface

I've always thought that the preface of a book was a waste of space. When I bought a book I always skipped the preface and rushed right into the good stuff.

Then I put together this book.

Now I realize how important it is. A preface is to be read, not when sitting comfortably in your chair at home, but while standing up in a bookstore. It provides a vital link from the mind of the author to the wallet of the potential reader. The preface enables the author to tell you why this book is a useful addition to your library. If you buy it, you can go home and sit down and read the good stuff.

So, where did this book come from? Well, about nine years ago, I realized that I had accumulated a largish bag of smallish computer graphics tricks. I had cute algorithms for clipping, viewing, lighting, and rendering certain types of images. I had ways of explaining homogeneous coordinates gleaned from years of teaching. I had simple databases for various interesting shapes. I had examples of tricky special cases that cause conventional algorithms to fail. All these tricks were too small to publish in a SIGGRAPH conference paper, but too interesting to let die. At the time, there was no *Graphics Gems* book series and no *Journal of Graphics Tools*. There was, however, the *IEEE Computer Graphics and Applications*. A column in this magazine would be the ideal way to share my bag of tricks with other computer graphicists. Coincidentally, the editorial board of that very journal had also thought of my writing a column. Norman Badler approached me on behalf of the board and was perhaps somewhat surprised when I agreed so readily.

It was pretty much a perfect match, although the contents of the columns were a little bit different from what either of us had expected. I had recently been producing compilation videos from my *Mechanical Universe* work with a rather, shall we say, lighthearted style, and I think the IEEE expected me to continue in this vein. This was made apparent by the original announcement of the column in the preceding issues: "Laugh while you learn! Read Jim Blinn's Corner, coming soon!" Laugh … hmmm. Well, the style I wound up using is certainly lighter than a typical SIGGRAPH paper, both in depth and in attitude.

*homogeneous coordinates.*

The results have proved fairly popular. But articles in a journal are somewhat ephemeral. Those readers who have become interested in the series recently might not be able to find the older issues. Those who have been following it from the beginning might not want to devote an entire shelf to them. It's time to collect the articles together in book form. I first became aware of this incremental approach to book writing with Martin Gardner's books taken from his column "Mathematical Recreations" in *Scientific American,* a source that inspired me greatly in my youth. More recent examples that I've admired are Jon Bently's *Programming Pearls* and Michael Abrash's *Zen of Graphics Programming.* I now feel that I am in some sense a part of that august community.

Over the last nine years I have accumulated about 45 articles, but the publishers and I decided that about 20 of them would make a good book-sized book. As it happens, the articles pretty much divide into two categories: those dealing with geometry and the graphics pipeline and those dealing with image processing and pixel arithmetic (with a few miscellaneous uncategorizable articles). So, we've chosen to gather the graphics pipeline articles into the current book. If there is sufficient interest, we'll put the pixel arithmetic articles out as a second book.

If you've gotten this far while still standing, you can stop. I'll just close by mentioning some stuff you might want to know if you've decided to read the whole book.

Individual columns in a magazine are written to be somewhat self-contained. They are also published in the order it occurred to the author to write them, not necessarily in the order the author would choose in writing a book. I have chosen to keep my columns here pretty much intact and in the order published (their original date of publication is printed at the beginning of each chapter). This leads inevitably to a bit of repetition among some of the chapters. This is not all bad, though, since it makes it easier to pick up the book in the middle and not need to read the whole book to get the context of what I'm talking about. Over the last nine years, though, my mathematical notation has drifted a bit, so I have done a small amount of work to try to normalize the notation and naming conventions. Keeping the columns in their original order also means that the best introduction to the relationships between the graphics pipeline and the chapters in the book is in the beginning of Chapter 14. Rather than reproduce it here, why don't you just take a look at that first.

I'd like to acknowledge the help of the *IEEE CG&A* editorial staff in getting these articles into print for the first time. These people include managing editors Margaret Neal and Nancy Hays, assistant editors Tom Culviner and Michael Haggerty, and associate editor Linda World. They have shown the utmost patience and confidence in me by routinely waiting until the absolute last moment before publication to get my final manuscript. If they had been more hard-line about deadlines, most of these articles wouldn't exist.

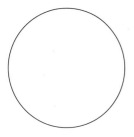

# CHAPTER ONE

# How Many Ways Can You Draw a Circle?

AUGUST 1987

I like to collect things. When I was young I collected stamps; now I collect empty margarine tubs and algorithms for drawing circles. I will presume that the latter is of most interest to you, so in this chapter I will go through my album of circle-drawing algorithms.

It's traditional at this point in any discussion of geometry to drag in the ancient Greeks and mention how they considered the circle the most perfect shape. Even though a circle is such an apparently simple shape, it is interesting to find how many essentially different algorithms you can find for drawing the Greeks' favorite curve.

I will be very brief about some pretty obvious techniques to leave space to play with the more interesting and subtle techniques. Note that many of these algorithms might be ridiculously inefficient but are included to pad the chapter. (OK, OK, they're included for *completeness*.)

I'm not sure where I first heard of some of these. I will cite inventors where known, but let me just thank the world at large in case I've missed anybody.

A word about the programming language used: I am not using any formal algorithm display language here. These algorithms are meant to be read by human beings, not computers, so the language is a mishmash of several programming constructs that I hope will be perfectly clear to you.

The collection can be categorized by the two types of output, line endpoints or pixel coordinates. This comes from the general dichotomy of curve representation—parametric versus algebraic.

# Line Drawings

first let's look at line output. All these algorithms will operate in floating point and generate a series of *x*, *y* points on a unit radius circle centered at the origin. You then play connect-the-dots.

*[handwritten: 13 June 2004]*

*[handwritten: Instead of evaluating it why not do a fast table look-up the way we did in IDACS?]*

*[handwritten: This way round off error can't accumulate.]*

## (1) Trigonometry

Evaluate sin and cos at equally spaced angles.

```
MOVE(1,0)
FOR DEGREES = 1 to 360
    RADIANS = DEGREES * 2 * 3.14159/360.
    DRAW(COS(RADIANS),SIN(RADIANS))
```

This has to evaluate the two trig functions at each loop; ick.

*[handwritten: This is funny!]*

## (2) Polynomial Approximation

You can get a fair approximation to a circle by evaluating simple polynomial approximations to sin and cos. The first ones that come to mind are the Taylor series.

$$\cos a \approx 1 - 1/2a^2 + 1/24a^4$$
$$\sin a \approx a - 1/6a^3 + 1/120a^5$$

These require fairly high-order terms to get very close, partly because the Taylor series just fits the position and several derivatives at *one* endpoint.

A better approach is to fit lower-order polynomials to both desired endpoints and end slopes. This is effectively what is happening with various commonly used Bézier curves. For example, the four control points (1, 0), (1, .552), (.552, 1), (0, 1) describe a good approximation to the upper-right quarter of a circle. You can get the other three quadrants by rotating the control points.

When transformed to polynomial form, the first quadrant is

$$x(t) = 1 - 1.344t^2 + .344t^3$$
$$y(t) = 1.656t - .312t^2 - .344t^3$$

with the parameter *t* going from 0 to 1.

```
MOVE(1,0)
FOR T = 0 TO 1 BY .01
    X = 1 + T * T * (-1.344 + T * .344)
    Y = T * (1.656 - T * (.312 + T * .344)
    DRAW(X,Y)
```

This makes a pretty good circle. The maximum radius error is about .0004 at $t = .2$ and $t = .8$.

## (3) Forward Differences

Polynomials can be evaluated quickly by the technique known as Forward Differences. Briefly, for the polynomial

$$f(t) = f_0 + f_1 t + f_2 t^2 + f_3 t^3$$

if you start at $t = 0$ and increment by equal steps of size $\delta$, the forward differences are

$$\Delta f = f_1 \delta + f_2 \delta^2 + f_3 \delta^3$$
$$\Delta\Delta f = 2 f_2 \delta^2 + 6 f_3 \delta^3$$
$$\Delta\Delta\Delta f = 6 f_3 \delta^3$$

Then, for our polynomials stepping in units of .01,

```
X = 1; DX = -.000134056; DDX = -.000266736; DDDX =  .000002064
Y = 0; DY =  .016528456; DDY = -.000064464; DDDY = -.000002064
MOVE(X,Y)
FOR I = 1 TO 100
    X = X + DX; DX = DX + DDX; DDX = DDX + DDDX
    Y = Y + DY; DY = DY + DDY; DDY = DDY + DDDY
    DRAW(X,Y)
```

Trust me, I'm a doctor. If you don't believe it, look up Forward Differences in Newman and Sproull's book[1]—I'm not going to do *all* the work here.

Notice the number of significant digits in the constants. It might seem that that many digits would require double precision, but, in practice, the accumulated roundoff error using single precision is less than the error due to the polynomial approximation.

## (4) Incremental Rotation

Let's back off from the approximation route and try another approach. Start with the vector (1, 0) and multiply it by a one-degree rotation matrix each time through the loop.

```
DELTA = 2 * 3.14159/360.
SINA = SIN(DELTA)
```

---

1  William M. Newman and Robert F. Sproull, *Principles of Interactive Computer Graphics*, 2nd ed. (New York: McGraw-Hill, 1979), page 328.

```
COSA = COS(DELTA)
X = 1;   Y = 0
MOVE(X,Y)
FOR I = 1 TO 360
     XNEW = X * COSA - Y * SINA
     Y    = X * SINA + Y * COSA
     X    = XNEW
     DRAW(X,Y)
```

## (5) Extreme Approximation

If the incremental angle is small enough, we can approximate cos $a$ = 1 and sin $a$ = $a$. The number of times through the loop is $n$ = $2\pi/a$ or, contrariwise, the angle is $a$ = $2\pi/n$, depending on which you want to use as input.

```
A = .015;   N = 2 * 3.14159/A
X = 1; Y = 0
MOVE(X,Y)
FOR I = 1 TO N
     XNEW = X - Y * A
     Y    = X * A + Y
     X    = XNEW
     DRAW(X,Y)
```

But there's a problem. Each time through the loop we are forming the product

$$\left[x_{new}, y_{new}\right] = \left[x_{old}, y_{old}\right]\begin{bmatrix} 1 & a \\ -a & 1 \end{bmatrix}$$

The matrix is almost a rotation matrix, but its determinant equals 1 + $a^2$. This is bad. It means that the running [$x$, $y$] can be magnified by this amount on each iteration, so what we get is a spiral that gets bigger and bigger. How to fix this? Introduce a bug into the algorithm.

## (6) Unskewing the Approximation

Since vector multiplication and assignment don't occur in one statement, we had to calculate $y$ carefully, using the old value for $x$. Suppose we were dumb and did it the naive way.

```
A = .015;   N = 2 * 3.14159/A
X = 1;      Y = 0
MOVE(X,Y)
FOR I = 1 TO N
```

```
X = X - Y * A
Y = X * A + Y
DRAW(X,Y)
```

Now, what is the effect of this? Really what we get is

$$x_{new} = x_{old} - y_{old}a$$
$$y_{new} = x_{new}a + y_{old} = x_{old}a + y_{old}(1-a^2)$$

In other words,

$$\left[x_{new}, y_{new}\right] = \left[x_{old}, y_{old}\right]\begin{bmatrix} 1 & a \\ -a & 1-a^2 \end{bmatrix}$$

This matrix has a determinant of 1, and there is no net spiraling effect. What you get is actually an ellipse that is stretched slightly in the northeast-southwest direction and squeezed slightly in the northwest-southeast direction. The maximum radius error in these directions is approximately $a/4$.

Now comes the interesting part. Since you can start out with any vector, let's try (1000, 0). Now, cleverly select $a$ to be an inverse power of 2 and the multiplication becomes just a shift. For example, a value of $a = 1/64$ is just a right shift by 6 bits. This generates the circle in about 402 steps. So, you can do this all with just integer arithmetic and no multiplication. This, children, is how we used to draw circles quickly—and in fact do rotation incrementally—before the age of hardware floating point and even hardware multiplication. (I understand that this was invented by Marvin Minsky.)

## (7) Rational Polynomials
Another polynomial tack can be taken by looking in our hat and pulling out the following rabbit:

$$\text{if} \qquad x = (1-t^2)/(1+t^2)$$
$$\text{and} \qquad y = 2t/(1+t^2)$$
$$\text{then} \qquad x^2 + y^2 = 1$$

no matter what $t$ is (or *identically*, as the mathematicians would say). Running $t$ from 0 to 1 gives the upper-right quadrant of the circle. We can again evaluate these polynomials by forward differences, stepping $t$ in increments of .01, and get

```
X = 1;   DX = -.0001;   DDX = -.0002
Y = 0;   DY =  .02
W = 1;   DW =  .0001;   DDW = .0002
```

```
MOVE(X,Y)
FOR I = 1 TO 100
    X = X + DX;   DX = DX + DDX
    Y = Y + DY
    W = W + DW;   DW = DW + DDW
    DRAW(X/W,Y/W)
```

Note that this is *not* an approximation like the last few tries. It is exact—except for roundoff error. Even roundoff error can be removed, either by calculating the polynomials directly or by scaling all numbers by 10000 and doing it with integers. (The division *x/w* must still be done in floating point.)

This one has always amazed me: you get to effectively evaluate two transcendental functions *exactly* with only a few additions. What's the catch? It's an application of the No-Free-Lunch Theorem—you don't get to pick the angles. If you watch the points, you see that they are not equally spaced around the circle. In fact, as *t* goes to infinity, the point keeps going counterclockwise but slows down, finally running out of juice at (–1, 0). If you go backwards to minus infinity, the point goes clockwise, finally stopping again at (–1, 0). (Yet more evidence that –∞ = +∞.) To draw a complete circle, you are best advised to run *t* from –1 to +1, which draws the whole right half, and then mirror it to get the left half.

## (8) Differential Equation

An entirely different technique is to describe the motion of [*x*, *y*] dynamically. Imagine the point rotating about the center as a function of time *t*. The position, velocity, and acceleration of the point will be

$$[x, y] = [\cos t,\ \sin t]$$
$$[x', y'] = [-\sin t,\ \cos t] = [-y, x]$$
$$[x'', y''] = [-\cos t,\ -\sin t] = [-x,\ -y]$$

You can cast these into differential equations and use any of several numerical integration techniques to solve them.

The dumbest one, Euler integration, is just

$$x_{new} = x_{old} + x'_{old}\Delta t = x_{old} - y_{old}\Delta t$$
$$y_{new} = y_{old} + y'_{old}\Delta t = y_{old} + x_{old}\Delta t$$

This looks a lot like Algorithm 5, and it has the same spiraling-out problem. You can generate better circles by using better integration techniques. My two favorites are the leapfrog technique and the Runge-Kutta technique.

*Leapfrog* calculates the position and acceleration at times

$$t, \quad t+\Delta t, \quad t+2\Delta t, \quad \dots$$

but calculates the velocity at times halfway between them:

$$t+\tfrac{1}{2}\Delta t, \quad t+\tfrac{3}{2}\Delta t, \quad \dots$$

Advancing time one step then looks similar to Euler, with just the evaluation times offset:

$$x_{t+\Delta t} = x_t + x'_{t+\frac{1}{2}\Delta t}\Delta t$$
$$x'_{t+\frac{3}{2}\Delta t} = x'_{t+\frac{1}{2}\Delta t} + x''_{t+\Delta t}\Delta t$$

(with similar equations for $y$). The position and velocity "leapfrog" over each other on even/odd half-time steps, so you have to keep separate variables for the velocities, $x'$ and $y'$. The code has a lot in common with Algorithm 6, and probably for good reason.

```
X   = 1;              Y = 0
VX = -SIN(DT/2);   VY = COS(DT/2)
MOVE(X,Y)
FOR I  = 1 TO N
    X  = X  + VX * DT   "update posn"
    Y  = Y  + VY * DT
    VX = VX - X  * DT   "update veloc, AX = -X"
    VY = VY - Y  * DT              "AY = -Y"
    DRAW(X,Y)
```

*Runge-Kutta* is a slightly involved process that takes a fractional Euler step, reevaluates the derivatives there, applies the derivative at the original point, steps off in this new direction, generally screws around, and finally takes some average between all these to get the new time step. Plugging our differential equation into the formulas and simplifying requires about a page of algebra. You can look up the actual equations;[2] they're not *incredibly* complicated but their *derivation* is "beyond the scope" of almost all numerical analysis textbooks I have seen.

One advantage of Runge-Kutta is that it finds the position and velocity at the same time step, so for circles you can generate $x$ and $y$ with the same computation. Another advantage is that it comes in second-order, third-order, fourth-order, etc., versions for higher orders of precision than leapfrog.

---

2  Runge-Kutta equations can be found in any numerical analysis text; e.g., Francis Scheid, *Schaum's Outline Series, Theory and Problems of Numerical Analysis* (New York: McGraw-Hill, 1968).

Plugging in for second-order Runge-Kutta, the ultimate result is

$$x_{new} = x_{old} \left(1 - \tfrac{1}{2}\Delta t^2\right) + y_{old} \left(-\Delta t\right)$$
$$y_{new} = x_{old} \left(\Delta t\right) + y_{old} \left(1 - \tfrac{1}{2}\Delta t^2\right)$$

Does this look familiar? It's just the Taylor series approximation to sin and cos again. The third-order Runge-Kutta and another page of algebra leads to

$$x_{new} = x_{old} \left(1 - \tfrac{1}{2}\Delta t^2\right) + y_{old} \left(-\Delta t + \tfrac{1}{6}\Delta t^3\right)$$
$$y_{new} = x_{old} \left(\Delta t - \tfrac{1}{6}\Delta t^3\right) + y_{old} \left(1 - \tfrac{1}{2}\Delta t^2\right)$$

Guess what fourth-order Runge-Kutta gives. . . . You're right. I won't even bore you with the code.

## (9) Half Interval

Another idea is the half interval method suggested by Jim Kajiya. This assumes you have two endpoints of an arc and wish to fill in the middle with points on the circle. At each step you insert a new point between two others. Assuming a circle centered at origin, the new point will be approximately halfway between the surrounding ones:

$$\left[x_m, y_m\right] = \left[\frac{x_1 + x_2}{2}, \quad \frac{y_1 + y_2}{2}\right]$$

It just needs to be moved outwards to lie on the circle. This involves scaling the above to length 1. If the original points are at unit distance from the origin, this means dividing by $\sqrt{1 + x_1 x_2 + y_1 y_2} \, / \sqrt{2}$.

By doing this recursively, you can keep splitting until some error tolerance is met. The code is something like

```
X1 = 1; Y1 = 0
X2 = 0; Y2 = 1
MOVE(X1,Y1)
SPLIT(X1,Y1,  X2,Y2)
```

where we define SPLIT(X1,Y1,  X2,Y2) to be

```
D  = SQRT(.5 * (1 + X1 * X2 + Y1 * Y2))
XM = (X1 + X2)/D
YM = (Y1 + Y2)/D
IF error tolerance ok
    DRAW(XM,YM)
    DRAW(X2,Y2)
```

```
ELSE
    SPLIT(X1,Y1,    XM,YM)
    SPLIT(XM,YM,    X2,Y2)
```

The error tolerance could be just a recursion depth counter, stopping at a fixed recursion depth. This is nice because, for a given pair of initial points, the value of D is just a function of recursion depth and can be precomputed and placed in a table.

# Pixel-Based Techniques

The other major category of algorithms involves output more directly suited to raster displays. Here the question is not where to move the "pen" next, but which of the grid of pixels to light up. The above algorithms can of course be applied to pixels by generating coordinates and feeding them to a line-to-pixel drawing routine, but we won't pursue those. Let's just look at ways to generate the desired pixels directly. For simplicity we will assume we are drawing a 100-pixel-radius circle with pixels addressed so that (0, 0) is in the center and negative coordinates are OK. The algorithms operate in integer pixel space, assuming square pixels. Note that the variables below start with I, indicating that they are integers.

### (10) Fill Disk

Perhaps the dumbest algorithm is just to see how far each pixel is from the center and color it in if it's inside the circle:

```
FOR IY = -100 TO 100
FOR IX = -100 TO 100
    IF (IX * IX + IY * IY < 10000) SETPXL(IX,IY)
```

This of course fills in the entire disk instead of just drawing lines, but who's being picky?

You would be correct in assuming that this might be a bit slow. Some quick speedups: calculate the value of $x^2$ by forward differences; calculate the allowable range of $x^2$ outside the $x$ loop (forward differences probably aren't worth the trouble for this latter calculation).

```
FOR IY = -100 TO 100
    IX2MAX = 10000 - IY * IY
    IX2 = 10000;  IDX2 = -199;  IDDX2 = 2
    FOR IX = -100 TO 100
        IF (IX2 < IX2MAX) SETPXL(IX,IY)
        IX2 = IX2 + IDX2;  IDX2 = IDX2 + IDDX2
```

### (11) Solve for x Range Covered

The above still examines every pixel on the screen. We can skip some of this by explicitly solving for the range in $x$.

```
FOR IY = 100 TO -100 BY -1
    IXRNG = SQRT(10000 - IY * IY)
    FOR IX = -IXRNG TO IXRNG
        SETPXL(IX,IY)
```

Or just plot the endpoints instead of filling in the whole disk.

```
FOR IY = 100 TO -100 BY -1
    IX = SQRT(10000 - IY * IY)
    SETPXL(-IX,IY)
    SETPXL(IX,IY)
```

This leaves unsightly gaps near the top and bottom.

### (12) Various Approximations to SQRT

Make a polynomial or rational polynomial approximation to $\sqrt{10000 - y^2}$ that is good for the range $-100 \ldots 100$. Evaluate it with forward differences.

### (13) Driving x Away

Let's do only the upper-right quarter of the circle and follow the point [0, 100]. For each downwards step in $y$, we move to the right some distance in $x$. Start at the $x$ that's left over from last time and step it to the right until it hits the circle, leaving a trail of pixels behind.

```
IX = 0
FOR IY = 100 TO 0 BY -1
    IX2MAX = 10000 - IY * IY
    DO UNTIL (IX * IX) > IX2MAX
        SETPXL(IX,IY)
        IX = IX + 1
```

Calculation of IX2MAX and $IX^2$ can be done by forward differences.

```
IX = 0
IX2 = 0;       IDX2 = 1;       IDDX2 = 2
IX2MAX = 0;  IDX2MAX = 199;  IDDX2MAX = -2
FOR IY = 100 TO 0 BY -1
    DO UNTIL IX2 > IX2MAX
        SETPXL(IX,IY)
        IX = IX + 1
```

```
        IX2  =  IX2 + IDX2;   IDX2  =  IDX2 + IDDX2
    IX2MAX   = IX2MAX  +  IDX2MAX
    IDX2MAX  = IDX2MAX  +  IDDX2MAX
```

This still has a few problems, but we won't pursue them because the next two algorithms are so much better.

## (14) Bresenham

The above begins to look like Bresenham's algorithm—this is the top of the line in pixel-oriented circle algorithms. It endeavors to generate the best possible placement of pixels describing the circle with the smallest amount of (integer) code in the inner loop. It operates with two basic concepts.

First, the curve is defined by an "error" function. For our circle, this is $E = 10000 - x^2 - y^2$. For points exactly on the circle, $E = 0$. Inside the circle $E > 0$; outside the circle $E < 0$.

Second, the current point is nudged by one pixel in a direction that moves "forward" and in a direction that minimizes $E$. We will consider just the octant of the circle from (0, 100), moving to the right by 45 degrees. At each iteration we will choose to move either to the right (R), $x = x + 1$, or diagonally (D), $x = x + 1$ and $y = y - 1$.

The nice thing about this is that the value of $E$ can be tracked incrementally. If the error at the current [$x, y$] is

$$E_{cur} = 10000 - x^2 - y^2$$

then an R step will make

$$E_{new} = 10000 - (x+1)^2 - y^2$$
$$= E_{cur} - (2x+1)$$

and a D step will make

$$E_{cur} = 10000 - (x+1)^2 - (y-1)^2$$
$$= E_{cur} - (2x+1) + (2y-1)$$

Now, for the octant in question,

$$x \leq y$$
$$x \geq 0$$
$$y > 0$$

So an R step subtracts something from $E$, and a D step adds something to $E$. The naive version of the algorithm determines which way to go by looking at the current sign of $E$, always striving to drive it towards its opposite sign.

```
IX = 0;   IY = -100
IE = 0
WHILE IX <= IY
     IF (IE < 0)
          IE = IE + IY + IY - 1
          IY = IY - 1
     IE = IE - IX - IX - 1
     IX = IX + 1
     SETPXL(IX,IY)
```

## (15) Improved Bresenham

We can do better. What we want to do at each step is actually to pick the direction that generates the smallest size error, $|E|$. We want to look ahead at the two possible new error values:

$$E_R = E - (2x + 1)$$
$$E_D = E - (2x + 1) + (2y - 1)$$

and test the sign of $|E_D| - |E_R|$. The trick is to avoid calculating absolute values. Look at the possibilities in Table 1.1.

Now comes the tricky part. We can define a "biased" error from the (+ −) case

$$G = E_D + E_R$$

and use this as the test for *all three* cases. This works for the following reason. In the (+ +) case, $|E_D| - |E_R| = 2y - 1$ is positive, but so is $G$. In the (− −) case, $|E_D| - |E_R| = -(2y - 1)$ is negative, but so is $G$.

$G$ can be calculated incrementally, just like $E$ was. The new values due to R and D steps are

$$G_R = G - 4x - 6$$
$$G_D = G - 4x + 4y - 10$$

**Table 1.1** *Possible signs of $E_D$ and $E_R$*

| $E_D$ | $E_R$ | $\|E_D\| - \|E_R\|$ |
|:---:|:---:|:---|
| + | + | $E_D - E_R = 2y - 1$; always positive |
| + | − | $E_D + E_R$ |
| − | + | Can never happen |
| − | − | $-E_D + E_R = -(2y - 1)$; always negative |

Further, the increments to $G$ can be calculated incrementally. You get the idea by now . . .

```
IR = 100
IX = 0; IY = IR
IG = 2 * IR - 3
IDGR = -6; IDGD = 4 * IR - 10
WHILE IX <= IY
    IF IG < 0
        IG = IG + IDGD    "go diagonally"
        IDGD = IDGD - 8
        IY = IY - 1
    ELSE
        IG = IG + IDGR    "go right"
        IDGD = IDGD - 4
    IDGR = IDGR - 4
    IX = IX + 1
    SETPXL(IX,IY)
```

Whew!

# Why Bother?

**W**hy is all this interesting—aside from the pack rat joy of collecting things?

Well, you can certainly use the algorithms to optimize your circle-drawing programs, if you're into circles. Each algorithm has its own little niche in the speed/accuracy/complexity trade-off space. Sometimes economy is misleading—the SETPXL routine often gobbles up any time you saved being clever with Bresenham's algorithm. Let's face it: unless there's something very time-critical, I usually use Algorithm 1 because it's easiest to remember.

The really interesting thing about all these is the directions they lead you when you try to generalize them. Algorithms 2 and 7 lead to general polynomial curves. Algorithm 4 leads to iterated function theory. Algorithm 5 leads to the CORDIC method of function evaluation.[3] Algorithm 11 has to do with rendering spheres. (I wonder what happens to Algorithm 15 if you use some other simple functions of $x$ and $y$ for $G$, $G_R$, and $G_D$.) In fact, although many of these algorithms look quite similar when applied to circles, their generalizations lead to very different things.

CORDIC?

---

3  Kenneth Turkowski, Anti-aliasing through the use of coordinate transformations, *ACM Transactions on Graphics* 1(3):215–234, July 1982.

It sort of shows the underlying unity of the universe. Maybe the Greeks had something there.

That's all for now. If you know of any essentially different circle-drawing algorithms, let me know.

# Ellipses

A reader named D. Turnbull wrote and asked about the generalization of Bresenham's algorithm to ellipses. Here's my reply.

The problem of ellipses is in fact also applicable to the problem of circles if you have non-square pixels. The Bresenham algorithm can be extended to any conic section by roughly the following process. The error function for an arbitrary conic section in an arbitrary orientation is

$$E = ax^2 + bxy + cy^2 + dx + ey + f$$

As usual, at each step you advance one pixel in the $x$ or $y$ direction or in both directions. If, for example, you step to the right one unit in $x$, the error becomes

$$E_R = a(x+1)^2 + b(x+1)y + cy^2 + d(x+1) + ey + f$$
$$= E + (2ax + by + d) + a$$

Likewise, after an upwards vertical step, the error becomes

$$E_U = E + (bx + 2cy + e) + c$$

Let's give names to the values in parentheses.

$$F = 2ax + by + d$$
$$G = bx + 2cy + e$$

A negative step in $x$ or $y$ requires subtraction of $F$ or $G$.

These increments can themselves be calculated incrementally. A step to the right changes $F$ and $G$ by

$$F_R = F + 2a$$
$$G_R = G + b$$

A step upwards changes $F$ and $G$ by

$$F_U = F + b$$
$$G_U = G + 2c$$

The actual loop then incrementally keeps track of $E$, $F$, and $G$ as the point crawls around the curve. The decision of whether to increment or decrement $x$ and/or $y$ comes from the signs of $F$ and $G$. Note that all arithmetic is still integer arithmetic as long as the coefficients $a$ through $f$ are integers. If they aren't, you can make them integers by scaling them all by the same factor.

A simple version of this technique that steps only horizontally or vertically is described in Cohen's paper.[4] A somewhat better version that steps diagonally and optimizes the magnitude of $E$ is described in Jordan et al.'s paper.[5] Ideally, we would like to reduce the inner loop calculation to an absolute minimum. The Jordan algorithm requires explicit testing of absolute values of the error in the three potential step directions (horizontal, vertical, and diagonal). It was possible to get rid of most of this for the final circle algorithm in this chapter. I don't know if it's possible for the general case here, though.

4   E. Cohen, A method for plotting curves defined by implicit equations, *SIGGRAPH '76 Conference Proceedings* (New York: ACM), pages 263–265.

5   B. W. Jordan et al., An improved algorithm for generation of nonparametric curves, *IEEE Transactions on Computers*, C-22(12):1052–1060, December 1973.

# CHAPTER TWO

# What, Teapots Again?

## The Teapot

In the January 1987 issue of *IEEE Computer Graphics and Applications*, Frank Crow published an article that gave the history of Martin Newell's teapot. He also included a database as an unstructured list of Bézier surfaces. There *is* some structure to the teapot though, and it allows a much more compact representation. Here it is.

### The Body

The body of the teapot is a surface of revolution with an outline consisting of three Bézier curves in the $xy$ plane. The surface is generated by rotating this outline curve about the $y$ axis. The control point coordinates are

| point nbr | $x$ | $y$ |
|---|---|---|
| 1 | 1.4000 | 2.25000 |
| 2 | 1.3375 | 2.38125 |
| 3 | 1.4375 | 2.38125 |
| 4 | 1.5000 | 2.25000 |
| 5 | 1.7500 | 1.72500 |
| 6 | 2.0000 | 1.20000 |
| 7 | 2.0000 | 0.75000 |
| 8 | 2.0000 | 0.30000 |
| 9 | 1.5000 | 0.07500 |
| 10 | 1.5000 | 0.00000 |

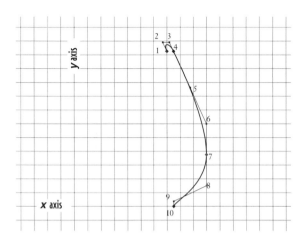

**Figure 2.1**  *Outline of the body*

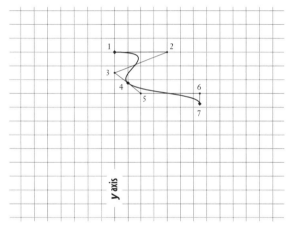

**Figure 2.2**  *Outline of the lid*

The three curves are generated by points (1, 2, 3, 4), (4, 5, 6, 7), and (7, 8, 9, 10). Note that points 3, 4, 5 are colinear, as are points 6, 7, 8, in order to make the segments blend together. A picture of the curve appears in Figure 2.1.

## The Lid

The lid is also a surface of revolution with a similar geometrical construction as the body. A picture of the lid outline appears in Figure 2.2. The control point coordinates are

| point nbr | x | y |
|---|---|---|
| 1 | 0.0 | 3.00 |
| 2 | 0.8 | 3.00 |
| 3 | 0.0 | 2.70 |
| 4 | 0.2 | 2.55 |
| 5 | 0.4 | 2.40 |
| 6 | 1.3 | 2.40 |
| 7 | 1.3 | 2.25 |

## The Handle

The handle is symmetrical about the $z = 0$ plane, so I'm only showing half of it—mirror it in $z$ to get the other half. Each half consists of two patches; each patch has two (opposite) edges in the $z = 0$ plane. A picture of these four curves (two per patch) appears in Figure 2.3. The control point coordinates are

| point nbr | x | y |
|---|---|---|
| 11 | -1.60 | 1.8750 |
| 12 | -2.30 | 1.8750 |
| 13 | -2.70 | 1.8750 |
| 14 | -2.70 | 1.6500 |
| 15 | -2.70 | 1.4250 |
| 16 | -2.50 | 0.9750 |
| 17 | -2.00 | 0.7500 |

| 21 | -1.50 | 2.1000 |
|----|-------|--------|
| 22 | -2.50 | 2.1000 |
| 23 | -3.00 | 2.1000 |
| 24 | -3.00 | 1.6500 |
| 25 | -3.00 | 1.2000 |
| 26 | -2.65 | 0.7875 |
| 27 | -1.90 | 0.4500 |

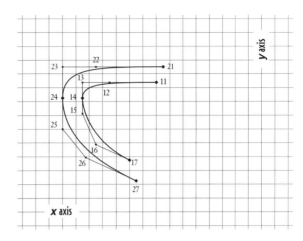

**Figure 2.3**  *Outline of the handle*

To generate a whole patch, you need four columns of four control points each. The two outer columns come from the above curves. One patch uses points (11, 12, 13, 14) and (21, 22, 23, 24). The other patch uses (14, 15, 16, 17) and (24, 25, 26, 27). In order to satisfy the smoothness constraint across the mirror plane, the two middle columns must have the same $x$, $y$ coordinates as their adjacent outer columns. The $z$ coordinates, though, are 0.3 instead of 0.

To be perfectly explicit, the patch for the top half of the handle has, as its 16 control points, the following coordinates. (The notation for each point is $p$, $z$ where $p$ is the point number to use for the $x$, $y$ coordinates.)

| 21,.0 | 21,.3 | 11,.3 | 11,.0 |
|-------|-------|-------|-------|
| 22,.0 | 22,.3 | 12,.3 | 12,.0 |
| 23,.0 | 23,.3 | 13,.3 | 13,.0 |
| 24,.0 | 24,.3 | 14,.3 | 14,.0 |

## The Spout

The spout is similar to the handle, except that all the $z$ coordinates of the middle columns don't happen to be the same. A picture of the edge curves appears in Figure 2.4. The control point coordinates are

| point nbr | x | y |
|-----------|------|---------|
| 11 | 1.700 | 1.27500 |
| 12 | 2.600 | 1.27500 |
| 13 | 2.300 | 1.95000 |
| 14 | 2.700 | 2.25000 |
| 15 | 2.800 | 2.32500 |
| 16 | 2.900 | 2.32500 |
| 17 | 2.800 | 2.25000 |

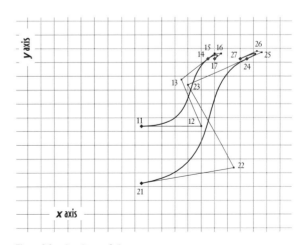

**Figure 2.4**  *Outline of the spout*

| 21 | 1.700 | 0.45000 |
|----|-------|---------|
| 22 | 3.100 | 0.67500 |
| 23 | 2.400 | 1.87500 |
| 24 | 3.300 | 2.25000 |
| 25 | 3.525 | 2.34375 |
| 26 | 3.450 | 2.36250 |
| 27 | 3.200 | 2.25000 |

Again, in order to satisfy the smoothness constraint, the middle columns of the patch control points must have the same $x$, $y$ coordinates as their adjacent outer columns. For these middle columns the $z$ coordinates are

```
adjacent
point nbr    z
  11,21     0.66
  12,22     0.66
  13,23     0.25
  14,24     0.25
  15,25     0.25
  16,26     0.15
  17,27     0.15
```

# Spillage

The original design of the teapot was a bit taller than the one everybody uses today. This is because once, during a demo for ARPA, we scaled the whole object by .75 in the $y$ direction. We thought at the time that they would be so impressed by this capability that they would give us lots more research money. (They didn't.) Anyway, we thought that the low-profile teapot looked prettier so we kept it that way. So, if you scale all the above $y$ coordinates by 1.33333, you will see that the numbers get much rounder.

# Leakage

Yes, in the original database the bottom of the teapot is missing. You can add a disk of radius 1.5 in the $xz$ plane if that is really important to you.

And yes, as a matter of fact, the volume of the teapot *is* almost 42 (but only before it was squashed).

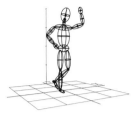

# CHAPTER THREE

# Nested Transformations and Blobby Man

O C T O B E R  1 9 8 7

There are a lot of interesting things you can do with transformation matrices. Later chapters will deal with this quite a bit, so I will spend some time here describing my notational scheme for nested transformations. As a non-trivial example I will include the database for an articulated human figure called *Blobby Man*. (Those of you who already know how to do human articulation, don't go away. There are some cute tricks here that are very useful.)

## The Mechanism

This is an implementation of the well-known technique of nested transformations. (Don't you just hate it when people call something "well known" and you have never heard of it? It sounds like they are showing off how many things they know. Well, admittedly we can't derive *everything* from scratch. But is sure would be nice to find a less smug way of saying so.)

For those for whom this is not so well known, the basic idea behind nested transformations appears in several places, notably in Foley and van Dam[1] and in Glassner.[2] It is just an organizational scheme to make it easier to deal with a hierarchy of accumulated transformations. It shows up in various software systems and has hardware implementations in the E&S Picture System or the Silicon Graphics IRIS.

1 James D. Foley and Andries van Dam, *Fundamentals of Interactive Computer Graphics* (Reading, Mass.: Addison-Wesley, 1984).

2 Andrew S. Glassner, *3D Computer Graphics: A User's Guide for Artists and Designers* (New York: Design Press, 1989).

Briefly, it works like this. We maintain a global $4 \times 4$ homogeneous coordinate transformation matrix called the *current transfomation*, $\mathbf{C}$, containing the transformation from a primitive's *definition space* onto a desired location in *screen space*. I will assume a *device-independent* (buzz, buzz) screen space ranging from $-1$ to $+1$ in $x$ and $y$ and where $z$ goes *into* the screen. This is a *left-handed* coordinate system.

Each time a primitive is drawn, it is implicitly transformed by $\mathbf{C}$. For example, the transformation of a (homogeneous) point is accomplished through simple matrix multiplication.

$$[x, y, z, w]_{scrn} = [x, y, z, w]_{defn} \mathbf{C}$$

Other primitives can be transformed by some more complex arithmetic involving this matrix.

$\mathbf{C}$ is typically the product of a perspective transformation and various rotations, translations, and scales. It is built up with a series of matrix multiplications by simpler matrices. Each multiplication *premultiplies* a new matrix into $\mathbf{C}$.

$$\mathbf{C} \leftarrow \mathbf{T}_{new} \mathbf{C}$$

Why in this order? Because a collection of objects, subobjects, subsubobjects, etc., is thought of as a tree-like structure. Drawing a picture of the scene is a top-down traversal of this tree. You encounter the more global of the transformations first and must multiply them in as you see them. The transformations will therefore seem to be applied to the primitives in the *reverse* order to that in which they were multiplied into $\mathbf{C}$. Another way you can think of it is that the transformations are applied in the *same* order stated, but that the *coordinate system* transforms along with the primitive as each elementary transformation is multiplied. At each node in the tree, of course, you can save and restore the current contents of $\mathbf{C}$ on a stack.

# The Language

The notational scheme I will use is not just a theoretical construct, it's what I actually use to do all my animations. It admittedly has a few quirks, but I'm not going to try to sanitize them because I want to be able to use databases I have actually tried out and to show listings that I know will work. I have purposely made each operation *very* elementary to make it easy to experiment with various combinations of transformations. Most reasonable graphics systems use something like this, so it shouldn't be too hard for you to translate my examples into your own language.

   The depth transformation is specified by two values—$z_n$ (the location of the *near* clipping plane) and $z_f$ (the location of the *far* clipping plane). The matrix transforms $z_n$ to $+0$, and $z_f$ to $+1$. I know that the traditional names for these planes are *hither* and *yon*, but for some reason I always get these words mixed up, so I call them *near* and *far*.

   Precalculate the following quantities (note that far clipping can be effectively disabled by setting $z_f = \infty$, which makes $Q = s$).

$$s = \sin(\alpha/2)$$
$$c = \cos(\alpha/2)$$
$$Q = \frac{s}{1 - z_n/z_f}$$

The matrix is then

$$\mathbf{C} \leftarrow \begin{bmatrix} c & 0 & 0 & 0 \\ 0 & c & 0 & 0 \\ 0 & 0 & Q & s \\ 0 & 0 & -Qz_n & 0 \end{bmatrix} \mathbf{C}$$

## Orientation

```
ORIE a, b, c, d, e, f, p, q, r
```

Sometimes it's useful to specify the rotation (orientation) portion of the transformation explicitly. There is nothing, though, to enforce it being a pure rotation, so it can be used for skew transformations.

$$\mathbf{C} \leftarrow \begin{bmatrix} a & d & p & 0 \\ b & e & q & 0 \\ c & f & r & 0 \\ 0 & 0 & 0 & 1 \end{bmatrix} \mathbf{C}$$

## Transformation Stack

```
PUSH
POP
```

These two commands push and pop $\mathbf{C}$ on/off the stack.

## Primitives

```
DRAW name
```

A primitive could be a list of vector endpoints, points-and-polygons, implicit surfaces, cubic patches, blobbies, etc. This command means "pass the elements in primitive *name* (however it's defined) through **C** and onto the screen."

# Example

A typical scene will consist of an alternating sequence of **C**-alteration commands and of primitive-drawing commands. At the beginning of the command list, **C** is assumed to be initialized to the identity matrix.

Here is a typical sequence of commands to draw a view of two cubes sitting on a grid plane. The primitive GPLANE consists of a grid of lines in the *xy* plane covering –2 to +2 along each axis, along with some labels and a tick-marked pole in the +*z* direction that is placed at *y* = 2. The primitive CUBE consists of a cube whose vertices have coordinates $[\pm 1, \pm 1, \pm 1]$ —that is, it is centered at the origin and has edge length equal to 2. Notice the scale by –1 in *z* to convert from the right-handed system in which the scene is defined to the left-handed system in which it is rendered.

```
PERS 45, 6.2, 11.8
TRAN 0, -1.41, 9
ROT -80, 1
ROT 48, 3
SCAL 1, 1, -1
DRAW GPLANE
PUSH
TRAN 0, 0, 1
ROT 20,3
DRAW CUBE
POP
PUSH
SCAL .3, .4, .5
TRAN -5, -3.8, 1
DRAW CUBE
POP
```

The results of executing these instructions appear in Figure 3.1.

Notice that the $z_n$ and $z_f$ variables are selected to bound the scene as closely as possible so that depth cueing will work. And, hey, it's called depth *cueing*, not depth *queueing* as I've seen some people write. (Depth queueing *could* perhaps be used to refer to a depth-priority rendering algorithm . . . hmmm.)

# Possible Implementations

There are several ways you could perform the operations described by these lists of commands.

- Translate them into explicit subroutine calls in some language implementation and compile them.

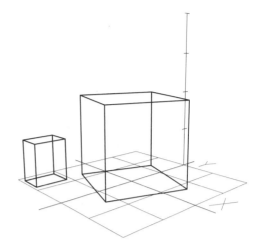

**Figure 3.1** *Cubes on parade*

- Read them through a "filter"-type program that executes the commands as they are encountered. This is the way most of my rendering programs work.

- Read them into an "editor"-type program that tokenizes the commands into some interpreter data structure and reexecutes the sequence upon each frame update. This is the way my animation design program works.

# Advanced Commands

The simple commands above can be implemented in about two pages of code. The enhancements below are a little more elaborate. The following constructions make sense only in the "editor" mode of operation.

### Parameters

Any numeric parameter can be given a symbolic name. A symbol table will be maintained and the current numeric value of the symbol used when the instruction is executed. For example, our cube scene could be

```
PERS FOV, ZN, ZF
TRAN XSCR, YSCR, ZSCR
ROT BACK, 1
ROT SPIN, 3
SCAL 1, 1, -1
DRAW GPLANE
PUSH
TRAN X1, Y1, Z1
```

```
ROT ANG, 3
DRAW CUBE
POP
PUSH
SCAL .3, .4, .5
TRAN -5, -3.8, Z1
DRAW CUBE
POP
```

By setting the variables

```
FOV = 45     ZN = 6.2     ZF = 11.8
XSCR = 0     YSCR = -1.41 ZSCR = 9
BACK = -80   SPIN = 48
X1 = 0       Y1 = 0       Z1 = 1
ANG = 20
```

and executing the command list, the same results would be generated. The same symbol can appear in more than one place, allowing a certain amount of constraint satisfaction.

## Abbreviations

Each time a subobject is positioned relative to a containing object, the instructions usually look something like

```
PUSH
   :
   :
various TRAN, ROT, SCAL commands
   :
   :
DRAW primitive
POP
```

While explicit, the above notation is sometimes a bit spread out and hard to follow. This sort of thing happens so often that it's helpful to define an abbreviation for it. We do so by following the DRAW command (on the same line) by the list of transformation commands, separated by commas. An implied PUSH and POP encloses the transformation list and DRAW. Our cube scene now looks like

```
PERS FOV, ZN, ZF
TRAN XSCR, YSCR, ZSCR
ROT BACK, 1
```

```
ROT SPIN, 3
SCAL 1, 1, -1
DRAW GPLANE
DRAW CUBE, TRAN,X1,Y1,Z1, ROT,ANG,3
DRAW CUBE, SCAL,.3,.4,.5, TRAN,-5,-3.8,Z1
```

## Subassembly Definitions

These are essentially subroutines. A subassembly is declared and named by bracketing its contents by the commands

```
DEF name
  :

any commands
  :
----
```

Once defined, a subassembly can be thought of as just another primitive. In fact, the "designer" of a list of commands should not know or care if the thing they are drawing is a primitive or a subassembly, so a subassembly is "called" by the same command as a primitive.

```
DRAW assy_name
```

The subassembly calling and return process is completely independent of the matrix stack PUSH and POP process. Interpretation of commands begins at the built-in name WORLD.

I typically organize my definitions so that WORLD contains only the *viewing transformation*, i.e., its rotations and transformations tell where the "camera" is and in which direction it is looking. My favorite all-purpose viewing transform is

```
DEF WORLD
PERS FOV, ZN, ZF
TRAN XSCR, YSCR, ZSCR
ROT BACK, 1
ROT SPIN, 3
ROT TILT, 1
TRAN -XLOOK, -YLOOK, -ZLOOK
SCAL 1, 1, -1
DRAW SCENE
----
```

The variables XLOOK, YLOOK, and ZLOOK determine the "look-at" point. BACK, SPIN, and TILT tumble the scene about this point. Then XSCR,

YSCR, and ZSCR position the "look-at" point on the screen. XSCR and YSCR might very well be zero, but ZSCR needs to be some positive distance to move the scene away from the eye.

The assembly SCENE contains the contents of the scene and can be designed independently of how it is being viewed. Our cube scene again:

```
DEF SCENE
DRAW GPLANE
DRAW CUBE, TRAN,X1,Y1,Z1, ROT,ANG,3
DRAW CUBE, SCAL,.3,.4,.5, TRAN,-5,-3.8,Z1
----
```

# Blobby Man

A few years ago I made a short animation of a human figure called Blobby Man to illustrate a new surface modeling technique.[4] Leaving aside issues of modeling, the figure itself is an interesting example of nested transformations. I have, in fact, used it as a homework assignment for my computer graphics class. (Gee, I guess I can't do that any more.)

Blobby Man's origin is in his stomach, and he stands with the z axis vertical. The only primitive element is a unit radius SPHERE centered at the origin. The parameterized variables are all rotation angles. Their usage is defined in Table 3.1.

The WORLD is the standard one given above. SCENE looks like

```
DEF SCENE
DRAW GPLANE
DRAW TORSO, TRAN,XM,YM,ZM, ROT,RZM,3,
----
```

The actual articulated parts are

```
DEF TORSO
DRAW LEFTLEG, TRAN,-0.178,0,0,
DRAW RGHTLEG, TRAN,0.178,0,0,
DRAW SPHERE, TRAN,0,0,0.08, SCAL,0.275,0.152,0.153,
DRAW BODY, ROT,EXTEN,1, ROT,BTWIS,2, ROT,ROT,3,
----
```

4  J. F. Blinn, A generalization of algebraic surface drawing, *ACM Transactions on Graphics* 1(3): 235–256, July 1982.

**Table 3.1**  *Meanings of Blobby Man variables*

| | |
|---|---|
| EXTEN | Extension. A dancers' term for bending forwards and backwards (*x* axis) |
| ROT | Rotation. A dancers' term for rotating the body and shoulders left and right about the vertical (*z*) axis |
| BTWIS | Angle of body leaning left and right (*y* axis) |
| NOD | Head nod |
| NECK | Head shake |
| LHIP,RHIP | Angular direction that the leg is kicked |
| LOUT,ROUT | Angular distance that the leg is kicked |
| LTWIS,RTWIS | Angle the leg is twisted about its length |
| LKNEE,RKNEE | Knee bend |
| LANKL,RANKL | Ankle bend |
| LSID,RSID | Arm rotation to side |
| LSHOU,RSHOU | Arm rotation forwards and back |
| LATWIS,RATWIS | Arm rotation about its own length |
| LELBO,RELBO | Elbow angle |

```
DEF BODY
DRAW SPHERE, TRAN,0,0,0.62, SCAL,0.306,0.21,0.5,
DRAW SHOULDER, TRAN,0,0,1, ROT,EXTEN,1, ROT,BTWIS,2, ROT,ROT,3,
----


DEF SHOULDER
DRAW SPHERE, SCAL,0.45,0.153,0.12,
DRAW HEAD, TRAN,0,0,0.153, ROT,NOD,1, ROT,NECK,3,
DRAW LEFTARM, TRAN,-0.45,0,0, ROT,LSID,2, ROT,LSHOU,1, ROT,LATWIS,3,
DRAW RGHTARM, TRAN, 0.45,0,0, ROT,RSID,2, ROT,RSHOU,1, ROT,RATWIS,3,
----


DEF LEFTLEG            DEF RGHTLEG
PUSH                   PUSH
ROT LHIP, 3,           ROT RHIP, 3,
ROT LOUT, 2,           ROT ROUT, 2,
ROT -LHIP, 3,          ROT -RHIP, 3,
ROT LTWIS, 3,          ROT RTWIS, 3,
```

```
DRAW THIGH              DRAW THIGH
TRAN 0, 0, -0.85,       TRAN 0, 0, -0.85,
ROT LKNEE, 1,           ROT RKNEE, 1,
DRAW CALF               DRAW CALF
TRAN 0, 0, -0.84,       TRAN 0, 0, -0.84,
ROT LANKL, 1            ROT RANKL, 1
DRAW FOOT               DRAW FOOT
POP                     POP
----                    ----


DEF LEFTARM             DEF RGHTARM
PUSH                    PUSH
DRAW UPARM              DRAW UPARM
TRAN 0, 0, -0.55,       TRAN 0, 0, -0.55,
ROT LELBO, 1,           ROT RELBO, 1,
DRAW LOWARM             DRAW LOWARM
TRAN 0, 0, -0.5,        TRAN 0, 0, -0.5,
DRAW HAND               DRAW HAND
POP                     POP
----                    ----
```

Some primitive body parts are defined as translated and squashed spheres as follows:

```
DEF HEAD
DRAW SPHERE, TRAN,0,0,0.4, SCAL,0.2,0.23,0.3
DRAW SPHERE, TRAN,0,-0.255,0.42, SCAL,0.035,0.075,0.035,
DRAW SPHERE, TRAN,0,0,0.07, SCAL,0.065,0.065,0.14
DRAW SPHERE, TRAN,0,-.162,.239, SCAL,.0533,.0508,.0506,
----


DEF UPARM
DRAW SPHERE, TRAN,0,0,-0.275, SCAL,0.09,0.09,0.275,
----


DEF LOWARM
DRAW SPHERE, TRAN,0,0,-0.25, SCAL,0.08,0.08,0.25,
----


DEF HAND
DRAW SPHERE, TRAN,0,0,-0.116, SCAL,0.052,0.091,0.155,
----
```

```
DEF THIGH
DRAW SPHERE, TRAN,0,0,-0.425, SCAL,0.141,0.141,0.425,
----


DEF CALF
DRAW SPHERE, SCAL,0.05,0.05,0.05,
DRAW SPHERE, TRAN,0,0,-0.425, SCAL,0.1,0.1,0.425,
----


DEF FOOT
DRAW SPHERE, SCAL,0.05,0.04,0.04,
DRAW SPHERE, TRAN,0,0.05,-0.05, SCAL,0.04,0.04,0.04,
DRAW SPHERE, TRAN,0,-0.15,-0.05, ROT,-10,1, SCAL,0.08,0.19,0.05,
----
```

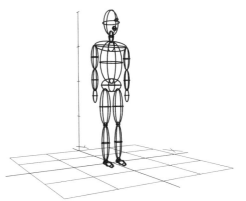

A picture of the result appears in Figure 3.2. The viewing parameters are

```
ZN = 5.17     ZF = 10.7
XSCR = -.1    YSCR = -1.6    ZSCR = 7.9
BACK = -90    SPIN = -30     TILT = 0
XLOOK = 0     YLOOK = 0      ZLOOK = 0
XM = 0        YM = 0         ZM = 1.75
```

All other angles are 0.

A picture of the man gesturing is in Figure 3.3. The view is the same, but the body angles are

**Figure 3.2** *Blobby Man*

```
NOD = -25    NECK = 28
RHIP = 105   ROUT = 13    RTWIS = -86    RKNEE = -53
LHIP = 0     LOUT = 0     LTWIS = 0      LKNEE = 0
LSID = -45   LSHOU = 0    LATWIS = -90   LELBO = 90
RSID = 112   RSHOU = 40   RATWIS = -102  RELBO = 85
```

There are several tricks in the model of Blobby Man that are especially notable.

## Cumulative Transformations

It is not necessary to POP a transformation just after it is used to DRAW something. Sometimes it is useful to continuously accumulate translations and rotations. For example, Blobby Man's leg could have looked like

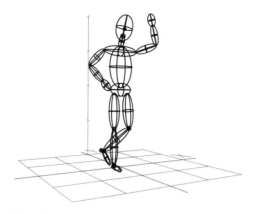

**Figure 3.3** *Blobby Man waving*

```
DEF LLEG
DRAW THIGH
DRAW CALFETC, TRAN,0,0,-0.85,
ROT,LKNEE,1
----

DEF CALFETC
DRAW CALF
DRAW FOOT, TRAN,0,0,-0.84, ROT,LANKL,1
----
```

As long as there are no transformed objects after the last one, some of the nesting can be dispensed with, leaving . . .

```
DEF LLEG
PUSH
DRAW THIGH
TRAN 0, 0, -0.85
ROT LKNEE, 1
DRAW CALF
TRAN 0, 0, -0.84
ROT LANKL, 1
DRAW FOOT
POP
----
```

## Repeated Variables

The variables EXTEN, BTWIS, and ROT are used twice, once to flex the BODY relative to the TORSO and once to flex the SHOULDER relative to the BODY. This gives a minimal simulation of a flexible spine for the figure.

## Rotated Rotations

The transformation of the (left) leg relative to the torso contains the sequence

```
ROT LHIP, 3
ROT LOUT, 2
ROT -LHIP, 3
```

This is something I'm especially proud of. It is a not-completely-obvious variation of a common technique—using simple transformations to build rotations or scalings about points other than the origin. For example, if you wanted to rotate a primitive about a point at coordinates (DX, DY), the commands would be

```
TRAN DX, DY, 0
ROT ANGLE, 3
TRAN -DX, -DY, 0
```

In other words, you translate the desired rotation center to the origin, rotate, and then translate the center back to where it used to be. (Remember that the transformations will be effectively carried out in sequence in the *reverse* order from that seen above.) The rotation sequence used for the leg enables us to rotate the leg about a rotated coordinate axis. The purpose of this is to make the foot always point forwards, no matter what LHIP and LOUT are. Figure 3.4 shows how this works. It is a top view of just the legs and hips, and the dark line shows the axis of rotation by the angle LOUT. A similar technique could have been used for the arm-shoulder joints, but I didn't happen to need that much flexibility in the animation.

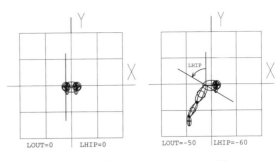

**Figure 3.4** *Top view of leg rotation*

# Addendum

I received a letter from Nelson Max about this chapter. He pointed out that the rotation trick for making the foot always point forwards does not keep it *exactly* forwards (with an *x* component of 0). It still has some small sideways component. This is, of course, quite true. My intention was just to keep it approximately pointing forwards (with a negative *y* component). This works best for the expected range of values $-90 <$ LOUT $< 0$ and $-90 <$ LHIP $< 90$. All other rotation combinations I tried made it too easy to get the foot pointing completely backwards, amusing perhaps, but a real nuisance for animation.

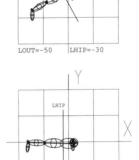

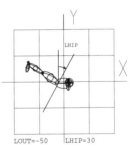

# CHAPTER FOUR

# Platonic Solids

I t is not often that major long-standing theories in geometry are over-thrown. Since the time of Plato, it has been thought that there were only five regular solids. Recently, however, James Arvo and David Kirk of Apollo have discovered a sixth. The new shape—the teapotahedron—is illustrated on the back cover of the SIGGRAPH '87 conference proceedings. Since I dealt with this shape in Chapter 2, I thought I would share some observations on databases of the other five Platonic solids.

Constructing a database for these shapes is a good basis for exploring the various sorts of symmetry they have. The main problem is to find explicit coordinates for the vertices. A cube or an octahedron uses pretty simple numbers. The other shapes, made of equilateral triangles or pentagons, might at first seem to require strange numbers as coordinates, but the messiness of the values depends on the orientation of the shape. My object here is to find orientations that allow the vertex coordinates to be as simple as possible. It turns out to be possible to construct all five shapes using only the numbers 0, 1, and the golden ratio $\varphi$. This latter is defined by the equation

Is this phi?

$$\frac{1}{\varphi} = \frac{\varphi}{1+\varphi}$$

which works out to

$$\varphi = \frac{1+\sqrt{5}}{2} \approx 1.618034$$

Now some notational conventions. Each point (vertex) is numbered, and the coordinates are declared by a line of the form

PNT n, x, y, z

After the points are defined, the polygons (faces) are described by a sequence of point numbers denoted

```
POLY n1, n2, n3, ...
```

Each polygon is carefully constructed so that the points are named going in a consistent clockwise order as seen from the outside (if you are left-handed) or counterclockwise order (if you are right-handed).

## The Cube

*14 June 2004*

*The top plane has odd numbered points. The bottom plane has even numbered? points*

The cube is centered at the origin, has an edge length of 2, and uses only the numbers +1 and −1 as coordinates.

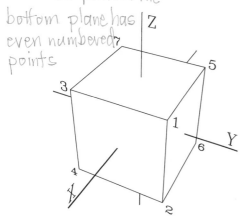

```
PNT 1,   1.,   1.,   1.
PNT 2,   1.,   1.,  -1.
PNT 3,   1.,  -1.,   1.
PNT 4,   1.,  -1.,  -1.
PNT 5,  -1.,   1.,   1.
PNT 6,  -1.,   1.,  -1.
PNT 7,  -1.,  -1.,   1.
PNT 8,  -1.,  -1.,  -1.
POLY 2, 1, 3, 4
POLY 5, 6, 8, 7
POLY 1, 2, 6, 5
POLY 4, 3, 7, 8
POLY 3, 1, 5, 7
POLY 2, 4, 8, 6
```

**Figure 4.1** *The cube*

A picture appears in Figure 4.1.

I am including decimal points in the coordinates, even though they happen to be integers, to emphasize the fact that they are floating-point numbers—a little readability trick. All the point numbers are integers and are essentially just names or labels. (In fact, many polygon modeling systems actually allow symbolic names here.)

*He names his points with numbers.*

*Phew! I'm not the only one to do this.*

## The Octahedron

This database is just as easy. Here we use the numbers +1, 0, and −1. See Figure 4.2.

```
PNT 1,   1.,   0.,   0.
PNT 2,  -1.,   0.,   0.
```

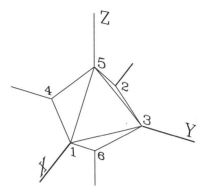

```
PNT 3,   0.,   1.,   0.
PNT 4,   0.,  -1.,   0.
PNT 5,   0.,   0.,   1.
PNT 6,   0.,   0.,  -1.
POLY 1, 3, 5
POLY 3, 1, 6
POLY 4, 1, 5
POLY 1, 4, 6
POLY 3, 2, 5
POLY 2, 3, 6
POLY 2, 4, 5
POLY 4, 2, 6
```

**Figure 4.2**  *The octahedron*

The octahedron is what is known as the "dual" shape of the cube. That is, each vertex of the octahedron lies at the center of a face of the cube, and each vertex of the cube corresponds to a face of the octahedron. (Scaling the cube uniformly by 1/3 makes its vertices lie exactly in the center of the octahedron's faces.) In fact, even though we are not numbering polygons explicitly, the polygons and points of the above databases have been carefully ordered so the $i$th point of the octahedron lies at the center of the $i$th polygon of the cube. Likewise, the $j$th point of the cube (times 1/3) lies at the center of the $j$th polygon of the octahedron.

So all right . . . the octahedron is balancing on its nose. To get it to lie with one face on, say, the $z = 0$ plane, you have to rotate and translate it. I have chosen to do this by selecting the final polygon (that is, points 2, 4, and 6) and solving for a rotation and translation matrix that makes all three points have a $z$ coordinate of 0. First rotate by 45 degrees around $y$ to get the points to have coordinates

```
2:   -R,   0,  -R
4:    0,  -1,   0
6:    R,   0,  -R
```

where $R = \sqrt{2}\,/\,2$. Then rotate about $x$ by an angle $\alpha$, putting the points at

```
2:   -R,   -R sinα,  -R cosα
4:    0,    -cosα,     sinα
6:    R,   -R sinα,  -R cosα
```

To make the $z$ coordinates the same, the angle and $z$ value must be

$$\alpha = \arctan \frac{-\sqrt{2}}{2} \approx -35.2644°$$
$$z = -\sqrt{3} \approx -.57735$$

*Neat!*

Using the notation for transformations developed in Chapter 3, the face-
on octahedron is

```
PUSH
TRAN 0, 0, .57735
ROT -35.2644, 1
ROT  45.0000, 2
DRAW OCTAHEDRON
POP
```

# The Tetrahedron

This is the first tricky one. The first thought is to put one of the triangles in, say, the $z = 0$ plane, but the coordinates are non-obvious. It happens, though, that a tetrahedron can fit entirely inside of a cube with its edges lining up with the diagonals to the cube's faces (abracadabra). The database is

```
PNT 1,  1.,   1.,   1.
PNT 2,  1.,  -1.,  -1.
PNT 3, -1.,   1.,  -1.
PNT 4, -1.,  -1.,   1.
POLY 4, 3, 2
POLY 3, 4, 1
POLY 2, 1, 4
POLY 1, 2, 3
```

No muss, no fuss. See Figure 4.3.

Admittedly the tetrahedron is in a bit of a weird orientation, sitting on one edge instead of one face. You can make it facedown by putting it through exactly the same transformation that made the octahedron facedown (double abracadabra).

```
PUSH
TRAN 0, 0, .57735
ROT -35.2644, 1
ROT  45.0000, 2
DRAW TETRAHEDRON
POP
```

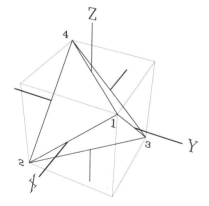

**Figure 4.3**  *The tetrahedron*

# The Icosahedron

This can also be done most easily edge-on. In this case, the 12 vertices of the icosahedron happen to lie at the corners of three golden rectangles that are symmetrically intertwined, as in Figure 4.4. A golden rectangle has a height-to-width ratio of 1:$\varphi$, where the aforementioned $\varphi \approx 1.618034$. Admittedly this is an irrational number, but it seems to be a popular one in nature. Generating the numbers and tying them together into polygons gives the database:

```
PNT 11,   1.618034,   1.,  0.
PNT 12,  -1.618034,   1.,  0.
PNT 13,   1.618034,  -1.,  0.
PNT 14,  -1.618034,  -1.,  0.

PNT 21,   1.,  0.,   1.618034
PNT 22,   1.,  0.,  -1.618034
PNT 23,  -1.,  0.,   1.618034
PNT 24,  -1.,  0.,  -1.618034

PNT 31,  0.,   1.618034,   1.
PNT 32,  0.,  -1.618034,   1.
PNT 33,  0.,   1.618034,  -1.
PNT 34,  0.,  -1.618034,  -1.

POLY 11, 31, 21 ! 1
POLY 11, 22, 33 ! 2
POLY 13, 21, 32 ! 3
POLY 13, 34, 22 ! 4
POLY 12, 23, 31 ! 5
POLY 12, 33, 24 ! 6
POLY 14, 32, 23 ! 7
POLY 14, 24, 34 ! 8

POLY 11, 33, 31 ! 11
POLY 12, 31, 33 ! 12
POLY 13, 32, 34 ! 13
POLY 14, 34, 32 ! 14

POLY 21, 13, 11 ! 21
POLY 22, 11, 13 ! 22
POLY 23, 12, 14 ! 23
POLY 24, 14, 12 ! 24
```

14 June 2004

He seems to have numbered the pnts using 3 planes numbered 1, 2 & 3 Then since each plane section has 4 pnts, we have 21, 22, 23, 24 11, 12, 13, 14 & 31, 32, 33, 34 Notice he doesn't go around the rectangles clockwise or counter clockwise but dashes across one long diagonal from 32 to 33 say. Can't quite see yet why he does it this way, but he must have a reason.

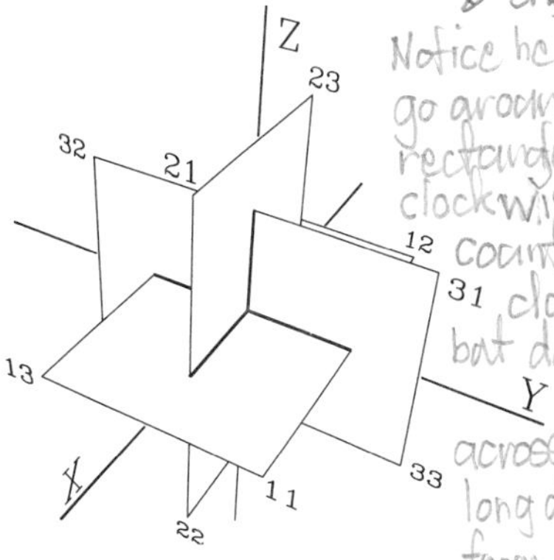

**Figure 4.4**  *Three intersecting golden rectangles*

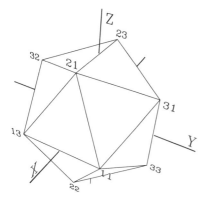

**Figure 4.5** *The icosahedron*

```
POLY 31, 23, 21 ! 31
POLY 32, 21, 23 ! 32
POLY 33, 22, 24 ! 33
POLY 34, 24, 22 ! 34
```

See Figure 4.5. The points have been number-named non-consecutively in an attempt to show which golden rectangle they come from. The polygons are named in the comment field (after the "!") in a non-consecutive way also, which will be useful later.

Again, this orientation is unsatisfying if you want to set the shape on a table. To get it facedown, let's rotate it about the $x$ axis so that the vertices of polygon 34 (that is, points 34, 24, and 22) all have equal $z$ coordinates. The angle and $z$ turn out to be

$$\arctan \frac{-1}{\varphi^2} \approx -20.9051°$$

$$z = -\varphi^2 / \sqrt{3} \approx -1.51152$$

The stable icosahedron is then

```
PUSH
TRAN 0., 0., 1.51152
ROT -20.9051, 1
DRAW ICOSAHEDRON
POP
```

# The Dodecahedron

Once again, an edge-on orientation gives the easiest coordinatization. Here, we need to generate 20 vertices. The dodecahedron is the dual shape of the icosahedron. This means that each vertex of the dodecahedron can be calculated as the centroid of a face of the icosahedron. Doing this for each face yields coordinates that look a bit messy at first. But by using the following identities:

$$1 / \varphi = \varphi - 1$$

$$\varphi^2 = \varphi + 1$$

$$\varphi^3 = 2\varphi + 1$$

and scaling the whole shape by $1/\varphi^2$, you get points with coordinates that use only the values 0, 1, $\varphi$, and $1/\varphi$.

This process reveals another interesting property of the dodecahedron—it has a cube embedded in it. I will play with this property a bit in Chapter 19. Eight of the vertices are the same as the eight vertices of our cube. The other 12 come from a set of three rectangles, intertwined in a similar fashion to those in the icosahedron; except that in this case the rectangles have aspect ratio $\frac{1}{\varphi}:\varphi$. The shape is shown in Figure 4.6 and the database is

*Not the same as the icosahedron, the reciprocal.*

```
PNT 1,   1.,    1.,    1.
PNT 2,   1.,    1.,   -1.
PNT 3,   1.,   -1.,    1.
PNT 4,   1.,   -1.,   -1.
PNT 5,  -1.,    1.,    1.
PNT 6,  -1.,    1.,   -1.
PNT 7,  -1.,   -1.,    1.
PNT 8,  -1.,   -1.,   -1.

PNT 11,   .618034,   1.618034,  0.
PNT 12,  -.618034,   1.618034,  0.
PNT 13,   .618034,  -1.618034,  0.
PNT 14,  -.618034,  -1.618034,  0.

PNT 21,   1.618034,  0.,    .618034
PNT 22,   1.618034,  0.,   -.618034
PNT 23,  -1.618034,  0.,    .618034
PNT 24,  -1.618034,  0.,   -.618034

PNT 31,  0.,    .618034,   1.618034
PNT 32,  0.,   -.618034,   1.618034
PNT 33,  0.,    .618034,  -1.618034
PNT 34,  0.,   -.618034,  -1.618034

POLY 2, 11, 1, 21, 22 ! 11
POLY 5, 12, 6, 24, 23 ! 12
POLY 3, 13, 4, 22, 21 ! 13
POLY 8, 14, 7, 23, 24 ! 14

POLY 3, 21, 1, 31, 32 ! 21
POLY 2, 22, 4, 34, 33 ! 22
POLY 5, 23, 7, 32, 31 ! 23
POLY 8, 24, 6, 33, 34 ! 24
```

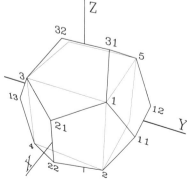

**Figure 4.6** *The dodecahedron*

```
POLY 5, 31, 1, 11, 12 ! 31
POLY 3, 32, 7, 14, 13 ! 32
POLY 2, 33, 6, 12, 11 ! 33
POLY 8, 34, 4, 13, 14 ! 34
```

Now the naming of the polygons of the icosahedron makes sense. Polygon $i$ of the icosahedron corresponds to point $i$ of the dodecahedron. Polygon $j$ of the dodecahedron corresponds to point $j$ of the icosahedron.

How to get it facedown? Rotate about $x$ to get all points of face 34 to have the same $z$ coordinate. The angle and $z$ are

$$\arctan(-\varphi) = -58.2825°$$
$$z = -\varphi^2 / \sqrt{\varphi + 2} \approx -1.37638$$

The net transformation is

```
PUSH
TRAN 0., 0., 1.37638
ROT -58.2825, 1
DRAW DODECAHEDRON
POP
```

# Other Ways

These databases have simple point coordinates, but they need to be rotated to get them facedown. It is still an interesting exercise to try to generate a database directly in another coordinate system, either face-on or vertex-on. I leave this as (ahem) an exercise for the reader.

Another way to generate these highly symmetric shapes is to use a single triangular polygon and place rotated copies of it in space to form the shape. In Chapter 9 I'll show the results of some such experiments.

# Applications

What good is this? Hey, it's abstract mathematics; it doesn't have to be practical. But actually there are practical applications. Geodesic domes are based on the icosahedron. You need to calculate locations of the vertices to build the dome. Knowledge of these coordinates also proved useful in the making of *The Mechanical Universe* telecourse. Several of the programs dealt with electric field lines radiating from point charges in space. A symmetric placement of starting points for these field lines was necessary. The vertex coordinates of an icosahedron or a dodecahedron proved exactly what was needed.

# Disclaimer

A simple proof can show that there are only five possible Platonic solids in three dimensions. The first paragraph of this chapter was a joke. I understand that after this chapter was first published in its previous incarnation as an *IEEE Computer Graphics and Applications* article, the IEEE offices received a letter from a very agitated mathematician. He did not realize this was a joke and thought a sixth solid really had been recently discovered.

# CHAPTER FIVE

# How to Write a Paper for SIGGRAPH

DECEMBER 1987

It's that time of year again. Snow is beginning to fall (I hear by rumor). Gold lamé pine trees adorn the shopping malls. Little fat men run around in red suits. Jack Frost nips at your toes. That's right, folks . . . it's SIGGRAPH paper deadline time. I thought that this month I would give my observations about the SIGGRAPH publishing process and what seems to get papers accepted and rejected. This comes from my experiences in writing papers as well as reviewing papers on the Papers Committee. I hasten to point out that what appears here is only my own viewpoint and not the official policy of SIGGRAPH.

## History

In the early days of computer graphics, the field was so new that it was not really considered a valid academic discipline. People wrote programs and solved problems but often didn't consider these solutions as something you would really publish.

After computer graphics became more respectable, people went around finally documenting and publishing things they had been doing for years. Many of the earlier papers were written after the ideas had had time to incubate and mature. In my own personal experience, on several occasions I did something, waited a year or two (OK, I'm lazy), found a better way to do it, and then published. For this reason, the first paper actually published on a subject usually presented a fairly refined solution.

Nowadays computer graphics is positively fashionable. There are university professors whose tenure depends on publication in this field. People are so eager to publish and so worried about being scooped that, as soon as they get the germ of an idea, they write it up and trot it out for publication. Then the following year, when they have had time to rethink the problem, they come up with the "correct" solution and submit a revised paper. Now it's rejected because the SIGGRAPH committee says, "We've seen this before." The result: the half-baked idea gets printed and the better idea doesn't. I don't know how to solve this problem.

There was another practice from the Middle Ages that I am happy to see disappearing. When SIGGRAPH had not yet established its reputation as *the* place to publish, the better papers accepted by SIGGRAPH were forwarded to the journal, *Communications of the ACM* (CACM), for publication there. Since CACM doesn't want to be a reprint service, these papers were not allowed to be in the SIGGRAPH conference proceedings. This has led to some curious incidents. For example, in 1978 I wrote a paper on a scan line algorithm for rendering patches that was accepted by SIGGRAPH. Since they especially liked it, they forwarded it to CACM (Yay!) . . . and CACM rejected it (Ouch!). And they weren't kind about it. (I remember reviewers' comments like "How dare you send such rubbish to CACM?") Whenever I tried to revise the paper according to the reviewers' comments I got so depressed that I put it right back on the shelf again. Meanwhile, the IEEE was publishing a volume of reprints of interesting papers, edited by John Beatty and Kelly Booth, and asked to include mine, thereby *re*printing the as yet *un*published paper. Furthermore, Turner Whitted and Jeff Lane and Loren Carpenter had come up with other algorithms for solving this same problem. Ultimately the four of us were going to put together a joint paper for CACM, but I was so discouraged that I withdrew my part. The other three were kind enough to include a brief description of my technique but didn't go into any detail. Finally, when the IEEE published the second edition of their reprint volume, they replaced my paper with the more up-to-date Lane et al. paper. As a result my algorithm now doesn't appear anywhere.

This is not an isolated incident. Similar things have happened to several other authors. I am happy to see that nowadays papers accepted by SIGGRAPH are published by SIGGRAPH.

# The Canonical Paper

Let us now look at the structure of a typical paper. A paper for SIG-GRAPH generally consists of three parts: the beginning, the middle, and the end.

### The Beginning

is where the author states some problem and offers a solution. Typically the solution will be a generalization of some current technique, a specialization of a current technique to make it faster, or a faster way to generate the same results. Then come some historical references about how people either have approached the problem in the past or have totally ignored it.

### The Middle

is where you give the problem solution. This should contain enough detail for the reader to be able to reproduce the results. In particular, you should endeavor to make the information useful to someone who does not have your exact system. Emphasize details that are exportable to other situations.

### The End

is where you point out obvious extensions and generalizations of the technique. This is where you can stake your intellectual claim to any and all generalizations of the technique.

# The Review Process

The Papers Committee gets about 250 papers (as of 1995), of which they must pick about 50, i.e., one out of five. The papers are first divided up among the 20 or so senior reviewers. These people then find two or three other people to review the papers, usually those who have done similar work in the past. Each paper is given a net score by the senior reviewer based on the reviews. The senior reviewer sends the scores to the Papers chair. The scores for all papers are then sorted in preparation for the meeting of the Papers Committee, where the final decisions are made. Usually the top scorers are accepted without much discussion. Likewise, the bottom scorers are rejected, unless one of the senior reviewers thinks it has special merit that was missed by the reviewers.

The big decisions are about the medium scorers. The committee members are very conscientious about being fair and not rejecting a paper for trivial reasons. But they are also sticklers for quality. To get in, you have to be better than you think you have to be. The committee is supposed to accept or reject papers on the basis of what it has actually received, not what it imagines the author could fix the paper up to be. There are always discussions about whether to accept a poorly written paper with great new ideas over a well-written paper that gives a good, accessible view of existing ideas.

# Advice

I have seen many papers go through this mill. Gone are the days when most anything with color pictures or a lot of equations would get in. Here are some of the things that are most likely to get papers rejected, sort of in order of frequency.

### Not New or Different Enough

Obviously SIGGRAPH is not in business to republish existing results. Sometimes someone will innocently rediscover and submit an idea that had been thought of 10 or 20 years earlier. It's not plagiarism; they just never heard of the earlier discovery. If it was an early enough result, it might never have been published but just passed around by word of mouth. You gotta know the territory. The most common phrase heard at Papers Committee meetings is "Didn't so-and-so do this 10 years ago?" Now if you have referenced so-and-so's paper (or at least shown knowledge of the technique) and explicitly told why your idea is different, you may head off such objections. Which leads us to . . .

### Improper References

Here is where you have to do your homework. While making sure that someone else has not already solved your problem, you must also make appropriate reference to those ideas that are precursors to your idea. I have actually reviewed papers where the author only references his own previous work. This tends to evoke a very negative emotional response in the reviewers. And furthermore, when you refer to Obscurovich's algorithm but don't describe it in your paper, you must give a (findable) reference for those of us who have never heard of Obscurovich.

### Too Little Detail

Some papers show a lot of pretty pictures and make a lot of claims about the applicability of an algorithm, but a reader simply cannot figure out how the author did it. The common test applied by the committee is "Could a reasonably intelligent graduate student be able to replicate these results just from the description in the paper?" Remember, SIGGRAPH is not an advertising agency. You can't just write a lot of hype and say the details are proprietary. I have seen papers rejected because they were about some mathematical simulation of lighting but did not contain a single equation.

### Unsupported Outrageous Claims

Many writers claim great speed advantages for their algorithm. The trouble is, they have never actually compared it with anything else, or only compared it in a trivial way. Someone will lovingly craft their implementation of their algorithm over a period of months or years. Then they feel they have to compare it with something, so they spend a weekend tossing together a crude implementation of some older algorithm. Lo and behold, their algorithm is faster! This simply won't do. Speed claims are an emotional topic. I have seen (verbal) fights break out in conferences over this. When you say your algorithm is faster, it makes people want to challenge you. Speed claims must be supported by some more controlled experiments and theoretical justifications of *why* it's faster.

### Bad English

Kids today don't know how to write good. If English is not your native language, have someone who does speak it check over your grammar and usage. The committee has also received (and almost rejected) some startlingly bad English from native speakers. This might seem like nit-picking, but it is surprisingly difficult to read such stuff. Your eye is continually being snagged by these bloopers, and after awhile you give up. Remember, the panel is looking for a reason to reject your paper (they have to get rid of 4/5 of them). Don't give them one.

# Trends

Multidisciplinary papers are starting to become common. An example would be "Applications of Dynamics Simulations to Computer Animation." This situation raises its own set of questions, since importation of ideas from another field usually starts with the simpler ideas. Should a paper be published if it brings in trivial results from some other field but is new to computer graphics? It's good for CG people to know about other fields, but is SIGGRAPH the place for tutorials?

There is always a cry for good applications papers. These basically take the form of "How I Used CG to Solve This Real-World Problem." If you have done such work, SIGGRAPH is interested in hearing from you.

In the early days, when all the easy problems hadn't been solved, the research was devoted to algorithmic tricks for finding a cheap, approximate solution for complex problems (an example of this would be bump mapping). Nowadays it seems we have passed the era of approximations. If you want to simulate second-order diffuse reflections from extended light sources in variable density fog, there seems to be no alternative to following zillions of light rays around the scene. Rendering research consists of finding more and more subtle lighting effects to simulate by using more and more brute force.

In fact, it seems that the hardest problem in computer graphics is finding something that hasn't been done already. That is your challenge.

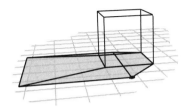

# Me and My (Fake) Shadow

J A N U A R Y   1 9 8 8

**E**arly computer images suffered from lack of gravity. Objects seemed to be floating above the ground plane. One way to solve this is to make the objects cast shadows; the shadow seems to "tie the object down." It also helps to separate the object from the background. A general shadow-casting algorithm is not trivial, but it is often not necessary for the shadows to be perfect to give the right visual effect. Approximations to shadows are quite adequate, as conventional animators have known for years, and it is possible to generate approximate shadows easily by some mathematical tricks.

One of the most common tricks is to cast shadows on a flat ground plane by redrawing the objects of the scene scaled by zero in the vertical direction. I will present two ways to do this here, one that works for parallel light rays and another that works for localized light sources. This latter illustrates some subtleties in the use of homogeneous coordinates and clipping.

I will use the notation developed in Chapter 3 for representing the scene. A subassembly called GROUND defines the ground plane that lies at $z = 0$. It is just a grid in the examples below. A subassembly called STUFF contains all the objects sitting on the ground, just a cube in the examples here. A scene without shadows would then be defined as

```
DEF SCENE
DRAW GROUND !ground plane at z = 0
DRAW STUFF !collection of objects
----
```

# Simple Shadows

If illumination comes from a single point source infinitely far away, all the light rays will be parallel to this direction, which we will call $[x_L, y_L, z_L]$. A point $[x_P, y_P, z_P]$ on some object of the scene will cast a shadow on the ground plane at $[x_S, y_S, 0]$. The cast shadow starts at P and moves away from the light source in the opposite direction of L by some amount $\alpha$, until it hits $z = 0$.

$$S = P - \alpha L$$

Solve for $\alpha$ by the requirement that $z_S = 0$. This results in

$$0 = z_P - \alpha z_L$$

or

$$\alpha = \frac{z_P}{z_L}$$

The $x$ and $y$ coordinates of the shadow point are then

$$x_S = x_P - \frac{z_P}{z_L} x_L$$

$$y_S = y_P - \frac{z_P}{z_L} y_L$$

While this is all very nice for computing individual points, it becomes exciting when written as a matrix multiplication:

$$[x_S, y_S, 0, 1] = [x_P, y_P, z_P, 1] \begin{bmatrix} 1 & 0 & 0 & 0 \\ 0 & 1 & 0 & 0 \\ -x_L/z_L & -y_L/z_L & 0 & 0 \\ 0 & 0 & 0 & 1 \end{bmatrix}$$

Now shadow generation can be performed by the standard transformation and viewing process. Simply draw the scene once normally, and then draw it again transformed by the above matrix.

```
DEF SCENE
DRAW GROUND
DRAW STUFF
PUSH
ORIE 1, 0, -XL/ZL, 0, 1, -YL/ZL, 0, 0, 0,
DRAW STUFF
POP
----
```

An example of this appears in Figure 6.1. The light comes from the direction [1.45, –.8, 2]. The cube is centered at the origin in $x$ and $y$ and stretches from 0 to 2 in $z$. Point P is at [1, 1, 2].

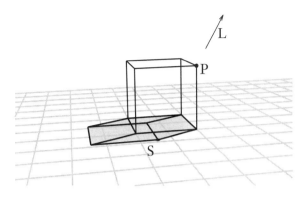

**Figure 6.1** *Light source at infinity*

# Perspective Shadows

**n**ow what about local light sources? Here the light position $[x_L, y_L, z_L]$ is an actual location in space, not a vector. The shadow is then a perspective projection of the object from the point of view of the light source.

The shadow of a point P is cast in the direction P – L so that

$$S = P - \alpha(P - L)$$

Again, putting in $z_S = 0$ and solving for $\alpha$ gives

$$\alpha = \frac{-z_P}{z_P - z_L}$$

The shadow coordinates turn out to be

$$x_S = \frac{x_L z_P - x_P z_L}{z_P - z_L}$$

$$y_S = \frac{y_L z_P - y_P z_L}{z_P - z_L}$$

Believe it or not, this can also be done with a matrix multiplication. The division can be accomplished by utilizing homogeneous coordinates and taking advantage of the implied division by the fourth coordinate. First, define

$$x_S = \tilde{x}_S / \tilde{w}_S$$

$$y_S = \tilde{y}_S / \tilde{w}_S$$

Then the shadow of point P is found by the matrix multiplication

$$[\tilde{x}_S, \tilde{y}_S, 0, \tilde{w}_S] = [x_P, y_P, z_P, 1] \begin{bmatrix} -z_L & 0 & 0 & 0 \\ 0 & -z_L & 0 & 0 \\ x_L & y_L & 0 & 1 \\ 0 & 0 & 0 & -z_L \end{bmatrix}$$

Now there is a bit of a nuts and bolts problem. We know each element of the desired $4 \times 4$ matrix; the problem is expressing it to our transformation system. There is no command for explicitly specifying all 16 elements of a matrix. The most straightforward solution might be to implement a new command similar to ORIE that allows 16 parameters. However, I regarded it as an intellectual challenge to come up with a series of PERS, TRAN, ROT, and SCAL transformations that, when multiplied together, yield exactly the above matrix.

How to do this? First, reexamine the PERS transformation. (I have, in fact, received some questions concerning an ambiguity in its description in Chapter 3.) By way of review and clarification, the perspective command

PERS $\theta$, $z_n$, $z_f$

performs a perspective projection from the origin with a pyramid of view having an apex angle $\theta$. The associated matrix is constructed by precalculating

$$s = \sin(\theta/2)$$
$$c = \cos(\theta/2)$$
$$Q = \frac{s}{1 - z_n/z_f}$$

The matrix is then

$$\begin{bmatrix} c & 0 & 0 & 0 \\ 0 & c & 0 & 0 \\ 0 & 0 & Q & s \\ 0 & 0 & -Qz_n & 0 \end{bmatrix}$$

The transformation effectively generates a screen $x$ and $y$ by dividing by $z$ and then scaling by the cotangent of half the field of view (i.e., the angle subtended from the center of the screen to the edge). The $z$ coordinate is also transformed in a way that won't concern us here. We will therefore simplify matters by setting $z_n = 1$ and $z_f = 1,000,000$, effectively making $Q = s$.

The basic strategy for using this transform to construct the shadow transform is

1. Translate the light source to the origin.
2. Apply a PERS transform by some angle.
3. Translate back to the original light source location.
4. Scale by 0 in $z$ to squash the shadow down onto the ground plane.

To find the angle, I multiplied the above transformations together (symbolically) and solved for a $\theta$ that causes the net matrix to be equal to the desired one. The result is

$$\cot(\theta/2) = -z_L$$

This may seem a bit strange since the field of view is negative, but it *does* generate the proper matrix. In fact, the trigonometry can be avoided by noting that you get the same effect by using a perspective field of view of 90 degrees and then scaling the result in $x$ and $y$ by the above cotangent, $-z_L$. The final transformed scene is then

```
DEF SCENE
DRAW GROUND
DRAW STUFF
PUSH
SCAL 1, 1, 0,
TRAN XL, YL, ZL,
SCAL -ZL, -ZL, 1
PERS 90, 1, 1000000
TRAN -XL, -YL, -ZL
DRAW STUFF
POP
----
```

So, I coded it up, put it into the machine, and presto . . . no shadows. What went wrong?

The problem has to do with a subtlety in the clipping algorithm used with homogeneous perspective transformations. This problem is described in more detail in an old paper by Martin Newell and myself.[1] I also touch on it here in Chapter 13. It concerns the situation when the $w$ coordinate of a homogeneous point is negative. Notice that this will be the case if the light source is higher than the object ($z_L > z_P$), the expected situation.

Normally the clipping condition is defined such that a point is "visible" if its location after the homogeneous division lies within the standard screen boundaries, i.e.,

1  J. F. Blinn and M. E. Newell, Clipping using homogeneous coordinates, *SIGGRAPH '78 Conference Proceedings* (New York: ACM), pages 245–251.

$$-1 < \frac{x}{w} < 1$$

Since clipping is done before division, this is rewritten to say that a point is visible if

$$0 < w - x$$
$$\text{and } 0 < w + x$$

This not quite correct, however; it's only right if $w > 0$. If $w$ is negative, a point might still project onto the visible region of the screen but be declared invisible by the above criterion. This ordinarily doesn't matter because, in the normal usage of the perspective transform, negative $w$'s only come from perspective projections of points that were behind the viewer, and we want to clip them off anyway. Here, however, we have negative $w$'s that we want to keep.

The matrix we are using generates a sort of "anti-shadow." If you move the light source below the object, a projected image appears on the ground plane that is the object projected through the light point. This is shown in Figure 6.2. The local light coordinates are [2.25, 0, 1], and the light is sitting on a "lamppost" just to make it easier to see where it is situated in three dimensions. Notice that the example point P = [1, 1, 2] projects on a straight line through the light source to the point S = [3.5, –1, 0].

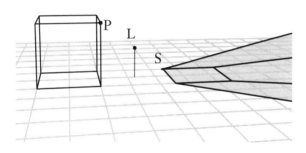

The solution to the anti-shadow problem is to avoid the negative $w$'s while retaining the same geometrical projection. This is done by multiplying the entire fake perspective matrix by –1. Usually, any non-zero scalar multiple of a homogeneous quantity represents exactly the same quantity. However, due to the asymmetry in clipping, this is not the case here. The correct shadow transform matrix is

**Figure 6.2** *Antishadow*

$$\begin{bmatrix} z_L & 0 & 0 & 0 \\ 0 & z_L & 0 & 0 \\ -x_L & -y_L & 0 & -1 \\ 0 & 0 & 0 & z_L \end{bmatrix}$$

Now we again have the intellectual challenge of constructing this matrix using only our defined operations. The sequence is

1. Translate light source to origin.
2. Turn around to look at the scene (rotate 180° in $y$).
3. Perspective projection by positive angle, $2\cot^{-1}z_L$.
4. Reverse the $y$ rotation.
5. Reverse the translation.
6. Scale by 0 in $z$.

Translating it into our command language gives

```
DEF SCENE
DRAW GROUND
DRAW STUFF
PUSH
SCAL 1, 1, 0,
TRAN XL, YL, ZL,
ROT 180, 2,
SCAL ZL, ZL, 1,
PERS 90, 1, 1000000,
ROT 180, 2,
TRAN -XL, -YL, -ZL
DRAW STUFF
POP
----
```

If you multiply all these matrices together in the indicated order, you find that you do indeed get the desired matrix with all signs flipped properly. The result is shown in Figure 6.3. The light is at [2.25, .5, 5].

Now I admit that I wasn't nearly that organized the first time I tried this. At first, I tried various hack and bash mechanisms for mixing available matrices to get the desired result. The solution I came up with is especially weird since the near clipping plane is set farther away than the far clipping plane. Here is that first attempt, which does indeed generate the identical desired matrix, but in a far less intuitive way.

```
DEF SCENE
DRAW GROUND
DRAW STUFF
PUSH
SCAL 1, 1, 0,
PERS 90, 1000000, 1,
TRAN 0, 0, ZL,
ORIE ZL, 0, -XL, 0, ZL, -YL, 0, 0, -1,
DRAW STUFF
POP
----
```

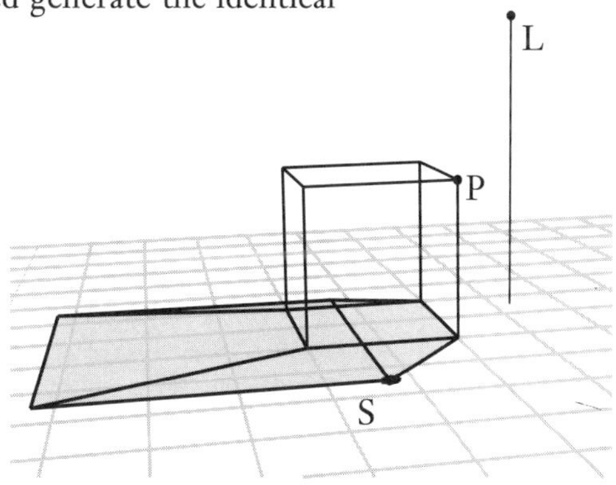

**Figure 6.3** *Correct perspective shadow*

Notice that, in a complete scene, we are using the perspective transform twice. We use it once as part of the viewing transformation, and a second time embedded in the model, to distort STUFF into the properly shaped shadow. When I first came up with this, I was very proud of myself. Awhile later I happened to be talking to Martin Newell on the phone and described it to him. He said, "Oh yes, that's how we used to make shadows in the late 60s in the CAD lab in England." Oh well. I guess it just goes to show you:

> Nobody ever does anything *first*.

# General Shadows

It is interesting at this point to compare the perspective shadow matrix with a variant of the infinite-light-source shadow matrix. The latter can be rewritten as

$$
\begin{bmatrix}
z_L & 0 & 0 & 0 \\
0 & z_L & 0 & 0 \\
-x_L & -y_L & 0 & 0 \\
0 & 0 & 0 & z_L
\end{bmatrix}
$$

In other words, we can come up with a general-purpose matrix that works for both cases:

$$
\begin{bmatrix}
z_L & 0 & 0 & 0 \\
0 & z_L & 0 & 0 \\
-x_L & -y_L & 0 & -w_L \\
0 & 0 & 0 & z_L
\end{bmatrix}
$$

where $w_L = 0$ for infinite light sources and $w_L = 1$ for local light sources.

How might we have found this to begin with? First, let's treat the relevant points P, L, and S as four-element homogeneous row vectors. An arbitrary point on the line connecting P and L can be represented in homogeneous coordinates as

$$
\alpha P + \beta L
$$

where the pair $[\alpha, \beta]$ forms a sort of one-dimensional homogeneous coordinate for points on the line.

Now represent the desired ground plane G as a four-element column vector. In our case, for $z = 0$, we have been using

$$G = \begin{bmatrix} 0 \\ 0 \\ 1 \\ 0 \end{bmatrix}$$

but it can be any plane in general.

The point on the shadow line that intersects the ground plane is given by the $[\alpha, \beta]$ that satisfy

$$(\alpha P + \beta L) \cdot G = 0$$

or

$$\alpha(P \cdot G) + \beta(L \cdot G) = 0$$

This can be satisfied by the pair of values

$$\alpha = (L \cdot G)$$
$$\beta = -(P \cdot G)$$

or any scalar multiple of it. The shadow point, S, is then

$$S = P(L \cdot G) - (P \cdot G)L$$

Now we must write this as a matrix multiplication. Behold the following trick. The expression

$$(P \cdot G)L$$

is a row vector times a column vector times a row vector. Matrix multiplication is associative, so it can be written

$$P(GL)$$

Now realize that, while $(L \cdot G)$ is a number, the quantity $(GL)$ is a $4 \times 4$ matrix according to the rules of vector product conformability. This is sometimes called the "outer product" of the vectors, in contrast to the ordinary "inner product." The construction of S can then be written

$$S = P[(L \cdot G)\mathbf{I} - GL]$$

where $\mathbf{I}$ is a $4 \times 4$ identity matrix. The perspective matrix itself is

$$[(L \cdot G)\mathbf{I} - GL]$$

If you plug in the $z = 0$ plane for G, you will get the matrix we derived above. In general, however, you can use this to perspectively project on any plane.

# CHAPTER SEVEN

# Things I Hope Not to See or Hear at SIGGRAPH

MAY 1988

No, I'm not going to talk about flying logos or glass balls. I am going to talk about that special form of performance art known as "Giving a Technical Presentation." These ideas apply to speakers in panels and tutorials as well. I realize that there is a somewhat small direct audience for this, but others of you might be able to use this information in your own talks elsewhere. Also, you should expect this from presentations you hear at SIGGRAPH.

SIGGRAPH sends out a lot of stuff about how to prepare visuals, etc., although from what I see, not many people read it. Reading this chapter does not excuse you from reading SIGGRAPH's materials, though; the following ideas are just my own personal biases. I will phrase them as things *not* to say/do because, let's face it, it's a lot easier to complain.

## Talks Read Verbatim

A technical talk is just one facet of a multimedia event built on your work. An adventure story appears differently in the film version and the book version. Likewise, different things are appropriate for the spoken version and the printed version of your paper. A much more conversational style is best for the talk. Tell a story about what got you interested in the problem in the first place. Briefly relate some dead ends that you tried that didn't work. But please don't read your paper verbatim. We are people out here in the audience; we're all your friends, just talk to us. The only exception to

*Tell a story . . .*

this rule is if you are not a native English speaker. If you are not fluent in English, it is probably best to have your words already prepared.

# Illegible Slides

The most important part of your talk is the visuals; this is SIG*GRAPH* after all. I am sometimes amazed at how many illegible slides are shown, most especially by representatives of organizations (who shall remain nameless) that sermonize about high-quality imaging. Here are some things that have disturbed me most about slides I have seen.

### Microtext

Many of you are involved in the microcircuit revolution and tend to think this also applies to the text on your slides. It doesn't. My personal rule is to put no more than six lines of text on any one slide. And while you're at it, use the biggest font you can that will fit on the slide. Six lines of teeny-weeny text with gigantic borders is still not readable. But, you may ask, what if I have more than six lines? Well . . . just use more than one slide. See? Simple.

A good check for readability of slides is to hold them at arm's length and see if they are still readable. (That is what I do, and my arms are probably longer than yours.) Believe me, that is how small they look from the back of the room. In fact, I make all my slides on my animation system that only has video resolution. This may seem to be a disadvantage, but it's not. It forces me keep the slides simple enough to be legible from a long distance.

One effect of this restriction concerns equations. You simply can't have a complex equation on a slide. Even if you shrink its many terms down so they will fit, it will look like gray noise from the back of the room. Recast your equations into simpler chunks and give each chunk its own name. Make one master slide with the basic equation in terms of these names. Then make a separate slide to define each chunk. Don't put more than one equation on a slide unless it is fantastically necessary. Use separate slides for each equation; it focuses attention while you are talking and gives you more room for each one.

### Magenta Lines on a Cyan Background

Another design issue concerns colors and contrast. Your best bet is to use some dark background (like blue) with very light color text (like white or yellow) on it. Alternatively you could use a light background and dark lines.

Even then, I have seen some terrible slides that use black letters on a white background. Even though the letters were big, the slides were illegible because the lines were too thin. Light areas seem to expand visually, so dark lines tend to get eaten up by a white background. If you must use light backgrounds, use a much thicker line width for the dark lines to compensate for this phenomenon.

If you want to emphasize some items on the slide, make them in a *lighter* color than the rest (not just in a *different* color).

## The Entire Text of the Talk Echoed on Slides

The audience is not going to want to read a lot of text while simultaneously trying to pay attention to what you are saying. Text on slides should just consist of section headings. If you have a section of your talk that you don't have any obvious graphics for, don't feel compelled to put the text you are reading on a slide just to have something there. The days of silent movies are over. If you must have something, try showing a picture of a pretty waterfall.

And remember, folks, no overhead transparencies allowed. There is a reason for this: they look terrible no matter what you do.

## "I'm Sorry These Slides Are So Dark."

I don't think I have ever seen a slide at SIGGRAPH that is overexposed. When you film your efforts, make several exposures and pick the brightest one. In general, err on the side of overexposure; make the exposures longer than you think will be necessary.

But for heaven's sake if, despite my sage advice, your slides don't come out bright enough, don't make a big production out of apologizing for them. It doesn't make them any more readable, and it may just call attention to problems that may not be as noticeable as you thought. Your view of the slides from where you speak is not the best one. The slides will look a lot brighter to the audience than they do to you. Just show them and get on with the talk.

Likewise, don't spend a lot of time fiddling with the focus (which requires shouting at the AV people in the back of the room). In the first place, your slides should be big and bold enough that a little bit of out-of-focus shouldn't bother them. Remember, from the back of the room the screen looks like a postage stamp. Problems with focus that appear bad to you, with your nose three feet from the screen, won't show up to the audience.

Talking about, and taking time with, these issues distracts attention from your presentation.

# The Floating Head

Because of the size of the auditorium, your face will probably be televised on a large TV screen behind you. The AV people set up the lighting to make your face optimally visible. This often has the effect that dark-colored clothing completely disappears into the background. This gives the impression of just your face floating in a sea of black. So . . . wear light-colored clothing. Your shoulders and arms will then show up and your audience will be able to tell that you are a whole person.

Additionally it would probably help to remove your plastic name badge holder while you are speaking. The television lights often reflect disturbingly off its shiny surface.

# The Tops of Speakers' Heads

No, I'm not saying this because I'm tall. I mean that speakers should look straight out at the audience instead of burying their noses in their notes. I know it looks like a black hole out there, what with the dim house lights and the spotlight on you. You can't really see the audience, but there *are* people there. If you look down all the time, all that people will see is the top of your head. This is so important that I'll say it again. Look up at the audience; it looks a lot better for the TV cameras.

Also, don't turn around to admire your face on the big TV screen. It just won't work; all people will see is the back of your head. Likewise, don't turn around and look at your slides all the time (except maybe for a brief glance to make sure you are on the one you expect). Traditionally, people really are more used to seeing the front of people's heads than any other side.

# The Fading Voice

Another reason not to turn around a lot is sound. There is a microphone in front of you, not behind you. A lot of speakers start out saying something into the microphone like "And as you see in this slide . . ." Then they turn around and look at the slide and say " . . . the secret of the universe is revealed." Only they aren't speaking into the microphone anymore. What comes out is "mumble mumble mumble." Speak consistently into the microphone. Let your secrets be revealed.

# Wiggly Pointerism

You will probably have a laser pointer to use during your talk. Since the screens are so large and so far away from you, a very slight motion of your hand will make the pointer jump around in a very distracting fashion. Try to keep your pointing hand as steady as possible to keep the audience from getting seasick. Or else turn it off when you aren't actually pointing at something.

# "I'm Almost Out of Time So I'll Just Run Through the Rest of These Slides Real Fast."

You are hereby warned: for a talk in the technical session you only have about 15 minutes to do your brain dump. The time you have is well known to you in advance; you must use it wisely. About all you can expect to do in this amount of time is give an overview of your paper and inspire those in the audience to read the paper itself for details.

Plan on spending most of your time talking about your new ideas. I have seen talks where the speaker spends 13 minutes giving a review of the field and a justification for why their specific problem is interesting. Then—what do you know—there's no time left for the meat of the talk. I think you can safely assume that most everyone in the audience thinks computer graphics is a good idea and that, in fact, the specific problem you are addressing is worth solving. You can probably do fine with about two minutes of introduction before getting to the good stuff.

Don't go into enormous detail in derivations of the math, just give the basic assumptions and the results. This simplification process goes hand-in-hand with the simplification of your equation slides. The general gist of the math should be describable without going into a lot of fine details that people will best get out of the paper.

If you have a videotape, time it and make sure it doesn't eat up the whole time for the talk. Speaking from experience, it is very embarrassing for a session chairman (whose main duty is as time police) to have to interrupt a nifty tape because there's no time left.

# "Uh, I Guess That's All I Have to Say."

Probably the most important parts of your talk are the first and last sentences. Have these all figured out before you go up to the podium. Try to have something snappy to end with rather than just drizzling off.

*First & last sentences...*

You also must give the audience a signal for when to applaud. Usually a simple "thank you" will suffice.

## Remember

Look up. Bright slides, big letters.
Uh, I guess that's all I have to say.
Thank you.

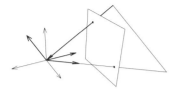

# CHAPTER EIGHT

# Where Am I?
# What Am I Looking At?

J U L Y  1 9 8 8

This chapter concerns a problem I originally had in making space movies that ultimately led to some interesting generalizations of the look-at transform. Besides, it lets me wallow in something I find vastly entertaining, vector algebra. It uses several general techniques that are useful in a lot of problems. The trick is to know how to use them and to recognize them when they occur.

## The Problem

The big problem in making the space movies is that of figuring out where to place the camera and in what direction to point it in order to get an interesting picture. Interesting pictures are those that have, say, the spacecraft in the foreground and a planet or moon somewhere in the background. This is doubly complicated since the two objects are each traveling along different curved paths.

The traditional approach to the look-at transformation is for the user to explicitly specify a viewing position and a viewing direction. My ultimate goal here is to be able to tell the program

> I want the spacecraft to be at location $[x_f, y_f]$ on the screen and $d$ meters away. I want the planet to be at location $[x_a, y_a]$ on the screen and I want a field of view of $\varphi$ degrees. Oh, and I want the spin axis of the planet to appear vertical on the screen.

and have it figure out where I must be standing and in what direction I must be looking for this to occur.

# The Standard Look-At Transformation

Let's first review the standard look-at transformation. We begin by giving explicit definitions to the three coordinate systems we are dealing with. Define *universe* space as the coordinate system that the scene and objects are defined in. Define *eye* space as a translation and rotation of universe space so that the desired eyepoint is at the origin and the desired viewing direction lies along the $z$ axis. This is the coordinate system *before* any perspective distortion is performed. Finally, define *screen* space as that *after* the perspective. It uses a canonical screen that stretches from –1 to +1 in $x$ and $y$ and where the $z$ axis points into the screen.

Now, for a traditional look-at transformation you specify an eye position, $P_{eye}$, and a location to look at, $P_{at}$ (both in universe coordinates). The idea is to construct a transformation consisting of only a translation and a pure rotation that generates a view sitting at point $P_{eye}$ and looking in a direction that puts $P_{at}$ in the center of the screen. The translation part is easy; it's just $-P_{eye}$. The rotation takes a bit more work. The idea is to find the matrix that rotates the vector $(P_{at} - P_{eye})$ to lie along the $z$ axis. There is still an arbitrary rotation about this look vector that is nailed down by another input variable, an *up* vector, $\hat{U}$. This is a vector in universe space that, when transformed to eye space, should point (as much as is possible) "up." That means that, in eye space, it has an $x$ component of 0. This up vector will have unit length, so I have written it with a hat. As a mnemonic aid I'll write all unit vectors in this chapter with hats.

Translating this into equations, first define the vector $\hat{T}$ as $P_{at} - P_{eye}$ scaled to unit length. The rotation matrix we seek, $M$, is that which transforms $\hat{T}$ and $\hat{U}$ as follows:

$$\hat{T}\,M = [0,0,1]$$
$$\hat{U}\,M = [0,V_y,V_z]$$

There are two ways commonly used to solve for $M$: by building it up out of simple rotations or by constructing the elements of $M$ directly with tricky algebra. I will be tricky. It shows off some techniques that are generally useful in solving vector equations.

For our first trick, let's try to find numerical values for $V_y$ and $V_z$. This is done with the aid of general technique #1:

Instructions for rendering a scene take the form of a list of commands and their parameters. These will be written here in TYPEWRITER type. All commands will have four or fewer letters. (The number 4 is used because of its ancient numerological significance.) Parameters will be separated by commas, not blanks. (Old-time FORTRAN programmers don't even see blanks, let alone use them as delimiters.) Don't complain, just be glad I'm not using O-Language (maybe I'll tell you about *that* sometime).

# Basic Command Set

These commands modify **C** and pass primitives through it. Each modification command premultiplies some simple matrix into **C**. No other action is taken. The command descriptions below will explicitly show the matrices used.

## Translation

TRAN *x, y, z*

premultiplies **C** by an elementary translation matrix.

$$\mathbf{C} \leftarrow \begin{bmatrix} 1 & 0 & 0 & 0 \\ 0 & 1 & 0 & 0 \\ 0 & 0 & 1 & 0 \\ x & y & z & 1 \end{bmatrix} \mathbf{C}$$

## Scaling

SCAL *sx, sy, sz*

premultiplies **C** by an elementary scaling matrix.

$$\mathbf{C} \leftarrow \begin{bmatrix} sx & 0 & 0 & 0 \\ 0 & sy & 0 & 0 \\ 0 & 0 & sz & 0 \\ 0 & 0 & 0 & 1 \end{bmatrix} \mathbf{C}$$

## Rotation

ROT $\theta$, *j*

The $j$ parameter is an integer from 1 to 3 specifying the coordinate axis ($x$, $y$, or $z$). The positive rotation direction is given via the Right-Hand Rule (if you are using a left-handed coordinate system) or the Left-Hand Rule (if you are using a right-handed coordinate system). This may sound strange, but it's how it's given in Newman and Sproull.[3] It makes *positive* rotation go *clockwise* when viewing in the direction of a coordinate axis. For each matrix below, we precalculate

$$s = \sin\theta$$
$$c = \cos\theta$$

The matrices are then
  $j = 1$ ($x$ axis)

$$\mathbf{C} \leftarrow \begin{bmatrix} 1 & 0 & 0 & 0 \\ 0 & c & -s & 0 \\ 0 & s & c & 0 \\ 0 & 0 & 0 & 1 \end{bmatrix} \mathbf{C}$$

  $j = 2$ ($y$ axis)

$$\mathbf{C} \leftarrow \begin{bmatrix} c & 0 & s & 0 \\ 0 & 1 & 0 & 0 \\ -s & 0 & c & 0 \\ 0 & 0 & 0 & 1 \end{bmatrix} \mathbf{C}$$

  $j = 3$ ($z$ axis)

$$\mathbf{C} \leftarrow \begin{bmatrix} c & -s & 0 & 0 \\ s & c & 0 & 0 \\ 0 & 0 & 1 & 0 \\ 0 & 0 & 0 & 1 \end{bmatrix} \mathbf{C}$$

## Perspective

PERS $\alpha$, $z_n$, $z_f$

This transformation combines a perspective distortion with a depth ($z$) transformation. The perspective assumes the eye is at the origin, looking down the $+z$ axis. The field of view is given by the angle $\alpha$.

---

3 William M. Newman and Robert F. Sproull, *Principles of Interactive Computer Graphics* (New York: McGraw-Hill, 1979).

*A pair of vectors that has a given dot product in one coordinate system has the same dot product when expressed in another coordinate system.*

So

$$[0,0,1]\cdot[0,V_y,V_z] = T\cdot\hat{U}$$

or

$$V_z = \hat{T}\cdot\hat{U}$$

We get $V_y$ by the requirement that $V$ be unit length.

$$V_y = \sqrt{1-V_z^2}$$

Whenever there are square roots about, it is necessary to worry about whether we want the positive or the negative square root. In this case we are talking about the $y$ coordinate of the up vector, something we earnestly wish to be positive.

Next, being a professional in this business, I happen to know that, since it's a pure rotation, the transpose of **M** equals the inverse of **M**. Multiplying this on both sides gives

$$\hat{T} = [0,0,1]\,\mathbf{M^t}$$

$$\hat{U} = [0,V_y,V_z]\,\mathbf{M^t}$$

This means that the bottom row of $\mathbf{M^t}$ (that is, the right column of **M**) is $\hat{T}$. So we already have one third of the elements of **M**. That was easy.

To do the rest of this, it will be convenient to give separate names to the rows of $\mathbf{M^t}$ (columns of **M**).

$$M_{i1} = \text{top row } \mathbf{M^t} = \text{left column } \mathbf{M}$$
$$M_{i2} = \text{middle row } \mathbf{M^t} = \text{middle column } \mathbf{M}$$
$$M_{i3} = \text{bottom row } \mathbf{M^t} = \text{right column } \mathbf{M}$$

Note that the left column of **M** is just the cross product of the other two columns (for the same reason that the $x$ axis is the cross product of the $y$ axis with the $z$ axis).

Now we can write the above equations as

$$\hat{T} = M_{i3}$$
$$\hat{U} = V_y\,M_{i2} + V_z\,M_{i3}$$

Simple algebra leads us to the expression of **M**:

$$M_{i3} = \hat{T}$$

$$M_{i2} = \frac{1}{V_y}\hat{U} - \frac{V_z}{V_y}\hat{T} = (\hat{U} - (\hat{U} \cdot \hat{T})\hat{T})/V_y$$

$$M_{i1} = M_{i2} \times M_{i3} = (\hat{U} \times \hat{T})/V_y$$

## Singularities

There are two deadly warning signs that something is going wrong in geometric calculations—attempting to take the square root of a negative number and attempting to divide by 0. What does it mean if there is a negative value under the square root sign for $V_y$? It means that $|\hat{T} \cdot \hat{U}| > 1$. Since $\hat{T}$ and $\hat{U}$ are supposed to be unit length, it means you cheated. Serves you right. You had better check, though, before diving into the square root routine, since roundoff error can make it negative.

Since we are going to divide by $V_y$, what if it's 0? This means that $\hat{T} = \hat{U}$ and the universe collapses. Many people panic in this situation, but I have not found it to be that much of a problem. While you have to make sure your program doesn't die hideously when this occurs, an interactive scene design program easily allows adjustment of $\hat{U}$ to something different from $\hat{T}$.

# Now, with One Hand Tied behind My Back

The homogeneous perspective matrix forces the use of a left-handed coordinate system for screen space. This is due to the fact that $x$ and $y$ are effectively divided by $z$ to get screen space. If you attempt to use a right-handed system, the $z$ axis points *out* of the screen and you must divide by $-z$ to get the perspective right. But you are effectively switching to a left-handed system when you do this division.

Coordinate systems defined for astronomical purposes, however, are right-handed. Since the $P_{at}$ and $P_{eye}$ are defined in the universe space, it is convenient to have eye space be right-handed and convert it to left-handed just before the perspective matrix multiplication.

The difference this makes algebraically is to cause a lot of minus signs to crop up. $\hat{T}$ must be rotated to coincide with the *negative z* axis, which we will call $\hat{L} = [0, 0, -1]$. This changes the solution for $(V_y, V_z)$ to read

$$\hat{L} \cdot \hat{V} = \hat{T} \cdot \hat{U}$$

so

$$V_z = -\hat{T} \cdot \hat{U}$$
$$V_y = \sqrt{1 - V_z^2}$$

and the solution for **M** to start with

$$\hat{T}\,\mathbf{M} = \hat{L}$$
$$\hat{U}\,\mathbf{M} = \hat{V}$$

which ultimately leads to

$$M_{i3} = -\hat{T}$$
$$M_{i2} = \frac{1}{V_y}\hat{U} + \frac{V_z}{V_y}\hat{T} = (\hat{U} - (\hat{U} \cdot \hat{T})\hat{T}) / V_z$$
$$M_{i1} = M_{i2} \times M_{i3} = -(\hat{U} \times \hat{T}) / V_z$$

This rotation must be followed by a scale of –1 in $z$ to switch to the left-handed system of the perspective.

# Truth in Advertising

Well, actually it wasn't really all that easy. This sort of thing is pretty error intensive. My original scheme did it the hard way by using the left-handed version of **M**. I then empirically found that I had to scale by –1 in $x$ instead of in $z$, and also to scale the $x_a$ and $x_f$ values by –1. (Basically I just put in enough minus signs after the fact to make it work.) Al Barr refers to this technique as "making sure you have made an even number of sign errors." Signs are always a nuisance in this business (e.g., clockwise/counterclockwise, inward/outward pointing normal vectors, etc.). You analyze and analyze and still only have a 50% chance of getting it right. That's why you have to try out your program instead of just theorizing. You have to test your program thoroughly to see if the signs are OK. Then, after the fact, you go back and derive why the minus sign had to be there anyway.

With some *very careful* examination of signs, you can see that the right-handed **M** is the same as the left-handed **M** with the signs of the first and third columns flipped. So scaling in $z$ for one generates the same net matrix as scaling in $x$ for the other.

Writing this chapter, in fact, motivated me to clean this up and do it right, as well as implement some other improvements described below. Writing has that effect on your thinking; I recommend it.

# The Final Frontier

The idea of a fly-by animation is to ride along with the spacecraft watching a planet or a moon go by. You can, of course, pick any object to ride along with and any other object to appear in the background. I will refer to the location of whatever is chosen for the "from" object as $P_{from}$, although I will often refer to it as "the spacecraft." Likewise I will give the name $P_{at}$ to the location of the background object, the "at" object, though I will often just call it "the planet." Some simple Keplerian calculations, which I won't go into here, can find the locations of the spacecraft, planet, and moons at any desired simulated time to be used for these vectors.

A first-order solution to the viewing problem is just to take the eye-point, $P_{eye}$, from the spacecraft location, $P_{from}$. The viewed point, $P_{at}$, is the location of the planet. This unfortunately makes rather boring pictures. It means that the planet is always exactly in the middle of the screen and that our eye is embedded in the middle of the spacecraft. To make a more interesting composition, I wanted to be able to generalize in two ways. First, pull back from the spacecraft by some offset, D, so it would be some small distance away from us, with $P_{eye} = P_{from} + D$. Second, rotate the eye slightly so that the background object isn't necessarily at the center of the screen, i.e., $P_{at} - P_{eye}$ no longer points exactly in the direction of $\hat{T}$. (We will give the new name $\hat{A}$ to the vector $P_{at} - P_{eye}$ scaled to unit length.)

Yuck! This is getting confusing. Let's make a table to keep all these vectors and coordinate systems straight (Table 8.1). See also Figure 8.1. The idea is to be able to calculate D and $\hat{T}$ from other vectors in the table. In fact, what we really want is to be able to specify the location of the spacecraft as $[x_f, y_f]$ in screen space and the planet as $[x_a, y_a]$ also in screen

**Table 8.1** *Vectors and coordinate systems used*

| Universe space | Eye space | Definition |
|---|---|---|
| $P_{eye}$ | $(0, 0, 0)$ | Eye location |
| $P_{from}$ | | From-body location |
| $P_{at}$ | | At-body location |
| $\hat{U}$ | $\hat{V}$ | Up vector (unit) |
| $\hat{T}$ | $\hat{L}$ | View direction (unit) |
| $\hat{A}$ | $\hat{H}$ | Eye to at-body (unit) |
| $Q = P_{at} - P_{from}$ | R | From-body to at-body |
| $D = P_{eye} - P_{from}$ | E | From-body to eye |

space, then have the program automatically calculate a desired D and $\hat{T}$ that will make them show up there.

Furthermore, for an entire space movie you may not always be tracking the same background object. For awhile you watch the spacecraft in the foreground with Saturn in the background. Then you pan over to watch a moon go by, letting the spacecraft slip out of the frame. Then you pan back to the spacecraft and Saturn. The pans are interpolations of D and $\hat{T}$ that may have been automatically calculated as the ending and beginning frames of sequences for other viewing modes. This explains the necessity of the four possible viewing modes:

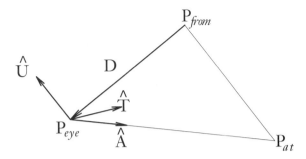

**Figure 8.1a**  *Universe space*

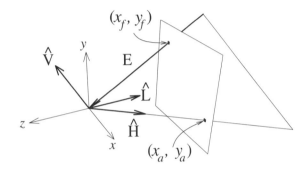

**Figure 8.1b**  *Eye space*

- Mode 1—Specify D and $\hat{T}$.
- Mode 2—Specify $[x_f, y_f]$ and $\hat{T}$; calculate D.
- Mode 3—Specify D and $[x_a, y_a]$; calculate $\hat{T}$.
- Mode 4—Specify $[x_f, y_f]$ and $[x_a, y_a]$; calculate D and $\hat{T}$.

Note that the screen positions may also be interpolated between keyframes.

Mode 1 is basically just the standard look-at transformation. Modes 2 through 4 each deserve a section of their own.

# I'm Looking over Here, Where Should I Stand?

In mode 2 the user is saying to the program, "Look in this given direction, $\hat{T}$, but position yourself so the spacecraft appears on the screen at $(x_f, y_f)$ but is *d* units in the distance." In this mode, fixing the spacecraft position and interactively adjusting $\hat{T}$ gives the impression of orbiting the spacecraft at a constant distance.

Since we are given $\hat{T}$, we can immediately calculate the rotation matrix **M**. The problem is to calculate D. To do this we first find its incarnation in eye space, which we'll call E. One way to do this is to multiply $(x_f, y_f, 0)$ by the inverse of the perspective and handedness-changing matrices. Another way to think of this is to imagine the screen (whose extent is

−1 to +1 in $x$ and $y$) as being at a distance $\cot(\frac{\varphi}{2})$ in front of the eye, where $\varphi$ is the field of view angle. The spacecraft then lies along the vector $(x_f, y_f, -\cot(\frac{\varphi}{2}))$ in eye space. Note the minus on the $z$ coordinate because of the right-handed system. This just gives the *direction* of E. It must be scaled to unit length and multiplied by $-d$ to make it the correct length. (The minus sign is because E must point *from* the spacecraft *to* the eye.)

You finally get D by multiplying E by the inverse (i.e., the transpose) of **M**, and then $P_{eye} = P_{from} + D$.

# Here I Am, Where Do I Look?

In mode 3 the user is telling the program, "Stand here and look in whatever direction puts the planet at $(x_a, y_a)$." In other words, you are given the viewing offset, D, and the desire to look in whatever direction causes the planet to be at the given location on the screen.

The first thing to do is to convert this screen location to a vector in eye space. This is similar to mode 2 in that the screen coordinates give us the direction vector from the eye to the at-body, called H, which is the eye space incarnation of $\hat{A}$. The unit vector $\hat{H}$ is then just

$$\left[ x_a, y_a, -\cot\frac{\varphi}{2} \right]$$

scaled to unit length. I also have included a feature to allow tracking of the limb of the planet instead of just its center. This takes the form of an offset to $[x_a, y_a]$ by an approximation to the expected screen size of the planet.

Now let's list the vectors, their coordinate systems, and whether we know them yet or not in Table 8.2. Remember we are trying to find $\hat{T}$. The known vectors are shaded. The general scheme is to start calculating unknown vectors in terms of known ones, until we finally find $\hat{T}$.

First, the vector $\hat{A}$ is just Q − D normalized to unit length.

**Table 8.2** *Input to mode 3*

| Universe space | Eye space | Definition |
|---|---|---|
| $\hat{U}$ | $\hat{V}$ | Up vector (unit) |
| $\hat{T}$ | $\hat{L}$ | View direction (unit) |
| $\hat{A}$ | $\hat{H}$ | Eye to at-body (unit) |
| Q | R | From-body to at-body |
| D | E | From-body to eye |

Next we get $\hat{V}$. This vector has only two unknown components (since $V_x = 0$), so we need to come up with only two equations containing it. One comes from the fact that it's a unit length vector, and the other from use of the dot-product constancy between coordinate systems.

$$\hat{V} \cdot \hat{V} = 1$$
$$\hat{V} \cdot \hat{H} = \hat{U} \cdot \hat{A}$$

Writing these in terms of coordinates, we get

$$V_y^2 + V_z^2 = 1$$
$$V_y H_y + V_z H_z - (\hat{U} \cdot \hat{A}) = 0$$

This can be interpreted geometrically as the intersection of a line in $(V_y, V_z)$ space with the unit circle. Let's temporarily generalize the parameters and solve it for the arbitrary line $(a, b, c)^t$. Fiddling with quadratic formulae and such ultimately results in intersections

$$\left( \frac{-ac \pm b\sqrt{a^2 + b^2 - c^2}}{a^2 + b^2}, \quad \frac{-cb \mp a\sqrt{a^2 + b^2 - c^2}}{a^2 + b^2} \right)$$

In our particular case, we turn these into $(V_y, V_z)$ by plugging in

$$a = H_y, \quad b = H_z, \quad c = -\hat{U} \cdot \hat{A}$$

There are two solutions to this intersection; which one should we use? As before, when we are finding the up vector, we want the one that has the largest (usually) positive value for $V_y$. Since $H_z = b$, this will come from the bottom sign in the $\pm$, $\mp$ expressions above.

Now (finally) for $\hat{T}$. We will construct it as a linear combination of $\hat{A}$, $\hat{U}$, and their cross product:

$$\hat{T} = \alpha \hat{A} + \beta \hat{U} + \gamma (\hat{A} \times \hat{U})$$

and solve for $\alpha$, $\beta$, and $\gamma$. We can get equations for these from our old friend, dot-product constancy.

$$\hat{H} \cdot \hat{L} = \hat{A} \cdot \hat{T}$$
$$\hat{V} \cdot \hat{L} = \hat{U} \cdot \hat{T}$$
$$(\hat{H} \times \hat{V}) \cdot \hat{L} = (\hat{A} \times \hat{U}) \cdot \hat{T}$$

Plugging in the definition of $\hat{T}$ on the right sides and explicit (known) components of the vectors for the left sides gives us

$$-H_z = \alpha + \beta(\hat{U} \cdot \hat{A})$$
$$-V_z = \alpha(\hat{U} \cdot \hat{A}) + \beta$$
$$-H_x V_y = \gamma(\hat{A} \times \hat{U}) \cdot (\hat{A} \times \hat{U})$$

Let me read into the record the following vector identity (remember that $\hat{A}$ and $\hat{U}$ are unit length):

$$(\hat{A} \times \hat{U}) \cdot (\hat{A} \times \hat{U}) = 1 - (\hat{U} \cdot \hat{A})^2$$

Dump this all in the linear equation solving machine, stir well, and out comes

$$\alpha = \left(-H_z + V_z(\hat{U} \cdot \hat{A})\right) / \Delta$$
$$\beta = \left(-V_z + H_z(\hat{U} \cdot \hat{A})\right) / \Delta$$
$$\gamma = \left(-H_x V_y\right) / \Delta$$
$$\Delta = 1 - (\hat{U} \cdot \hat{A})^2$$

## Singularities

As usual, you must check for bad square roots and bad divisions. These can come if

$$H_y^2 + H_z^2 - \hat{U} \cdot \hat{A} < 0$$

or if

$$\hat{U} \cdot \hat{A} = \pm 1$$

They essentially indicate an unsatisfiable set of conditions. For example, $[x_a, y_a]$ might be very large and generate an $\hat{H}$ that points so far to the side that the smallest angle with any possible $\hat{V}$ (in the $yz$ plane) is still bigger than the angle between $\hat{U}$ and $\hat{A}$. Or else $\hat{A}$ and $\hat{U}$ coincide and again the universe collapses.

## What Have We Learned from This?

I have given the above derivation, all the time charging ahead knowing where I was going. But how might you have figured out how to do it if you didn't know already? The next case is even trickier, so it's important to make sure we have learned as much as possible from this case. Let's look at the problem backwards. Ultimately we need to find $\hat{T}$. It can be constructed in terms of any two known vectors in universe space. But how do we know what the coefficients should be? In linear algebra you are taught to take dot products for such things. This seems boring and obvious until you use basis vectors that aren't necessarily unit length or perpendicular to each other as we have now done.

These dot products can be turned into known numbers if the dot products are also known in eye space. So the entire name of the game is

*Find a pair of vectors to use as basis vectors that are known in* both *universe and eye space.*

Proceed.

# Where Am I? Where Do I Look?

In mode 4 you are required to put the spacecraft at one given screen location $[x_f, y_f]$ and distance $d$, and put the planet at another screen location $[x_a, y_a]$. You must solve for the D and $\hat{T}$ that brings this about.

First off, turn the screen locations into eye space vectors E and $\hat{H}$ exactly as in the two previous cases.

Then what? Again let's list the vectors, their coordinate systems, and whether we know them yet or not. See Table 8.3. The known vectors are shaded.

This one had me stumped for quite awhile. Every time I tried to come up with an explicit solution for $\hat{T}$, I kept getting it in terms of vectors that hadn't been found yet. (It's easy to lose track of what's known and what you are solving for in this problem.) Finally, I gave up and solved for $\hat{T}$ numerically. The basic iteration was

1. Set D to 0.
2. Solve the mode 3 problem for **M**.

**Table 8.3**  *Input to mode 4*

| Universe space | Eye space | Definition |
|---|---|---|
| $\hat{U}$ | $\hat{V}$ | Up vector (unit) |
| $\hat{T}$ | $\hat{L}$ | View direction (unit) |
| $\hat{A}$ | $\hat{H}$ | Eye to at-body (unit) |
| Q | R | From-body to at-body |
| D | E | From-body to eye |

3. Transform E by inverse of **M**, getting a new approximation to D.
4. Goto 2.

This is the technique used for all of the space movies actually produced so far. There is a subtlety in the calculation that was necessary since it is being used for animation; the iteration was repeated exactly six times. For animation purposes it's better to use a fixed number of iterations, so there won't be a jump in the screen appearance if the number of iterations were to change from one frame to the next.

Well, I have been presenting this to my classes for several years as an unsolved problem. I wasn't even certain there was a closed form solution. Finally a student named Scott Hemphill came up with one. He did it an entirely different way, by composing rotation matrices and translations, but I was able to take his basic insight and adapt it to the formulation we are using here.

The nut that was cracked is the ability to solve for R. To do this we need the distance from the eyepoint, $P_{eye}$, to the at-point, $P_{at}$, a quantity we shall call $a$. The Law of Cosines tells us that, for the triangle formed from $(P_{eye}, P_{from}, P_{at})$, the lengths are

$$q^2 = d^2 + a^2 - 2ad\cos\theta$$

where $q = |Q|$ and $\theta$ is the angle subtended at the eye by the from-object and the at-object. But what is $\theta$? Remember we don't know $P_{eye}$ yet. I told you this was tricky.

We can get this crucial piece of information by looking at the same triangle in eye space. See Figure 8.2. Here we see that

$$\cos\theta = \frac{-E}{|E|} \cdot \hat{H}$$

Note that

$$|E| = d$$

Putting this together and solving the quadratic equation for $a$, we get

$$a = -(E \cdot \hat{H}) \pm \sqrt{(E \cdot \hat{H})^2 - d^2 + q^2}$$

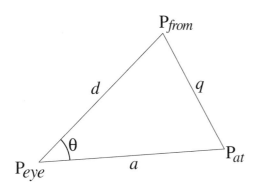

**Figure 8.2a**  *Universe space*

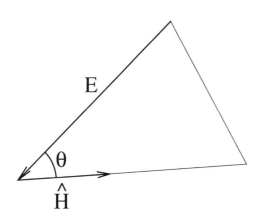

**Figure 8.2b**  *Eye space*

Which solution should we pick? Usually one of them will be negative, but in any event it is safe to use the largest one from the positive square root. Now we can say

$$R = E + a\hat{H}$$

Now we're home free. We proceed as in mode 3 with R taking the role of $\hat{H}$ and Q taking the role of $\hat{A}$. That is, solve for $\hat{V}$ by starting with the dot-product equivalence

$$\hat{V} \cdot R = \hat{U} \cdot Q$$

and use the unit-circle/line intersection formula with

$$a = R_y \qquad b = R_z \qquad c = -\hat{U} \cdot Q$$

Then construct $\hat{T}$ as

$$\hat{T} = \alpha Q + \beta \hat{U} + \gamma (Q \times \hat{U})$$

Taking all the appropriate dot products and fiddling leads to

$$\alpha = \left( -R_z + V_z(\hat{U} \cdot Q) \right) / \Delta$$
$$\beta = \left( -V_z(Q \cdot Q) + R_z(\hat{U} \cdot Q) \right) / \Delta$$
$$\gamma = \left( -R_x V_y \right) / \Delta$$
$$\Delta = Q \cdot Q - (\hat{U} \cdot Q)^2$$

Wrap up as usual; use $\hat{T}$ and $\hat{U}$ to find **M**, and multiply E by $\mathbf{M}^t$ to get D.

## Singularities

Here we can get in trouble due to negative square roots when solving for $a$. This again indicates an unsatisfiable set of conditions. It will happen only when the viewer is much farther from $P_{from}$ than the distance between $P_{from}$ and $P_{at}$. Effectively you have told it to separate the two objects on the screen, but you are so far away from them that their separation angle can't be that big.

This is a case where the numerical simulation wins. The closer the input conditions get to singularity, the more iterations it takes to get the correct answer. Using a program with a fixed number of iterations provides a smooth transition from the correct view for small distances to a reasonable compromise view for large distances.

# Look Again

To summarize, to define a scene you need to specify

- The field of view, $\varphi$
- An up vector in universe coordinates, $\hat{U}$
- Eyepoint location relative to a foreground object by either explicitly setting D or by giving $(x_f, y_f)$ and $d$ and having the program calculate D
- The view direction by either explicitly setting $\hat{T}$ or by giving $(x_a, y_a)$ and having the program calculate $\hat{T}$

I could include some color pictures of the results, but that would be gratuitous.

# CHAPTER NINE

# The Three-Dimensional Kaleidoscope

SEPTEMBER 1988

In Chapter 4 I talked about Platonic solids, concerning myself mostly with the coordinates of the vertices. This time, let's examine another way to construct Platonic solids that takes advantage of their symmetry. This works well with the coordinate transform system we have developed, since symmetry is based on coordinate transformations.

There are two ways to think of symmetry. First, the analytic approach: You start with some symmetrical shape and characterize its symmetries as the collection of transformations it can undergo that leave its shape unchanged. The allowable transformations we will consider here are pure rotations and mirror reflections. Second is the synthetic approach. You start with some asymmetrical seed shape, and apply the above collection of transformations to generate the whole symmetrical shape.

## The Cube

Let's begin with an analysis of the symmetries of a cube. A cube can be rotated by 90 degrees about, say, the $x$ axis, and the result looks identical to the original cube. Likewise it can mirrored along the $x$ axis without changing its shape. With a little organization and imagination you can discover that there are 48 different transformations that result in a cube indistinguishable from the original. These include 24 pure rotations, to whit:

- The identity
- Rotation of 90, 180, and 270 degrees about the $x$, $y$, and $z$ axes (nine total)

- Rotation of 120 and 240 degrees about the four diagonals (eight total)
- Rotation of 180 degrees about the axes connecting the center with the midpoints of each edge (six total)

The other 24 transformations are reflections or rotation/reflections:

- The point inversion (scale by –1 along each of $x$, $y$, and $z$ axes)
- Reflection along the $x$, $y$, or $z$ axes followed by rotation by 0, 90, or –90 degrees about that axis (nine total)
- Reflection along the four diagonals followed by rotation of $\pm 60$ degrees about that diagonal (eight total)
- Reflection through the planes $x = \pm y$, $x = \pm z$, and $y = \pm z$ (six total)

Next, let's switch to the synthetic approach. What is the minimal asymmetrical portion of a cube that can be transformed by all these rotations and reflections to regenerate the whole cube? One choice is the triangle shown in yellow in Figure 9.1 (color plates), having the following vertex coordinates:

```
Point 1:   (1, 1, 1)
Point 2:   (1, 0, 0)
Point 3:   (1, 0, 1)
```

Now how do we build up a cube from this seed shape? It is possible (but inconvenient) to individually apply all 48 transformations to the triangle. Instead let's build it up in modules. Here's one of the many ways to do it: First combine the triangle with its mirror image in the $xz$ plane to get the symmetrical triangle in Figure 9.2a (color plates). This can be described in our transformation system from Chapter 3 as

```
DEF QUADRANT
DRAW TRIANGLE
DRAW TRIANGLE, SCAL 1, -1, 1,
----
```

Then replicate this four times by 90-degree rotations about the $x$ axis to get one entire face of the cube. This is shown in Figure 9.2b (color plates) and defines CFACE:

```
DEF CFACE
DRAW QUADRANT
ROT 90, 1
DRAW QUADRANT
ROT 90, 1
DRAW QUADRANT
ROT 90, 1
```

```
DRAW QUADRANT
ROT 90, 1
----
```

Finally generate all six sides of the cube by 90-degree rotations about the $y$ and $z$ axes:

```
DEF CUBE
PUSH
DRAW CFACE
ROT 90, 2
DRAW CFACE
ROT 90, 2
DRAW CFACE
ROT 90, 2
DRAW CFACE
ROT 90, 2
ROT 90, 3
DRAW CFACE
ROT 180,3
DRAW CFACE
POP
----
```

What have we just done? The collection of 48 transformations of the cube makes up a mathematical entity known as a *group*. One property of such a group is that it is *closed*, that is, after performing any two transformations in sequence the net result is always another transformation in the group. Alternatively, you can often start with just a few seed transformations and generate all the rest with multiple products of the seeds. For example, you can generate all the pure rotations of the cube group using just two matrices, 90-degree rotation about $x$ (call this A) and 90 degrees about $y$ (call this B). I entertained myself for an entire weekend working out the combinations of A and B necessary for each of the other 22 transformations. It takes five, for example, to construct a 90-degree rotation about $z$ (ABAAA). I also found some surprising identities (ABA = BAB, AA = BAAB, etc.). You could even express these as rewriting rules in some kind of context-free grammar.

But I digress.

*Group theory*

*Nice*

# Other Related Shapes

Now that we have a way of generating the cube from transformations of our seed shape, what happens if we change the seed shape? For the time being, let's keep the shape such that its edges continue to match with the edges of its neighbors. That is, we will not introduce tears or gaps in the final shape. In order to do this, point 1 must remain on the $xyz$ diagonal, point 2 must remain on the $x$ axis, and point 3 must remain on the $xz$ plane. The point coordinates can be parameterized as

```
Point 1:   (a, a, a)
Point 2:   (b, 0, 0)
Point 3:   (c, 0, c)
```

My implementation of the transformation system doesn't allow changing shapes in this way. Instead I did it by starting with a slightly different seed shape called BTRIANG, expressed in point-polygon form as

```
PNT 1, 1., 0., 0.
PNT 2, 0., 1., 0.
PNT 3, 0., 0., 1.
POLY 1, 2, 3
```

then subjecting it to the transformation

$$\begin{bmatrix} a & a & a \\ b & 0 & 0 \\ c & 0 & c \end{bmatrix}$$

This appears in transformation language as

```
DEF TRIANG
PUSH
ORIE a,b,c, a,0,0, a,0,c,
DRAW BTRIANG
POP
----
```

If $a = b = c = 1$ we get our cube back (Figure 9.3a in the color plates). By playing with $a$, $b$, and $c$ you can get a variety of closed shapes, all sharing the same symmetry properties as the cube. What sort of other shapes can we get? One interesting shape comes from $a = \sqrt{2}, b = \sqrt{6}, c = \sqrt{3}$. Here, all points are equidistant from the origin and the object is roughly spherical (Figure 9.3b, color plates). Other shapes include the octahedron (the dual shape to the cube; Figure 9.3c, color plates) and the rhombic dodecahedron (a shape with 12 faces, each of which is a rhombus; Figure 9.3d, color plates).

How can we organize this collection? One interesting way is to observe the values of $a$, $b$, and $c$ that cause the seed triangle to be coplanar with its three neighbors. Referring to Figure 9.4 (color plates), the three neighbors are colored red, green, and blue. What restrictions on the values of $a$, $b$, and $c$ does coplanarity imply? The three points $(a, a, a)$, $(b, 0, 0)$, and $(c, 0, c)$ of the yellow triangle lie in the plane whose column vector is

$$\begin{bmatrix} ac \\ bc - ab \\ ab - ac \\ -abc \end{bmatrix}$$

The three conditions of coplanarity translate into

1. Red triangle is coplanar with yellow triangle. The point $(a, -a, a)$ lies on the plane. Dotting it with the plane vector and setting the result to 0 ultimately shows that $a = c$.
2. Blue triangle is coplanar with yellow. The point $(0, 0, b)$ lies on the plane, which implies $2c = b$.
3. Green triangle is coplanar with yellow. The point $(c, c, 0)$ is on the plane, which implies that $ac + bc = 2ab$.

We can visualize these conditions as curves in the "shape space" with axes $a$, $b$, and $c$. Since any scalar multiple of $a$, $b$, and $c$ generates the same shape (just larger or smaller), these numbers form a sort of homogeneous coordinate system. We will simplify the situation by fixing $c$ at the value 1. The three conditions translate into three lines in the $ab$ plane (see Figure 9.5). The lines are

1. $a = 1$
2. $b = 2$
3. $b = \dfrac{a}{2a - 1}$

Where lines 1 and 2 meet, you get the cube. Where lines 2 and 3 meet, you get the octahedron. Where lines 3 and 1 meet, you get the rhombic dodecahedron. This information is tabulated in Table 9.1.

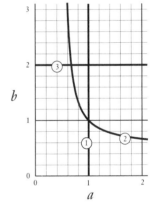

**Figure 9.5** *Parameter space for cube symmetry*

**Table 9.1** *Shape-space coordinates for the cube family*

| Conditions | $a$ | $b$ | $c$ | Shape |
|---|---|---|---|---|
| 1, 3 | 1 | 1 | 1 | Cube |
| 2, 3 | $\frac{2}{3}$ | 2 | 1 | Octahedron |
| 1, 2 | 1 | 2 | 1 | Rhombic dodecahedron |

Let's play with this a bit. If you slowly interpolate $a$ and $b$ from their cube values to their octahedron values, keeping condition 3 satisfied, you get a transformation of the cube shape to the octahedron shape that looks particularly interesting. Since the green triangle stays coplanar with the yellow one, each face of the cube breaks up into four quadrilaterals. The center point of each face bulges out while the vertices flatten in, always keeping the midpoints of the edges of the cube unchanged. This sequence appears in Figure 9.6 (color plates). An equivalent series can transform the octahedron to the rhombic dodecahedron and the rhombic dodecahedron to the cube.

# Kaleidoscope

Now let's go really wild! We can replace the seed triangle with any shape whatever, and all the replications will generate a result that also shares the symmetry of the cube. In Figure 9.7 (color plates) I have tried a few variations on this theme. Figure 9.7a is just the cube recolored with normal triangles blue and mirrored triangles yellow. In Figure 9.7b I stuck in the bizarre values of $(a, b, c) = (-1.15, 2, 1.41)$. Figure 9.7c relaxes the restrictions of triangle edges matching. Figure 9.7d replaces the triangle with a sort of blunted pyramid shape. Much more fun could be had using teapots, but you get the idea.

Furthermore, by making the seed shape rotate and move about in some random way, you can animate a changing shape that generates the three-dimensional kaleidoscope patterns of the chapter title. I have seen several interesting test animations done this way, but the names of the perpetrators escape me.

# The Tetrahedron

I will briefly go through this rigamarole for another simple shape, the tetrahedron. A tetrahedron is exactly half as symmetrical as a cube. This is because only half of the 48 cube transformations will leave the tetrahedron intact (and in its original orientation). For the tetrahedron shown in Figure 9.8a (color plates), they are

- The identity
- Rotations of 180 degrees about $x$, $y$, or $z$ (three total)
- Rotations of $\pm 120$ degrees about the diagonals of an enclosing cube (eight total)
- Reflections about the $x = \pm y$, $x = \pm z$, and $y = \pm z$ planes (six total)

# Color Plates

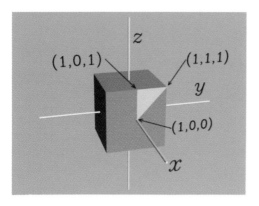

**Figure 9.1.** *Seed triangle for a cube*

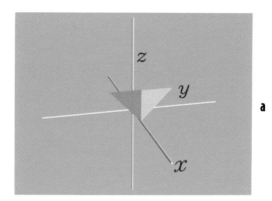

a

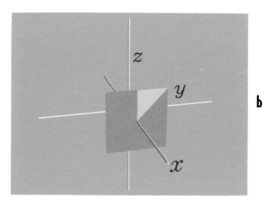

b

**Figure 9.2.** *Generating a cube face: a, seed triangle reflected; b, seed triangle reflected and rotated four times*

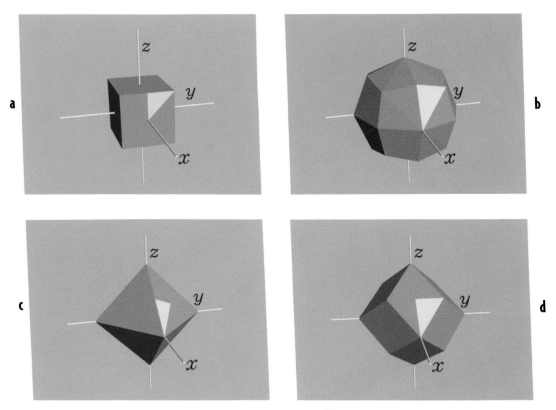

**Figure 9.3.** *Varying a, b, and c: a, $a = b = c = 1$ (cube); b, $a = \sqrt{2}$, $b = \sqrt{6}$, $c = \sqrt{3}$ (vertices on sphere); c, $a = \frac{2}{3}$, $b = 2$, $c = 1$ (octahedron); d, $a = 1$, $b = 2$, $c = 1$ (rhombic dodecahedron)*

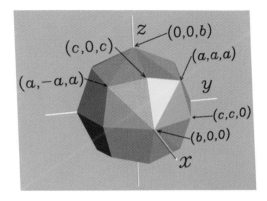

**Figure 9.4.** *Neighbors of the seed triangle*

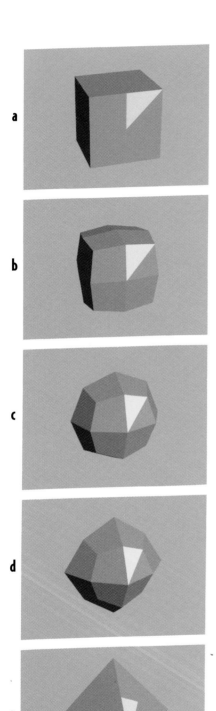

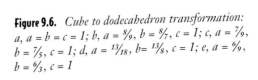

**Figure 9.6.** *Cube to dodecahedron transformation:*
*a, a = b = c = 1; b, a = ⁸⁄₉, b = ⁸⁄₇, c = 1; c, a = ⁷⁄₉,*
*b = ⁷⁄₅, c = 1; d, a = ¹³⁄₁₈, b= ¹³⁄₈, c = 1; e, a = ⁶⁄₉,*
*b = ⁶⁄₃, c = 1*

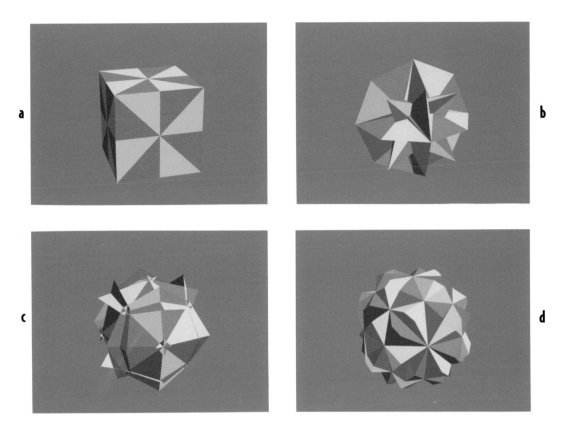

**Figure 9.7.** *Wilder variations: a, a = b = c = 1; b, a = −1.15, b = 2, c = 1.41; c, seed triangles don't match edges; d, seed shape is arbitrary polygon*

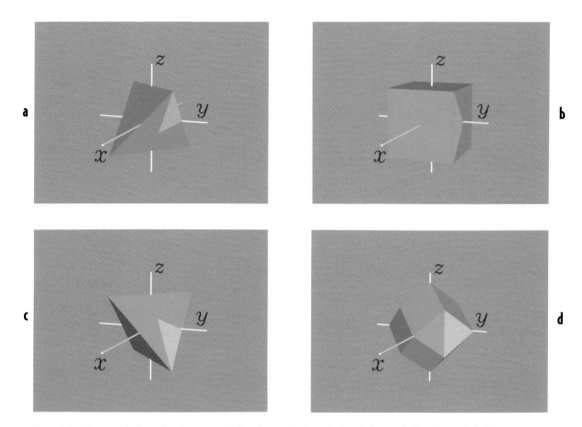

**Figure 9.8** *The tetrahedron family: a, a = 1, b = 1, c = ⅓ (tetrahedron); b, a = 1, b = 1, c = 1 (cube); c, a = ⅓, b = 1, c = 1 (tetrahedron); d, a = ½, b = 1, c = ½ (rhombic dodecahedron)*

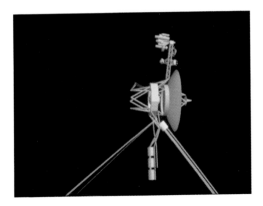

**Figure 11.1** *Voyager spacecraft*

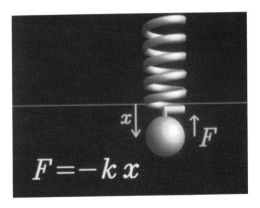

**Figure 11.8** *Helical spring*

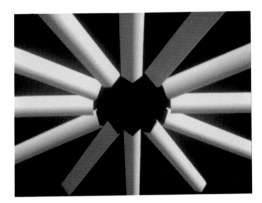

**Figure 11.6** *Test pattern of tubes*

**Figure 11.7** *Close-up of the Voyager spacecraft*

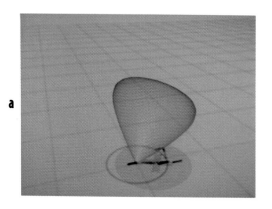

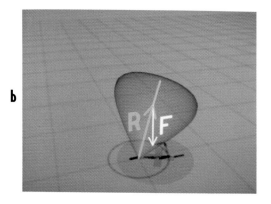

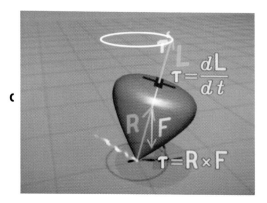

**Figure 19.5** *a, Back half of top; b, lines and text inside top; c, front half of top*

- Reflections through the $x$, $y$, and $z$ axes followed by rotations by $\pm 90$ degrees about that axis (six total)

We can synthesize the tetrahedron and its symmetric relatives by starting with a seed triangle whose vertices are

```
Point 1:   (a, a, a)
Point 2:   (0, b, 0)
Point 3:   (c, c,-c)
```

Combine this with its mirror image formed by reflecting across the $x = y$ plane. This generates one third of the equilateral triangle for one face.

```
DEF THIRD
DRAW SEED
PUSH
ORIE 0,1,0, 1,0,0, 0,0,1
DRAW SEED
POP
----
```

Generate the rest of the face by copies rotated 120 degrees about the center of the face, $(\frac{1}{3}, \frac{1}{3}, -\frac{1}{3})$. The matrix to do this is surprisingly simple:

$$\begin{bmatrix} 0 & 1 & 0 \\ 0 & 0 & -1 \\ -1 & 0 & 0 \end{bmatrix}$$

In transformation language:

```
DEF TFACE
PUSH
DRAW THIRD
ORIE 0,0,-1, 1,0,0, 0,-1,0
DRAW THIRD
ORIE 0,0,-1, 1,0,0, 0,-1,0
DRAW THIRD
POP
----
```

Finally copy this face four times to get the whole tetrahedron.

```
DEF TETRAHED
DRAW TFACE
DRAW TFACE, ROT, 180,1
DRAW TFACE, ROT, 180,2
```

```
DRAW TFACE, ROT, 180,3
----
```

Again, by varying $a$, $b$, and $c$, you can get various shapes that share the symmetry of the tetrahedron. A coplanar-neighbor analysis done in a similar manner to the cube case gives three conditions as follows. First fix $b = 1$. The conditions are

1. $a = 1$
2. $c = 1$
3. $c = \dfrac{a}{4a - 1}$

If both conditions 1 and 3 are met, you get the tetrahedron. If both conditions 2 and 3 are met, you get another tetrahedron upside down (the dual of the original one). If both conditions 1 and 2 are met, you get a cube. You can also get a rhombic dodecahedron if $a = c = 1/2$. See Figure 9.8 (color plates). Tabulating these conditions gives us Table 9.2.

Wait a minute . . . I just said that this group was only half as symmetrical as the cube. Now we have a cube coming out of it. What gives? Well, if $a = c$, the seed shape *itself* is now symmetrical (it has mirror symmetry along the $z$ axis). I leave it to you to figure out if we could have done a similar thing with the cube symmetry above.

# Further Ideas

*14 June 2004*

*Good research project*

The examples shown here are just two of the many three-dimensional point symmetry groups. The next logical candidate for exploration is the icosahedron-dodecahedron pair. What other shape does this generate in the same manner that the cube-octahedron pair generated the rhombic dodecahedron? What other non-Platonic shapes typify the other 3D point symmetry groups? If anybody out there generates some pictures of these, I will print them in a future book.

**Table 9.2** *Shape-space coordinates for the tetrahedron family*

| Conditions | $a$ | $b$ | $c$ | Shape |
|---|---|---|---|---|
| 1, 3 | 1 | 1 | $\frac{1}{3}$ | Tetrahedron |
| 2, 3 | $\frac{1}{3}$ | 1 | 1 | Tetrahedron |
| 1, 2 | 1 | 1 | 1 | Cube |
| 3 | $\frac{1}{2}$ | 1 | $\frac{1}{2}$ | Rhombic dodecahedron |

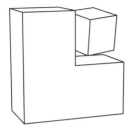

# CHAPTER TEN

# Fractional Invisibility

Isn't it great when you come up with an elegant solution to a particularly nasty problem? Isn't it terrible when you find a case that your elegant solution doesn't handle?

The particular problem I have in mind concerns getting rid of some special cases in a hidden line elimination (HLE) algorithm. I had my nose rubbed in this back in 1980 while animating a scene about human evolution for the *Cosmos* television series. The problem was to interpolate between various critters on the evolutionary chain. Each frame was a two-and-a-half-dimensional line drawing—so the moving arms and legs had to hide those parts of the body they moved in front of. I was able to adapt standard three-dimensional HLE algorithms to the task, but there have always been some annoying special cases in these algorithms. The problems occur when two distinct objects happen to exactly line up in such a manner that a vertex of one projects exactly on an edge of the other, as with the cube in Figure 10.1. Since I did my calculations in integer pixel coordinates, unfortunate coincidences were more likely than usual. To see why this is a problem, we must start with an understanding of how hidden line algorithms work.

## A Hidden Line Algorithm

Hidden line elimination was once one of the great classic problems of computer graphics. It receives less attention nowadays, partly because good solutions have been found and partly because color, shaded images

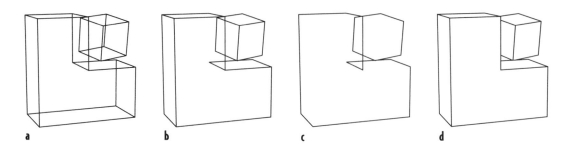

**Figure 10.1**  *a, wireframe; b, front faces; c, boundary edges; d, hidden line*

have captured the public fancy. It's still an important problem, though, because it's useful when using vector displays and because it underlies any correct solution to the aliasing problem for raster images. In addition, I personally see more magic in a moving hidden line image than in a realistic shaded image. You *expect* shaded images to move around; you see it in real life. A hidden line image is obviously artificial, so it's much more unexpected to see it move.

Let's begin, then, with a brief description of a typical hidden line algorithm, a distillation of the good ideas of others[1] with a few refinements of my own. I will omit some of the details for brevity, but you can get this detail by referring to any of the original papers.

First, a disclaimer: the algorithm described here suffers from square law time growth. Methods for changing this to $n\log n$ have been published and can be applied to this algorithm,[2] but the enhanced versions still make use of the same low-level calculations that we are going to talk about here.

### Scene Preprocessing

This algorithm deals only with collections of closed, nonintersecting polyhedra. The database must list the vertices of each polygon in a consistant (e.g., clockwise) direction as seen from the outside of the polyhedron.

1  A. Appel, The notion of quantitative invisibility and the machine rendering of solids, *Proc. ACM National Conference* (New York: ACM, 1967), pages 387–393.

B. G. Baumgart, Geometric modeling for computer vision, Stanford Artificial Intelligence Laboratory Memo AIM-249.

R. Galimberti and U. Montanari, An algorithm for hidden-line elimination, *Comm. ACM* 12(4):206, April 1969.

P. P. Loutrel, A solution to the hidden-line problem for computer-drawn polyhedra, Department of Electrical Engineering, New York University, Technical Report 400-167, September 1967 (available from University Microfilms, Ann Arbor, Mich.).

2  Baumgart, Geometric modeling.

I. E. Sutherland, R. F. Sproull, and R. A. Schumaker, A characterization of ten hidden-surface algorithms, reprinted in *Tutorial: Computer Graphics*, J. Beatty and K. Booth, editors (Los Alamitos, Calif.: IEEE Computer Society Press, 1982).

For a particular frame, transform all vertices by the desired viewing transformation and do the perspective division to project them into screen space. The occlusion problem now becomes a two-dimensional problem of overlap of polygonal areas. The $z$ (depth) coordinate in screen space determines which of two overlapping regions is closer to the viewer.

Apply the standard backface cull to remove all polygons that face away from the viewer. Only edges of the frontfaces remain as candidates for drawing, as shown in Figure 10.1b.

Form an auxiliary list of boundary (or silhouette) edges. These are edges that separate front-facing and back-facing polygons as in Figure 10.1c. An edge of another object can become hidden or be reexposed only by crossing behind one of these boundary edges.

## The Notion of Quantitative Invisibility

To draw the scene, trace along each edge of each front-facing polygon and determine where any nearer polygons overlap it. To do this, we keep track of a cumulative *quantitative invisibility* (*QI*) count—the total number of polygons hiding the test edge at any given point. Wherever this total is 0, the test edge is visible. Now why go to all this work? Isn't it enough to find whether there are *any* polygons hiding a stretch of the edge? Yes, but since the *QI* count goes up or down by 1 only at

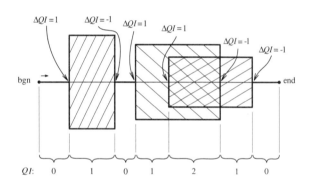

**Figure 10.2**  *Use of quantitative invisibility*

intersections with boundary edges, the total *QI* count is actually easier to calculate. See Figure 10.2.

## Basic Geometric Operations

The meat of the algorithm consists of two basic geometric operations: the *face-vertex compare* and the *edge-edge compare*.

The face-vertex compare comes from the need to initialize the *QI* count of an edge at its beginning vertex. We do this by testing that vertex against all polygonal faces in the scene. If the vertex lies inside the *xy* extent of a polygon *and* if it lies behind the plane of the polygon, add 1 to the initial *QI* count.

We use the edge-edge compare to test an edge for intersections with each of the boundary edges. Upon discovering an intersection, we determine whether it will decrease or increase *QI* by finding whether the test

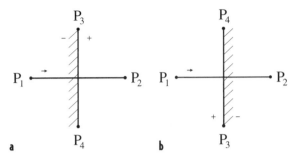

**Figure 10.3**  *Coming and going*

line *comes out* from behind the boundary edge (Figure 10.3a) or whether it *goes behind* the boundary edge (Figure 10.3b).

### Drawing the Visible Segments

If the initial *QI* count from the face-vertex compare is 0, generate a MOVE to the beginning point. Then place all boundary edge intersections in a list and sort them according to their proportional distance along the edge. Examine the intersection list in order and, at each intersection, increment or decrement the *QI* count (and thus the number of polygons hiding the test edge). Whenever *QI* transitions from 1 to 0, generate a MOVE instruction to that point; when it transitions from 0 to 1, generate a DRAW instruction (see again Figure 10.2). If the total ever gets negative, you did something wrong. After the last intersection in the list, we arrive at the final vertex of the test edge. If the total *QI* count is 0, generate a DRAW to the final vertex.

Then proceed to draw another edge. A new initial face-vertex compare may not be necessary. If the new edge begins at the final vertex of the old edge, just use the final *QI* count of the old edge as the initial *QI* count of the new edge. In this way, the algorithm can trace out the entire network of edges in the scene, one at a time, drawing those segments that are visible, but needing only a few initial face-vertex compares.

# Edge–Edge Comparison

Now let's look at the fundamental edge-edge comparison in more detail. We will test the edge from point $P_1$ to point $P_2$ against a boundary edge from point $P_3$ to point $P_4$. Assume the boundary edge is oriented in such a manner that the body of its polygon is on the right when the edge is viewed from $P_3$ to $P_4$. (This is easy to ensure if the original polygons were ordered consistently.) We must see whether segment $P_1...P_2$ intersects (in $x$ and $y$) segment $P_3...P_4$. This will happen if points $P_1$ and $P_2$ fall on opposite sides of the line formed by $P_3...P_4$, and if points $P_3$ and $P_4$ fall on opposite sides of the line formed by $P_1...P_2$. Points are on opposite sides of a line if their dot products with the homogeneous line equation have opposite signs. The homogeneous coordinates for a line in two dimensions are formed from the cross product of the homogeneous coordinates of two points on the line. What all this means is that the test depends on the quantities:

$$D_1 = P_1 \cdot (P_3 \times P_4)$$
$$D_2 = P_2 \cdot (P_3 \times P_4)$$
$$D_3 = P_3 \cdot (P_1 \times P_2)$$
$$D_4 = P_4 \cdot (P_1 \times P_2)$$

The line segments intersect if both $D_1$ and $D_2$ have opposite signs and $D_3$ and $D_4$ have opposite signs. Of course if $D_1$ and $D_2$ have the same sign, we don't even need to bother calculating $D_3$ or $D_4$.

A bit of algebraic shenanigans can boil these calculations down to

$$D_1 = (x_4 - x_3)(y_1 - y_3) - (x_1 - x_3)(y_4 - y_3)$$
$$D_2 = (x_4 - x_3)(y_2 - y_3) - (x_2 - x_3)(y_4 - y_3)$$
$$D_3 = (x_1 - x_3)(y_2 - y_3) - (x_2 - x_3)(y_1 - y_3)$$
$$D_4 = D_1 - D_2 + D_3$$

If the lines intersect, we must find $\alpha$, the proportional distance of the intersection from point $P_1$ (where $\alpha = 0$) to point $P_2$ (where $\alpha = 1$). $\alpha$ will be the sort key for the intersection list and will also be used to interpolate $x$ and $y$. Computation of $\alpha$ is very similar to that for clipping described in section 2 of my paper with Martin Newell.[3] The punchline is

$$\alpha = \frac{D_1}{D_1 - D_2}$$

Then we must find out whether the test edge is actually behind the boundary edge at the intersection or whether it's in front of the boundary edge and the whole thing was a false alarm. Do this by comparing the $z$ (depth) coordinates of the two edges at the intersection. The $z$ values come from linear interpolation between the two endpoints (this is something that appears obvious but is actually a slightly subtle property of the homogeneous perspective transformation). Calculate

$$z_i = z_1 + \alpha(z_2 - z_1)$$
$$z_j = z_3 + \beta(z_4 - z_3)$$

where

$$\beta = \frac{D_3}{D_3 - D_4}$$

3  J. F. Blinn and M. E. Newell, Clipping using homogeneous coordinates, *SIGGRAPH '78 Conference Proceedings* (New York: ACM), pages 245–251.

If $z_i < z_j$, then edge $P_1...P_2$ lies in front of boundary edge $P_3...P_4$ and the intersection is not counted.

If the intersection is a keeper, we must determine whether the line $P_1...P_2$ goes behind boundary $P_3...P_4$ ($\Delta QI = 1$) or comes out from behind it ($\Delta QI = -1$). By looking at Figure 10.3 you can see that the side of $P_3...P_4$ that generates a negative dot product is the side that the polygon lies on. Therefore the sign of $D_1$ will equal the sign of $\Delta QI$ due to the edge intersection.

# Face-Vertex Comparison

The face-vertex comparison determines whether a given polygon hides another given vertex point. This will happen if two conditions are met:

1. The vertex is behind the plane of the face. (This can be discovered by testing the point against the plane equation of the face.)
2. The vertex point lies within the polygon formed by projecting the face on the screen.

There are traditionally two ways to make this last test: by calculating the "winding number" of the vertices of the polygon about the point,[4] or by counting the number of intersections between the polygon and a line from the point to infinity. I will use this latter method.

Start at the test point and draw a line to infinity in the $-x$ direction. If this semi-infinite line intersects the boundary of the polygon an odd number of times, then the point is inside the polygon. Otherwise it is outside (see Figure 10.4). To turn this into formulae, define

$$\begin{aligned}
P_\infty &= (-1, 0, 0) && \text{Point at infinity in} - x \\
P &= (x, y, 1) && \text{The test point} \\
P_i &= (x_i, y_i, 1) && \text{The } i\text{th polygon vertex} \\
P_{i+1} &= (x_{i+1}, y_{i+1}, 1) && \text{Next clockwise vertex}
\end{aligned}$$

We must test the segment $P_\infty...P$ against each edge of the polygon, $P_i...P_{i+1}$. This is very similar to the calculation we did for the edge-edge comparison. Calculate

$$\begin{aligned}
D_\infty &= P_\infty \cdot (P_i \times P_{i+1}) \\
D &= P \cdot (P_i \times P_{i+1}) \\
D_i &= P_i \cdot (P_\infty \times P) \\
D_{i+1} &= P_{i+1} \cdot (P_\infty \times P)
\end{aligned}$$

---

4  W. Newman and R. Sproull, *Principles of Interactive Computer Graphics*, 2d ed. (New York: McGraw-Hill, 1979).

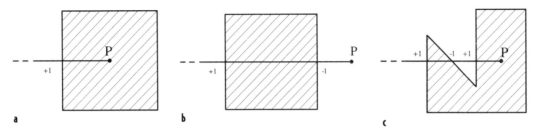

**Figure 10.4** *Face-vertex compare: a, one intersection (QI = 1); b, two intersections (QI = 0); c, three intersections (QI = 1)*

An intersection is counted if both $D_\infty$ and $D$ have opposite signs and $D_i$ and $D_{i+1}$ have opposite signs. More algebraic skulduggery can show

$$D_\infty = y_{i+1} - y_i$$
$$D = (y_{i+1} - y)(x_i - x) - (x_{i+1} - x)(y_i - y)$$
$$D_i = y_i - y$$
$$D_{i+1} = y_{i+1} - y$$

Since $D_i$ and $D_{i+1}$ are so simple, it's best to calculate them first. If they have the same sign, we don't need to bother calculating $D_\infty$ and $D$.

We don't actually need to count intersections and then test the count for evenness. It's simpler just to invert an "inside" flag whenever we discover an intersection. An even number of inversions, for example, results in a clear flag at the end.

# The Nasty Problem

The above algorithms work just dandy for most cases, but they screw up when faced with certain geometric accidents. Suppose the test edge passes exactly through a vertex joining two boundary edges, as in Figure 10.5a. The intersection test with either of the boundary edges becomes a little nebulous since the $D$ value for point $P_b$ is 0. If both are considered as intersections, the invisibility count goes up by 2; if neither are counted, the count goes up by 0. The actual count should go up by 1. (Anyone who thinks that this is too unlikely to worry about has never done any animation.)

Now look at Figure 10.5b. Here the same situation occurs, but the

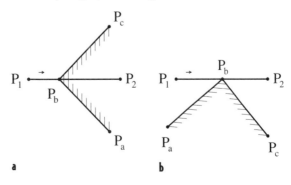

**Figure 10.5** *No picnic*

invisibility count should remain unchanged. These sorts of problems are mentioned in Loutrel's paper where he writes: "They all had to be solved in the program and that was no picnic."[5] It would seem that a correct determination of the change in $QI$ depends upon examination of the global environment in which the degeneracy occurs. No picnic.

# The Notion of Fractional Invisibility

Picnics can be restored by the following trick. We carefully assign a *fractional invisibility increment* to the situations designated above. If an edge passes exactly through one of the endpoints of another edge (signaled by one of the $D$ values being 0), we give it an invisibility change of $\frac{1}{2}$. We arrange the sign of the fractional invisibility change so that situations such as that shown in Figure 10.5a both have a value $+\frac{1}{2}$ (adding up to 1) and situations such as that shown in Figure 10.5b have $+\frac{1}{2}$ and $-\frac{1}{2}$ (adding up to 0). The trick is to make these calculations independently for each boundary edge without needing any information about the direction of any neighboring edges.

### Edge-Edge Solution

As a warm-up exercise, look at some edge-edge possibilities in Figure 10.6. To get the desired $\Delta QI$, first extract the signs of $D_3$ and $D_4$ into $J_3$ and $J_4$:

```
if (D_i < 0) then J_i = -1
if (D_i = 0) then J_i = 0
if (D_i > 0) then J_i = +1
```

The fractional invisibility is then just

$$\Delta QI = \frac{J_4 - J_3}{2}$$

So what happens in the reverse situation, where $P_1$ or $P_2$ lies exactly on the edge $P_3...P_4$? In fact there are 81 different combinations of values of

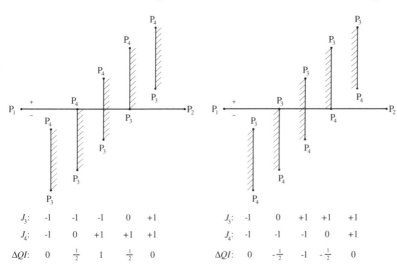

| $J_3$: | -1 | -1 | -1 | 0 | +1 |
| $J_4$: | -1 | 0 | +1 | +1 | +1 |
| $\Delta QI$: | 0 | $\frac{1}{2}$ | 1 | $\frac{1}{2}$ | 0 |

| $J_3$: | -1 | 0 | +1 | +1 | +1 |
| $J_4$: | -1 | -1 | -1 | 0 | +1 |
| $\Delta QI$: | 0 | $-\frac{1}{2}$ | -1 | $-\frac{1}{2}$ | 0 |

**Figure 10.6** *Fractional invisibility*

$J_1$, $J_2$, $J_3$, and $J_4$, but only about 41 of them are possible due to the fact that $D_1 + D_3 = D_2 + D_4$. I have made an exhaustive study of these possibilites but will spare you the details. The easiest general way I've found to calculate the desired $\Delta QI$ is

$$\texttt{if } (J_1 - J_2 > 0)$$
$$\texttt{then } \Delta QI = \frac{J_1 - J_2}{2}\frac{J_4 - J_3}{2}$$
$$\texttt{else } \Delta QI = -\frac{J_1 - J_2}{2}\frac{J_4 - J_3}{2}$$

The `if` statement could just as well test $J_4 - J_3$, as it happens that this has the same sign as $J_1 - J_2$ (unless one of them is 0).

By the way, it's not really necessary to use floating-point arithmetic for invisibility counts. Since $\frac{1}{4}$ is the smallest fraction that can occur, the $QI$ counts can be scaled everywhere by 4 and still remain integers. I did this in the actual implementation, but I'll continue to speak of fractional values here.

Figures 10.7 and 10.8 show two examples of fractional invisibility correctly solving some problems. Notice that in Figure 10.8, the $QI$ of the test edge can remain at a fractional value of $\frac{1}{2}$ if it runs exactly along a boundary edge for awhile. When it links to another edge not coincident with the boundary, the $QI$ increments/decrements back to an integral value. Neat.

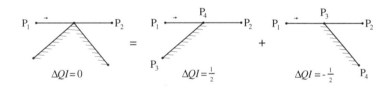

**Figure 10.7** *It works*

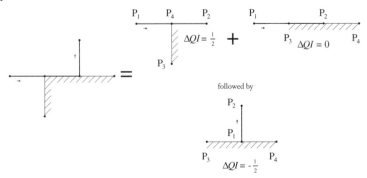

**Figure 10.8** *It still works*

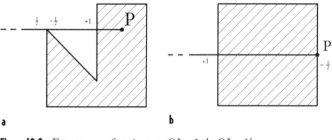

**Figure 10.9**   *Face-vertex fractions: a, QI = 1; b, QI = ½*

## Face-Vertex Solution

Problems with the face-vertex compare fall into two categories: In Figure 10.9a the line to infinity happens to pass through a vertex of the overlying polygon—this is just an accident of the orientation of the polygon. In Figure 10.9b, the point itself lies exactly on an edge of the polygon—its *QI* should be ½.

To solve these problems with fractional invisibility, we get rid of the "visible" flag and instead use a *QI* count—the sum of the $\Delta QI$ values (fractional or otherwise) from each edge intersection. After going through all edges of the polygon we will get a total *QI* of 0 (point outside polygon), +1 (point inside polygon), or ½ (point on edge of polygon); see again Figure 10.9. This last case will interface properly with subsequent edge-edge comparisons to generate the correct counts for any test edge starting from the test vertex.

Why are we so sure we can only get a positive count? Because a negative count would come from a backface that should have been culled from the database. In addition, a count of 2 or above can happen for certain self-intersecting polygons, which we should disallow. This summing of $\Delta QI$ values may have uses in detecting some of these cases.

# A Fly in the Ointment

Now what about the situations where we get ¼ for a $\Delta QI$? This occurs if either $P_1$ or $P_2$ happens to coincide with either $P_3$ or $P_4$. I originally thought that just adding up the ¼s would work just like it did for the ½s. Sad to say, it just isn't so. Why?

## Edge-Edge Problems

Look at the boundary edge pair in Figure 10.10, with a common vertex $P_b$. Any test edge that comes in and terminates with $P_2 = P_b$ should have its *QI* count incremented by ½ if $P_1$ is in the unshaded region, $-½$ if $P_1$ is in the shaded region (i.e., it's on its way out from under the boundary), or 0 if $P_1$ is exactly on one of the boundary edges. Now look at the pairs of $\Delta QI$ values (one due to each of the boundary edges) that label the four regions in the diagram. Just adding the two $\Delta QI$ values won't work; instead, we have to use the modified addition shown in Table 10.1. But this only works for

**Table 10.1** $\Delta QI$ *summation table for convex corner*

| $\Delta QI_b$ | $\Delta QI_a$ | | |
|---|---|---|---|
| | $-\frac{1}{4}$ | $0$ | $+\frac{1}{4}$ |
| $-\frac{1}{4}$ | $-\frac{1}{2}$ | $0$ | $\frac{1}{2}$ |
| $0$ | $0$ | $0$ | $\frac{1}{2}$ |
| $+\frac{1}{4}$ | $\frac{1}{2}$ | $\frac{1}{2}$ | $\frac{1}{2}$ |

**Table 10.2** $\Delta QI$ *summation table for concave corner*

| $\Delta QI_b$ | $\Delta QI_a$ | | |
|---|---|---|---|
| | $-\frac{1}{4}$ | $0$ | $+\frac{1}{4}$ |
| $-\frac{1}{4}$ | $-\frac{1}{2}$ | $-\frac{1}{2}$ | $-\frac{1}{2}$ |
| $0$ | $-\frac{1}{2}$ | $0$ | $0$ |
| $+\frac{1}{4}$ | $-\frac{1}{2}$ | $0$ | $\frac{1}{2}$ |

"convex" boundary corners. If the corner is "concave," as in Figure 10.11, the modified addition must be as shown in Table 10.2.

We can distinguish these two cases by examining the sign of $P_c \cdot (P_a \times P_b)$. Positive means concave ($P_c$ is on the outside of edge $P_a \ldots P_b$); negative means convex. Zero means that $P_a$, $P_b$, and $P_c$ are colinear and either case can be used. A symmetrical situation happens for the double degeneracy where $P_l$ coincides with the common vertex of the boundary edges.

This is all doable, but it's not nearly as elegant. Before, we only needed an undifferentiated list of boundary edges. Now, we need to detect double degeneracies (they always travel in pairs) and retain enough information to do the convexity test and funny addition. Oh, well.

## Face-Vertex Problems

There still remains the problem of double degeneracies in the face-vertex compare. This happens when the test point coincides exactly with one of the polygons' vertex points. Using funny addition as above will properly give the test point a value of $\frac{1}{2}$. Unfortunately this is not necessarily what we want. Suppose the test point is behind a mesh of polygons and happens to coincide with one of the interior vertices, like point P in Figure 10.12. Here, a contribution of

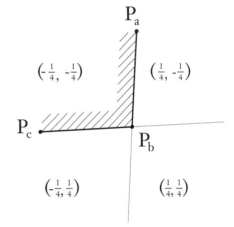

**Figure 10.10** *Convex corner*

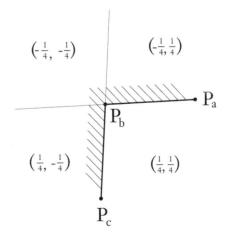

**Figure 10.11** *Concave corner*

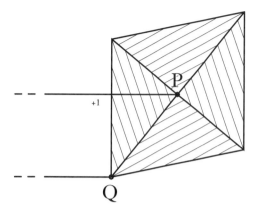

**Figure 10.12** *Face-vertex problems*

½ from each polygon and +1 from the left edge gives the totally wrong initial value of 3. Yuck. Ironically, just using normal addition here would give the correct answer—all the ¼s will cancel out, leaving just the +1 from the left-hand edge. But that won't work for point Q, which coincides with the lower-left vertex. Double yuck. Probably the only way to get around this is to form some sort of pseudo-polygon out of just the boundary edges of the mesh. Grumble.

# What Works and What Doesn't

Our elegant fix works *almost* all the time. (In fact, it worked well enough to get the evolution scene done.) While the original comparison tests work only if there are no geometric accidents, the fractional invisibility idea extends this to work if a point accidentally lies exactly on an unrelated edge. In the even more unlikely case of a point accidentally coinciding with another point, a more complex fix-up can handle edge-edge compares, but face-vertex compares are still a problem. But really, how often is this going to happen? Ha, ha.

There is also an important lesson here. The special cases all occur when some geometric test value is 0. This suggests the general principle that, when the sign of a quantity is being used to make a geometric test, it is unwise to treat 0 as just another positive number.

# CHAPTER ELEVEN

# Optimal Tubes

During the month of August, 1989, the Voyager spacecraft made its final planetary visit to the planet Neptune (see Figure 11.1 in the color plates). Over the years I've made a lot of pictures of this device, but when I first saw it I thought, Oh no, the spacecraft is all booms and struts. They're the most difficult things to render since they're long and skinny and will alias a lot. And they're going to be a pain to model.

I'll just briefly mention my antialiasing trick here. Most of the booms are pretty small, about ¼ inch in diameter. What I did was simply to increase their radius to 1 inch. This is sort of justified by the following idea: if a shape has high frequencies, one way to reduce aliasing is to reduce the high frequencies in the model. Sleazy, but it helps a lot.

But what I really want to talk about is optimal tubes. Sounds like a rock group, doesn't it? In fact, it's a little trick I devised to considerably cut down on the number of polygons required to model and render the Voyager spacecraft. It's an exercise in how much you can get away with and still make the pictures look more or less OK. The trick requires the solution of a simple geometric problem: find the tangent lines from a point to a circle. Now I don't feel I really understand a problem unless I can solve it several different ways. There are two ways to go about the problem, one using common garden-variety analytical geometry and the other using high-tech homogeneous coordinates. I'll do it the simple way first, but the homogeneous way gives us some useful generality so I'll do that too.

A word about typography: scalars are written in italics, homogeneous coordinates in lowercase italics, ordinary coordinates in uppercase italics. Point and line vector names are in roman type. Matrices are in boldface.

# Modeling

**B**ooms, struts, and tubes are just long skinny cylinders. Most any modeling system can place a cylinder at an arbitrary position with an arbitrary scale factor and orientation. It's just a nuisance.

The most convenient way to describe a tube is by just giving its endpoints and its radius. Tubes are built into my polygon description program as a sort of medium-level primitive. You give it a command to set the RADius of all subsequent tubes and then a list of MOVE and DRAW commands.

```
RAD  R
MOVE  X₁,  Y₁,  Z₁
DRAW  X₂,  Y₂,  Z₂
.
.
.
```

Each DRAW command generates a tube from the previous point to the current point. It's just like a line drawing with real solid lines.

# Positioning the Tube

**T**he program reads the commands and internally generates calls to position a canonical unit radius cylinder to form the tubes along each "line." This standard cylinder has its axis along $Z$, stretching from $Z = 0$ to $Z = 1$. We want to construct a transformation matrix that will turn this into a tube stretching from $[X_1, Y_1, Z_1]$ to $[X_2, Y_2, Z_2]$. First get the length of the line in the obvious way:

$$D = \sqrt{(X_1 - X_2)^2 + (Y_1 - Y_2)^2 + (Z_1 - Z_2)^2}$$

Scale the cylinder in $XY$ by the desired radius $R$ and in $Z$ by the length $D$. Rotate the cylinder to orient it along the line and then translate it to the point $[X_1, Y_1, Z_1]$. The following transformation calls, using the transformation notation described in Chapter 3, will do the trick:

```
PUSH
TRAN  X₁,  Y₁,  Z₁
ORIE  matrix M (see below)
SCAL  R,  R,  D
DRAW CYLINDER
POP
```

The translation and scaling part are pretty easy; it's the rotation part, **M**, that will take a bit of work. Start by finding the unit vector along the axis of the cylinder.

$$\left[X_a, Y_a, Z_a\right] = \left[\frac{X_2 - X_1}{D}, \frac{Y_2 - Y_1}{D}, \frac{Z_2 - Z_1}{D}\right]$$

We want something that rotates the axis of the standard cylinder, [0, 0, 1], to coincide with this axis. (It's sort of the inverse of a "look at" transformation.) We can do this two ways: by figuring out angles and axes to rotate them around, or by calculating the matrix elements directly. The latter is more edifying and points out some properties of rotation matrices that are convenient to know.

We want the matrix to do the following:

$$\left[0, 0, 1\right] \mathbf{M} = \left[X_a, Y_a, Z_a\right]$$

This gives the bottom row of **M** immediately. Now what about the other rows? Since we're drawing a cylinder, we don't really care about some random rotation about the cylinder, $Z$, axis. We only want the matrix **M** to be a pure rotation. A useful fact about rotation matrices is that each row can be thought of as a unit length vector, and that each of these vectors is perpendicular to the others. Now how can we come up with a vector that is perpendicular to $[X_a, Y_a, Z_a]$? Any ideas? Its dot product with $[X_a, Y_a, Z_a]$ must be 0. How about

$$\left[\frac{-Y_a}{d}, \frac{X_a}{d}, 0\right]$$

where

$$d = \sqrt{X_a^2 + Y_a^2}$$

Try it; it works.

Now how about the remaining row? It has to be perpendicular to the other two and have unit length. You can get it from the cross product of the other two:

$$\left[X_a, Y_a, Z_a\right] \times \left[\frac{-Y_a}{d}, \frac{X_a}{d}, 0\right] = \left[\frac{-X_a Z_a}{d}, \frac{-Y_a Z_a}{d}, \frac{X_a^2 + Y_a^2}{d}\right]$$

So, after a smidgen of simplification, the rotation matrix we want is

$$\mathbf{M} = \begin{bmatrix} -Y_a/d & X_a/d & 0 \\ -X_a Z_a/d & -Y_a Z_a/d & d \\ X_a & Y_a & Z_a \end{bmatrix}$$

We do have to watch out for $d = 0$. If this happens, it means that the tube axis already points along $Z$ (but it may point in the negative direction). In this case use the $X$ axis, $[1, 0, 0]$, for the first row of $\mathbf{M}$. Then the cross product of the third and first rows will still give a correct result for the second row.

# Polygonizing the Cylinder

Once the transformation is set up as above, the DRAW CYLINDER command just feeds our unit cylinder down the ol' graphics pipeline. For polygon-based systems, your first impulse might be to hack the cylinder up into, say, six or eight polygonal facets. With Gouraud shading this can look fairly respectable, but the silhouette edges and shading boundaries are only approximations. To get a better approximation we need more polygons.

The problem was, I was doing this on a PDP-11, and there was only room for about 1000 polygons total. So I tried to economize as much as possible by substituting intelligence for testosterone. Given the eyepoint and lighting direction, I carefully arranged to divide the cylinder into polygons at only "visually significant" places. I wound up only needing either two or three polygons for each tube and got better results than if I had used many more statically defined polygons.

Now visually significant places are of two kinds: the silhouette edges of the cylinder and breakpoints in the intensity of the cylinder.

### Silhouette Edges

The most important visually significant points are the silhouette edges of the tubes. These are the points where a line from the eye is tangent to the tube. They determine the visual extent of the tube on the screen. How do we calculate them?

The neat thing about this, the thing that really excited me, was the realization that if you do everything in the coordinate system of the unit cylinder, it all becomes a 2D problem. Why? Well, imagine an *infinite* cylinder centered on the $Z$ axis and being viewed from the point $[X_E, Y_E, Z_E]$. The planes through the eyepoint and tangent to the cylinder are parallel to the $Z$ axis. The intersection of these planes is the line through the eyepoint and parallel to the $Z$ axis. The $Z$ coordinate of the eye doesn't matter. Now, wonder of wonders, if the cylinder is back to its canonical extent of $0 < Z < 1$, the tangent planes don't change, even if $Z_E$ is way above or below the cylinder.

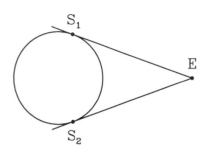

**Figure 11.2**  *Silhouette points of a circle*

So the technique is as follows. First transform the eyepoint by the inverse of the current viewing/modeling transformation into the coordinate system of the unit cylinder, yielding $[X_E, Y_E, Z_E]$. Throw away $Z_E$. Then find the 2D points of tangency from the point $E = [X_E, Y_E]$ to the unit circle at the origin; see Figure 11.2. (Later we will make polygon edges from these points, stretching from $Z = 0$ to $Z = 1$.) Let's start with a real simple special case. Suppose the eyepoint is on the $X$ axis a distance $E$ to the right, see Figure 11.3. By similar triangles, the dimensions of the small triangle (and thus the coordinate of the tangent points) are

$$\left[ \frac{1}{E}, \frac{\pm\sqrt{E^2-1}}{E} \right]$$

To get the silhouette points of a more arbitrary point $[X_E, Y_E]$, you just rotate. $E$ is still the distance from the eyepoint to the origin:

$$E = \sqrt{X_E^2 + Y_E^2}$$

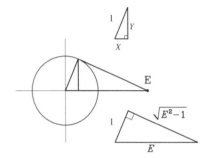

**Figure 11.3**  *Simple silhouette coordinates*

The sine and cosine of the rotation angle are $Y_E/E$ and $X_E/E$, respectively. Build a rotation matrix out of these and multiply by the simple silhouette points to get the general silhouette points.

$$\left[ \frac{1}{E}, \frac{\pm\sqrt{E^2-1}}{E} \right] \begin{bmatrix} X_E/E & Y_E/E \\ -Y_E/E & X_E/E \end{bmatrix} =$$

$$\left[ \frac{X_E \mp Y_E\sqrt{E^2-1}}{E^2}, \frac{Y_E \pm X_E\sqrt{E^2-1}}{E^2} \right] = [X_S, Y_S]$$

What happens if the eye is inside the tube? You wind up taking the square root of a negative number. Very painful.

Here's an outline of another solution. Parameterize points on the circle by $[\cos\theta, \sin\theta]$. The normal vector at a point on the circle has the same coordinates as the point itself. The silhouette points are where the normal vector is perpendicular to the line to the eyepoint; their dot product is 0.

$$[X_E - \cos\theta, Y_E - \sin\theta] \cdot [\cos\theta, \sin\theta] = 0$$

Solve this for $\cos\theta$ and $\sin\theta$. You get the same answer as above.

## Intensity Breakpoints

Now that we have the silhouette edges figured out, let's try to find where the shading might change and put edges there. You can define lots of such points, but I've done just fine with the following two types: the *terminator* (the boundary between the day side and night side) and the *maximum brightness point.*

For pure Lambert's law shading, this latter point is where the dot product of the surface normal vector and the light source direction is a maximum. If we transform the light source, L, into unit cylinder coordinates, getting $[X_L, Y_L, Z_L]$, the location of the maximum dot product is the point lying just under the light source.

$$B = \left[ \frac{X_L}{\sqrt{X_L^2 + Y_L^2}}, \frac{Y_L}{\sqrt{X_L^2 + Y_L^2}} \right]$$

We can find the terminator points by plugging $[X_L, Y_L]$ into the same formula we used to get silhouette points. But there are some additional considerations that make this formula not general enough. First, you get two terminator points from this calculation, but you only need to keep the ones that are on the visible side of the cylinder. So we will need an easy way to find whether a point is on the visible side. Also, the light source might very well be modeled as being at infinity (a common practice). So when we transform it into unit cylinder space we really get $[x_L, y_L, z_L, w_L]$ with $w_L = 0$. We need a homogeneous formula.

## The Homogeneous Way

First some review. A 2D homogeneous point is represented by a three-element row vector:

$$[x, y, w]$$

A 2D homogeneous line is a three-element column vector:

$$\begin{bmatrix} a \\ b \\ c \end{bmatrix}$$

A second-order curve (those points that satisfy the second-order equation $f(x, y, w) = 0$) can be written as a $3 \times 3$ symmetric matrix so that, for points on the curve,

$$f(x, y, w) = \begin{bmatrix} x, & y, & w \end{bmatrix} \mathbf{Q} \begin{bmatrix} x \\ y \\ w \end{bmatrix} = 0$$

A point on the curve has one tangent line at that point. The gradient of $f$ gives the coordinates of that line. From the above equation you can express the gradient as the matrix product

$$2 \begin{bmatrix} \dfrac{\partial f}{\partial x} \\[2mm] \dfrac{\partial f}{\partial y} \\[2mm] \dfrac{\partial f}{\partial w} \end{bmatrix} = \mathbf{Q} \begin{bmatrix} x \\ y \\ w \end{bmatrix} = \begin{bmatrix} a \\ b \\ c \end{bmatrix}$$

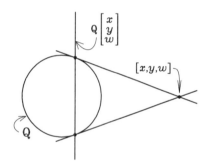

If you do this with a point *not* on the curve, you get another line called the *polar line* to the curve from the given point. This just happens to be the line connecting the two points of tangency. See Figure 11.4.

Now in our case, we have a particularly simple curve—the unit circle at the origin. Its matrix is

$$\mathbf{Q} = \begin{bmatrix} 1 & 0 & 0 \\ 0 & 1 & 0 \\ 0 & 0 & -1 \end{bmatrix}$$

**Figure 11.4**  *The polar line*

The polar line from the point $[x, y, w]$ is also particularly simple:

$$\mathbf{Q} \begin{bmatrix} x \\ y \\ w \end{bmatrix} = \begin{bmatrix} x \\ y \\ -w \end{bmatrix}$$

To get the two tangent points we just intersect the polar line with the unit circle. The easiest way to do this is to express the polar line parametrically in terms of two points on it. This will be

$$P(\alpha) = \begin{bmatrix} xw, & yw, & x^2 + y^2 \end{bmatrix} + \alpha \begin{bmatrix} -y, & x, & 0 \end{bmatrix}$$

How did I come up with these two points? You can see that they both lie on the polar line by direct substitution. Well, the first one is the point on the polar line that is closest to the origin. It will be midway between the tangent points. The second is the intersection of the line with the line at infinity. Anyway, plug this into P **Q** Pᵗ = 0 and solve for α. You get

$$\alpha = \sqrt{x^2 + y^2 - w^2}$$

If the stuff under the square root is negative, it means the point is inside the circle and you should bail out. Otherwise:

$$x_{tang} = xw \mp y\sqrt{x^2 + y^2 - w^2}$$
$$y_{tang} = yw \pm x\sqrt{x^2 + y^2 - w^2}$$
$$w_{tang} = x^2 + y^2$$

(You can also get this formula directly from the nonhomogeneous derivation by plugging in $X_E = x/w$ and $Y_E = y/w$ and fiddling a bit.) I implemented the formula as a subroutine that I call with point $[x_E, y_E, w_E]$ to get the silhouette points and with point $[x_L, y_L, w_L]$ to get the terminator points.

The polar line has another useful function. It gives us our simple way of separating the visible (eyepoint-facing) part of the tube from the nonvisible (back-facing) part. The polar line from the eyepoint will be

$$\mathbf{Q}\,E^t = \begin{bmatrix} x_E \\ y_E \\ -w_E \end{bmatrix} = V$$

Remember, the sign of the dot product of any point with a line will tell what side of the line the point is on (there are some subtleties here that won't bother us). So which sign means which? Try a test point. The dot product of the polar line with the eyepoint itself is

$$E \cdot V = \begin{bmatrix} x_E, & y_E, & w_E \end{bmatrix} \begin{bmatrix} x_E \\ y_E \\ -w_E \end{bmatrix} = x_E^2 + y_E^2 - w_E^2$$

This will be positive if the eyepoint is outside the circle (which it had better be). So, positive means visible.

# Algorithm

The whole thing wraps into an algorithm as follows:

1. Transform the eyepoint into unit cylinder space, getting $[x_E, y_E, w_E]$, and calculate the silhouette points $S_1$ and $S_2$.

2. Transform the light source into unit cylinder space, getting $[x_L, y_L, w_L]$, and calculate the silhouette points $T_1$ and $T_2$.
3. Calculate the sublight point B as above.
4. Output $S_1$.
5. If $(T \cdot V) > 0$, output $T_1$.
6. If $(B \cdot V) > 0$, output B.
7. If $(T_2 \cdot V) > 0$, output $T_2$.
8. Output $S_2$.

The output operation takes a 2D point, $[X, Y]$, on the unit circle and generates a polygon edge from $[X, Y, 0]$ to $[X, Y, 1]$. The normal vector along that edge to use for shading calculations is just $N = [X, Y, 0]$. Join consecutive edges into polygons in a more or less obvious way. You then pass the edge and the normal vector down the graphics pipeline to the screen. And don't forget that when you transform normal vectors, you must use the inverse of the point transformation matrix.

# Results

The results of this for two different light source directions are shown in 2D in Figure 11.5. The thick lines represent generated polygons. One required three polygons and the other only two. Note that usually only one of the terminator points will be on the visible side of the circle.

Figure 11.6 (color plates) shows a test pattern of tubes arranged like spokes in a wheel. The shading looks fine, but the endpoints of the tubes give away the game. Remember, this is all still a crude approximation to real cylinders and won't hold up if you get too near it, but it works just

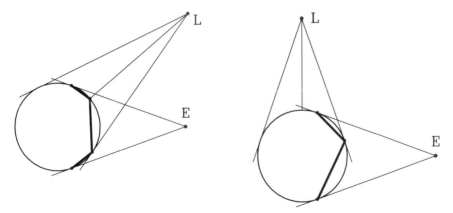

**Figure 11.5** *Generated polygons with two different light source directions*

dandy for reasonable viewing distances. Figure 11.7 (color plates) shows a close-up of some of the Voyager spacecraft made of tubes with the rings of Saturn in the background.

# Extensions

Now let's look at a (literal) extension to this trick. On some occasions I have used optimal tubes to approximate a circular extrusion along some space curve. I just give the space curve as a bunch of short line segments and the tube primitive will spit out cylindrical segments along it. But two consecutive segments will appear to have a crack between them. You can see this a little bit on the white tubes at the left of Figure 11.7 (color plates).

To avoid cracks I extended each tube segment a little bit until they abutted. You specify the amount of extension with another parameter, an extension ratio, $F$. This is the proportion of the radius to add on to each end of the tube. Its implementation just slightly modifies the cylinder transformation scheme

```
PUSH
TRAN  X₁ , Y₁ , Z₁
ORIE  matrix M
TRAN  0,0,-R*F
SCAL  R, R, D + 2*R*F
DRAW CYLINDER
POP
```

The numerical value to use for $F$ is determined experimentally. A more elaborate scheme might calculate it automatically from the surrounding points. An example is the helical spring in Figure 11.8 (color plates).

# Pick the Right Coordinates

When solving geometric problems, picking the right coordinate system helps a lot. In this case it reduced the dimension of the problem. For visibility and lighting threshold problems you can either transform the modeling primitive into eye space or you can transform the eyepoint and light source into the modeling primitives' definition space. I have often found that it's easiest to do the latter. This is because transforming a point (E or L) turns it into just another point, while transforming the primitive might give you a shape whose arithmetic is not so trivial.

# CHAPTER TWELVE

# The Ultimate Design Tool

NOVEMBER 1990

When I first came to Caltech I co-taught the computer graphics course with Ivan Sutherland. Near the beginning of the term he gave a lecture about philosophy of computer graphics. Then I chimed in with some blather about how *I* was going to talk about more concrete things, since younger practitioners were more practical while older ones became more philosophical. I think he was somewhat miffed at being labeled old. Well . . . I'm now as old as he was then. So I'm feeling philosophical.

When I was young and energetic I was primarily a tool builder. I still like to make my own tools, but now it's more of a hobby, sort of like gardening. I'm reminded of the story of the Chinese Mandarin visiting England for the first time. After observing a group of lords and ladies playing tennis, running all over the place and working up a sweat, he turned to his host and said, "In China we would have coolies to do that for us."

Nowadays I am mostly a tool user. I spend most of my time designing and implementing videos for the *Mathematics!* project at Caltech and writing the articles making up this book. And I find myself becoming more interested in getting a particular job done rather than showing off a particular tool. Here, then, are some musings on tool building from a tool user's point of view.

## The Creative Process

First, let's look at the creative process. That, after all, is the activity that tools are supposed to support. I find creation to be a two-phase process:

a progression from chaos to order, from ideation to implementation. In terms of graphics, the phases are deciding what to draw (a right brain activity) and figuring out how to draw it (a left brain activity).

In ideation or brainstorming mode, you are madly generating ideas and connections between ideas and don't want to worry about structure, coherance, or implementation details. In implementation mode, you are actually trying to make these ideas real.

This view of the creative process isn't new with me. An early animator named Shamus Culhane wrote about it in his book *Animation, from Script to Screen*.[1] His most sucessful technique of animation was to draw like crazy for hours at a stretch, making very crude and incomplete sketches. He writes:

> *I never stopped to number drawings; gave only a cursory glance at the exposure sheets; and forgot about spacing charts . . . None of the roughs were completed drawings. Some were just an eyeball; others were finished bodies, except for the head. It was a kind of shorthand . . . I realized that I had one strict rule: I never stopped drawing for any of the usual reasons for interrupting the work, that is, studying the exposure sheets, erasing mistakes, or checking the model sheets . . . The important thing was to keep going on my pell-mell roughing out.*
>
> *In the second stage, there were no impulsive moves; conscious thinking was my main effort. I was now totally involved in interpreting those drawings I had dashed out.*

Another author who writes about the creative process is Roger von Oech. In his book *A Kick in the Seat of the Pants*,[2] he breaks down creative thought into four stages: Explorer, Artist, Judge, and Warrior. The first two of these involve research and idea generation, respectively. I would group them in the ideation stage. The last two involve evaluation and implementation of ideas. I have grouped them into one implementation stage.

## Computer Graphics Tools

What does this have to do with computer graphics? Generally, computerized design tools are optimized for only the implementation part of the process. Sure, sure . . . one of the powers of computer graphics is that you can change things easily. And that's good for fine tuning. But none of the computer tools I have seen are real good for the crazy play-with-ideas part

---

1  New York: St. Martin's Press, 1988.
2  New York: Harper and Row, 1986.

of the process. Why do I say this? The ideation part of the process has to be quick and dirty. And when I'm talking about quick and dirty, I mean real quick and real dirty. Even a completely general sketch and paint program is orders of magnitude too slow, low rez, physically inconvenient, and makes you think too much about structure to be a useful tool for random idea generation.

# The Ultimate Design Tool

There *is* a tool that works perfectly fine for the ideation phase of creation. I know it might be heretical to say this, but the ultimate creative design tool is

*paper and pencil*

What are the advantages of using old-fashioned paper and pencil?

1. They're cheap.
2. They're quiet; there are no cooling fans.
3. They're portable; you can carry them wherever you go.
4. They're lightweight; you can sit with them in your lap or curl up with them on a couch.
5. There are no power requirements, no batteries to go dead, and no extension cords to trip over.
6. You can fit lots of little pictures on one page at high enough resolution to see them but still be able to stand back to get "the big picture."

The combination of paper and pencil works . . . I don't see computer graphics replacing it. *And that's OK.* I'm not being funny here. It's OK not to use a computer for absolutely everything.

Now computer tool builders don't want to hear this. Call me cynical but I find that the tool builders' only response to any problem is "Buy my tool." Even with noncommercial tool builders, their self worth is based on how many people they can get to use their tool. It may come as a shock to these people that someone would want to use anything other than the computer. If there is some part of the creative process that they haven't included in their tool, they start thinking about ways to simulate it on the computer. I myself have experimented with building automated storyboard aids, but I haven't really used them. But you don't have to do *everything* on the computer. I can still scribble sketchy notes or doodles faster than I can type or wiggle a mouse. And when writing longhand, I am less tempted to waste time correcting spelling errors and forget the thrust of what I was saying.

# How It Works

Here's how paper and pencil work for me and my projects.

## Writing

Here's the process I use to write English text—like the chapters of this book. The zeroth draft is just a jumble of random ideas. These usually come just as I am falling asleep or when I am walking or driving somewhere, so I keep a pad of paper by my bed and carry a small notebook wherever I go.

The first draft consists of making some vague order out of these ideas and scribbling a crude version onto paper with lots of cross-outs, insertions, and circled sentences connected with arrows. Even though it looks like a mess, it's very malleable. I can get lots on a page. And I can lie on a couch, sit in a corner, etc., to work on it.

For the next draft I type this all in and print it out on paper with pretty formatting. Then I crawl in a corner and scribble all over the printout with more cross-outs, insertions, and circled regions with arrows. Then I edit in the changes, sometimes extemporizing local improvements to the text as I am typing at the computer. Then back for another pretty draft.

I need to iterate this five or six times, expanding on brief notes to myself and rearranging the pieces, until it gets in a form that makes any sense at all to someone other than myself. So it's not always just one cycle of idea-and-implement. Sometimes it takes iteration between them. I might try something on the computer, not like it, and then go away and think about it to figure out why I don't like it. Even when I have something on the computer, if I find I don't like the design, it's still useful to go away somewhere and doodle.

## Animation

How does this work for animation? For the type of animation I do, the most important thing to me is to separate the essence of what I am trying to say from conventional visual representations of it. I can then try out new representations.

The analog to a rough draft of text is a set of storyboard sketches. The first draft of the storyboard is best done by hiding out where there's no computer and doodling on paper. This is because it's usually easier to draw one single frame by hand than with a computer (and even more so if you're an artist).

Computer graphics is useful mostly when you want to draw lots of slightly different frames. Only after I have identified *what* I want to draw do I go to the computer. While sketching storyboards you just concentrate on how the frame looks; you don't have worry about what parts are subobjects of what other parts. But one of the most important things about *implementing* an animation scene is to get the nesting structure of the objects right. Sure, with a flexible design system you can restructure the nesting levels if you get it wrong. But it's a lot quicker if, with a little bit of scribbling and doodling and thought, you can input the best nesting structure the first time.

## Mathematics

Even when I'm trying to work out some purely mathematical problem this two-step process happens. In the early stages I am scribbling all over the page. I get going on one development, get to the bottom of the page, bend it over so the last step is now visible on the back side of the page, and keep going on the back side with no interruption. If I find I'm going in a wrong direction, I go back to the middle of some derivation, cross out the parts below it, and resume in the margins. The result is a mess of equations, cross-outs, and circled results. Then I have to go back and recopy the useful results neatly so I can see what I did.

# Low Tech Works!

The creative process starts with random rapid idea generation and finishes with implementation. Computers help a lot with implementation, but idea generation is still done with pencil and paper. Can computers help here too? I don't think so. Why try to cram something on a computer when there is a cheap and effective alternative? Computers are wonderful production tools, but paper and pencil is my method of choice as an ideation tool. Maybe it's just a matter of looking down (as at a piece of scratch paper) to generate ideas and looking forward (as at a computer screen) to implement ideas.

And remember, even the best tools don't *generate* ideas. If they did, would they be your ideas or the tool builder's ideas?

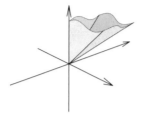

# CHAPTER THIRTEEN

# Line Clipping

JANUARY 1991

Teaching an introductory graphics class at Caltech has two benefits: it encourages me to read up on recent developments, and it gives me an excuse to sit and think about better ways of doing things. In particular, I've recently been lecturing about the standard computer graphics transform-clip-draw pipeline, so I diligently researched all the published clipping algorithms I could find and came to the conclusion that they all were . . . how shall I put this diplomatically . . . really terrible. They're way too complicated and have too many special cases. There *is* a good way to do clipping. I learned it at Utah but now realize that it hasn't made it into the published literature yet.

So this is the first of a series of chapters on the graphics pipeline. It's a bit of a personal journey since I will just concentrate on those techniques that I have found useful. This time out I am going concentrate on just the algorithmic aspects of the line clipping part of the pipeline. I will have to defer some juicy issues about how clipping interacts with transformations for later, so some of the things I say here will have to be taken on faith. Trust me.

## The Pipeline

The classic computer graphics pipeline is an assembly line–like process that geometric objects must experience on their journey to becoming pixels on the screen. There are many variants, but let's look at the four stages in Figure 13.1. Since we are all adults I won't mess around with 2D

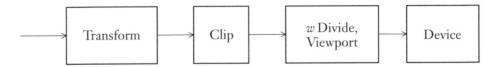

**Figure 13.1**  *The graphics pipeline*

versions of these routines; I'll deal directly with 3D homogeneous coordinates. I'll also follow my typical convention that homogeneous coordinates are in lowercase and real coordinates (the ones with the $w$ divided out) are in uppercase. We begin with some objects defined as collections of ($x$, $y$, $z$, $w$) points (often with $w = 1$), connected by line segments, and perform three types of operations on them (one of which is performed twice): transformation, $w$ division, and clipping.

> *Transform*—Takes ($x$, $y$, $z$, $w$) points and multiplies them by a $4 \times 4$ matrix to get them into a special clipping space.
> *Clip*—Takes ($x$, $y$, $z$, $w$) points in clipping space and clips lines against some set of boundary planes.
> *Viewport*—Takes ($x$, $y$, $z$, $w$) in clipping space, divides out the $w$, and transforms to hardware pixel space.
> *Device*—Takes ($X$, $Y$, $Z$) in the coordinate space of the hardware and does whatever is necessary to display lines.

## Transformations

I've talked about transformations in Chapter 3 and will say more about them in Chapters 14 through 18, but we need to review enough to see how they affect the clipper arithmetic.

There is conceptually one big transformation that takes coordinate points straight from their definitional space all the way to integer hardware pixel space. Since we want to minimize as much redundant transformation as possible, this whole thing could (if it weren't for clipping) be represented by multiplication by one single $4 \times 4$ matrix. After all, that's why mathematicians invented associativity, isn't it?

But we do have to do clipping, so we define an intermediate coordinate system—clipping space. The big transformation is broken into two pieces; the first maps definitional space to clip space (I'll call this $\mathbf{T}_1$), and the second maps clip space to pixel space (I'll call this $\mathbf{T}_2$). The $\mathbf{T}_1$ transformation typically contains modeling and viewing transformations and perspective. The $\mathbf{T}_2$ transformation is typically just a scale and translation. The product of the two should still equal the original complete transformation.

There are two reasons for using a separate clipping space. First, it can make the clipper arithmetic simpler, and second, it separates knowledge of the location of the boundaries from the code of the clipper. The idea is to make a clipper that clips to a simple built-in set of boundaries. Then the transforms are responsible for mapping the actually desired boundaries to the clipper's boundaries. In fact, the algorithm I will describe will work perfectly well for any boundaries, but the basic version wires in some simple ones.

To make the clipper and its arithmetic as simple as possible, we will pick a particularly convenient clipping space. The usual choice is to clip to the rectangular region $-1 \leq X \leq 1$, $-1 \leq Y \leq 1$, and $0 \leq Z \leq 1$. But wait a minute. The reason for using a special clipping space is to make the clipping arithmetic simple. But this isn't as simple as it could be. Let's face it, you're going to have to do the transformation anyway. Why not make it go to a *really* convenient clip space: the region $0 \leq X \leq 1$, $0 \leq Y \leq 1$, and $0 \leq Z \leq 1$. This single change made an almost 20% difference in the speed of my clipper.

Let me reassure you that a clipping region of (0...1) does not imply that, for perspective, the eye is looking at a corner of the screen. The actual clipping region is set up in the viewport initialization routine. It effectively appends an extra scale and translate onto the end of $\mathbf{T}_1$, and its inverse at the beginning of $\mathbf{T}_2$. This makes the location of the boundaries used internally by the clipper invisible to the caller of the pipeline. The punchline is that a clipper with built-in boundaries of (0...1) in $X$, $Y$, $Z$ can, when spliced between two transforms, serve for all rectangular or perspective pyramid boundaries.

## Connectivity

A typical database poured into this pipe consists of a bunch of points connected by line segments: a sequence of `MoveTo`, `DrawTo`, `DrawTo`... operations. All the clippers I have seen in the literature immediately break this down into a series of unconnected segments with calls such as `clip(endpoint0,endpoint1)`. I think this is a mistake for two reasons. First, you are destroying information about connectivity. Some output devices (like physical pen plotters—these still do exist) or output routines (like PostScript postprocessors) can make use of this connectivity. Second, some intermediate calculations (the *BC*s and outcodes described below) need be done only once per point if you maintain the connectivity.

So we've established that we want `MoveTo(point)` and `DrawTo (point)` calls. We could provide a separate `MoveTo` and `DrawTo` routine at each stage of the pipeline, but this is a bit of a nuisance since the transform and viewport stages of the pipe do the same operation on their parameters regardless of whether it's a `MoveTo` or `DrawTo` call. For this reason each stage of the pipeline consists of a single routine with two parameters: the new point and a flag that indicates `MoveTo` versus `DrawTo`. The clip and device stages keep an internal "current point" for joining up segments.

# Clipper Overview

A clipper is an example of a common type of computer graphics problem: one that does a lot of work to acomplish nothing. By this I mean that clippers are unnecessary a lot of the time, e.g, if the object is completely visible. Any time it takes to figure this out is wasted. So our main goal is for the clipper to quickly test when it isn't needed and step out of the way.

### History (?)

If you look in the literature at published line clippers, you will typically find the following three: Cohen-Sutherland (described in Newman and Sproull's book in 1979),[1] Cyrus-Beck (1978),[2] and Liang-Barsky (1984),[3] The algorithm I'm going to talk about doesn't present any stunning new concepts in clipping; it just contains all the best features of each of these algorithms. In addition I think it's a lot more general and more straightfor-ward. The interesting thing is that I learned the essence of this algorithm from Martin Newell in 1975! And I don't think he invented it either, it was just presented at Utah as a reasonable way to do clipping. I've been teach-ing it to my graphics classes for years but never realized it wasn't formally published.

Over the years I've tinkered with the algorithm, refining and simplify-ing it. Even while writing this chapter I've come up with some new simplifications. Simplification is something we need more of in this world. I don't really remember how much of it is mine and how much I got from others, so I won't try to accurately reproduce any particular historical algorithm here. I'll just present the most highly refined clipper that I've been able to come up with.

---

1  W. Newman and R. Sproull, *Principles of Interactive Computer Graphics*, 2d ed. (New York: McGraw-Hill, 1979).

2  M. Cyrus and J. Beck, Generalized two- and three-dimensional clipping, *Computers and Graphics* 3:23–28, 1978.

3  Yu-Dong Liang and Brian Barsky, A new concept and method for line clipping, *ACM Transactions on Graphics* 3(1):1–22, January 1984.

## Boundary Coordinates

We define our convex clipping volume as a set of bounding planes. In homogeneous coordinates, a plane is a column vector; the dot product of a point with this vector gives 0 if the point is on the plane. By picking the signs of the column vector properly, we can arrange for the dot product to be positive if it's on the visible side of the plane and negative if it's on the invisible side.

Here's where our special clipping space pays off. The two clip planes in the X direction, for example, are $X = 0$ and $X = 1$. These correspond to the column vectors

$$B_1 = \begin{bmatrix} 1 \\ 0 \\ 0 \\ 0 \end{bmatrix} \text{ and } B_2 = \begin{bmatrix} -1 \\ 0 \\ 0 \\ 1 \end{bmatrix}$$

Taking the dot product of $(x, y, z, w)$ with these is easy; it's just $x$ and $w - x$. We will call these values the *boundary coordinates* (*BC*). The expressions for each of the six boundary coordinates for the clipping boundaries are then as shown in Table 13.1. The first thing the clipper does to a new point is to calculate this vector of *BC*s. Due to our clever choice of boundaries, this only takes three subtractions. We will use these *BC* values at several places in the algorithm. A point is visible if all of its *BC*s are positive.

## Outcodes

We use the sign bits of the *BC*s to find where we need to do work. Assume we have the list of boundary coordinates for point P0, called *BC0*, and the list for point P1, called *BC1*. To see if the segment from P0 to P1 straddles boundary $i$, look at the sign bits of $BC0_i$ and $BC1_i$. See Table 13.2. Remember, a 1 bit means that the point is outside the particular boundary.

**Table 13.1** *Boundary coordinate values*

| *BC* | Homogeneous value | Real space plane |
|------|-------------------|------------------|
| $BC_1$ | $x$ | $X = 0$ |
| $BC_2$ | $w - x$ | $X = 1$ |
| $BC_3$ | $y$ | $Y = 0$ |
| $BC_4$ | $w - y$ | $Y = 1$ |
| $BC_5$ | $z$ | $Z = 0$ |
| $BC_6$ | $w - z$ | $Z = 1$ |

**Table 13.2** *Boundary coordinate sign bit meanings*

| Sign($BC0_i$) | Sign($BC1_i$) | Meaning |
|---|---|---|
| 0 | 0 | Whole segment visible with respect to this boundary |
| 1 | 0 | Straddles boundary, P0 is out |
| 0 | 1 | Straddles boundary, P1 is out |
| 1 | 1 | Whole segment outside boundary |

To make best use of these we construct a flag word for each point called an *outcode*. Each bit in the outcode is the sign bit of an element of the *BC* array. If the whole outcode is 0, the point is visible. But the really nifty thing about outcodes is that they enable us to test all clip planes in parallel using bitwise logical operations.

If both ends of a segment are outside at least one of the boundaries, the whole segment can be skipped. We can detect this "trivial reject" by taking the logical AND of the outcodes of the two endpoints. If the bit position of any boundary is 1 for both outcodes, the result will be non-zero. Next, if both endpoints are inside all boundaries, the whole segment is visible. We can detect this "trivial accept" by taking the logical OR of the outcodes and getting a result of 0. A lot of high-level languages don't seem to encourage this type of shenanigans. But it's so useful, it's worth coercing your program to do it. After all, if your computer can't do ANDs and ORs, who can?

I actually construct the outcode with a little assembly language routine that looks at the sign bits of the floating-point numbers. It requires no floating-point instructions at all, just six pairs of load and shift instructions. This is the ideal application for assembly language—small routines that do bit shuffling that compilers are crummy at. This type of solution may not appeal to everyone, but profiling tests showed me that this is where a lot of time was spent. You do have to be careful though; I have had problems under certain weird circumstances with getting a value of –0 for an element of *BC*, resulting in a bad outcode bit.

## Interpolation

If a line segment crosses a clipping plane, we must calculate the intersection. You can do this easily by doing parametric interpolation. The parameterized segment from point P0 to P1 is

$$P(\alpha) = P0 + \alpha(P1 - P0)$$

When $\alpha = 0$ we are at P0, and when $\alpha = 1$ we are at P1.

How to calculate $\alpha$? Dot the above equation with the column vector, $B_i$, of the straddled boundary plane:

$$P(\alpha) \cdot B_i = P0 \cdot B_i + \alpha(P1 - P0) \cdot B_i$$

Since we want $P(\alpha)$ to be on the boundary, its dot product should be 0. The dot products with P0 and P1 are just the boundary coordinates. This gives

$$0 = BC0_i + \alpha(BC1_i - BC0_i)$$

Then just solve for $\alpha$.

$$\alpha = \frac{BC0_i}{BC0_i - BC1_i}$$

Note that this expression is only in the range (0...1) if $BC0_i$ and $BC1_i$ have different signs. We will endeavor to calculate $\alpha$ only when actually necessary to do an interpolation, i.e., when we have previously determined that the $BC$ values for the endpoints of the segment have opposite signs.

This works in homogeneous coordinates for perhaps a somewhat subtle reason. Look at Figure 13.2a. Here we are clipping P0 = [–1, 0, 0, 1] to P1 = [1, 0, 0, 1]. The left edge $BC$ is just $x$ so $BC0_1 = -1$ and $BC1_1 = +1$—different signs indicating that the line crosses the left boundary, so $\alpha = -1/(-1 - (+1)) = \frac{1}{2}$ as you would expect. Now what if P0 = [–2, 0, 0, 2]? It's the same geometric location in space but represented homogeneously differently. Here the $BC$s are –2 and 1 and $\alpha = -2/(-2 - (+1)) = \frac{2}{3}$. You would think that the interpolated point would be wrong. But we are interpolating in *homogeneous* space, not real space. If you look at Figure 13.2b, you see that the point $\frac{2}{3}$ of the way from P0 to P1 in homogeneous space does indeed project onto the boundary, $X = 0$, when we (later) divide by $w$.

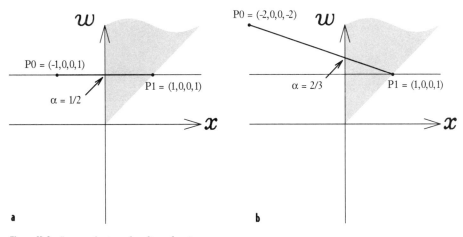

**Figure 13.2** *Interpolating the clipped point*

# The Algorithm

First a few conventions: the variables P0, P1, and P are homogeneous points (four elements: $x$, $y$, $z$, $w$). Any arithmetic done on them is assumed to be done for each element. The clip routine outputs its results to the next stage of the pipeline by calling the routine ViewPt.

Also, I have separated the code into bite-sized chunks with what appear to be subroutine calls connecting them. I don't suggest you make separate subroutines out of them; the subroutine call overhead would probably be excessive. I just split the pieces out to make the listing more understandable, all nice and top down.

### Outer Shell

The outer shell of the clip routine basically just takes care of connectivity. It maintains information about the "current point" in P0, BC0(1...6), and KODE0. (You'll have to excuse me for some of the variable names, but I get uneasy when I see integer type variables with names that don't start with the letters I, J, K, L, M, or N.) Note that the BC and KODE values are calculated only once per endpoint and saved from one call to another for DrawTo operations that are chained together.

```
Clip(P1, Flag)
    calculate BC1(1...6) and KODE1
    if Flag = 'MOVE'
        do MOVEstuff
    else
        do DRAWstuff
    copy P1, BC1, KODE1 to P0, BC0, KODE0
```

### Move

This part is simple, it just passes the MOVE operation down the pipe if the point is visible.

```
MOVEstuff
    if KODE1 = 0
        call ViewPt(P1, 'MOVE')
```

### Draw

First we do trivial reject and trivial accept tests using bitwise logical operations on the outcodes. If the logical AND of the outcodes is non-zero, we have trivial reject. Stated another way, a 0 result means no trivial reject. Next, if the logical OR is 0, we have trivial accept.

```
DRAWstuff
    if (KODE0 AND KODE1) = 0
        if (KODE0 OR KODE1) = 0
            call ViewPt(P1, 'DRAW')
        else
            do NontrivialStuff
```

Almost all line segments will be trivial accepts or trivial rejects, so the above covers the vast majority of cases. Once you have the outcodes, you only need one AND and one OR and you're outta there.

## Another Way

Modern computers have prefetch queues operating in parallel to their instruction execution. This queue must be flushed every time there is a branch instruction so, to really streamline things, we want to avoid branching. Let's reorganize this code to make the most commonly occurring situation (the trivial accept) fall through with straight line code. (If you assume trivial reject is the most common, a slightly different rearrangement would be necessary.) This is not so "structured," requiring horrible goto statements, but I think it is actually just as understandable.

```
Clip(P1, Flag)
    calculate BC1(1...6) and KODE1
    if Flag = 'MOVE' goto move
    if (KODE0 AND KODE1) ≠ 0 goto finish
    if (KODE0 OR  KODE1) ≠ 0 goto nontriv
    call ViewPt(P1, 'DRAW')
finish: copy P1, BC1, KODE1 to P0, BC0, KODE0
    return

move: if (KODE1 ≠ 0) goto finish
    call ViewPt(P1, 'MOVE')
    goto finish

nontriv: do NontrivialStuff
    goto finish
```

## Nontrivial Stuff

You get to `NontrivialStuff` only if the segment straddles at least one boundary. The individual bits of (`KODE0 OR KODE1`) give a mask for those boundaries the segment straddles, so we recalculate this value and store it as `KLIP`. It might seem strange to do this a second time, but remember, this is the rarely executed part of the code. We just avoided storing `KLIP` in the more often encountered case where we never use it.

While examining straddled boundaries, we keep track of the still-visible part of the segment with the two values $\alpha_0$ and $\alpha_1$. For each straddled boundary, we calculate the $\alpha$ value for the intersection and update whichever endpoint the outcodes tell us is the outside one. The loop variable `MASK` selects one bit at a time, so the innards of this loop is only executed for those bit positions of `KLIP` that are 1.

There are two subtleties. First, a point might be outside more than one boundary. Updating an $\alpha$ value must only be done if the new intersection shaves more off the segment than has been shaved off so far. For example, see Figure 13.3a, where we first test the right boundary and then the top boundary. This latter test generates an $\alpha$ that is closer to the endpoint, so no update happens. Figure 13.3b shows the second subtlety: if $\alpha_0$ ever gets greater than $\alpha_1$, we have a nontrivial reject.

```
NontrivialStuff
    KLIP = KODE0 OR KODE1
    α₀ = 0.0;   α₁ = 1.0;   MASK = 1
    for I = 1 to NbrClipPlanes
```

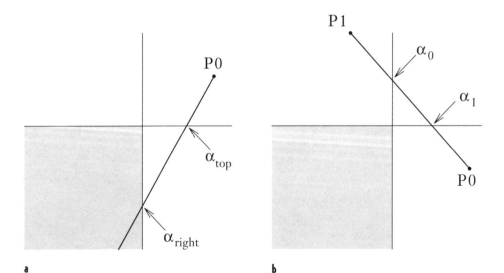

a                                                    b

**Figure 13.3**  *Nontrivial cases*

```
    if (KLIP AND MASK) ≠ 0
        α = BC0(I)/(BC0(I) - BC1(I))
        if (KODE0 AND MASK) ≠ 0
            α₀ = max(α₀, α)
        else
            α₁ = min(α₁, α)

        if (α₁ < α₀) goto NontrivReject

    shift MASK left one bit

if KODE0 ≠ 0
    P = P0 + α₀ (P0 - P1)
    call ViewPt(P, 'MOVE')

if KODE1 ≠ 0
    P = P0 + alpha1 (P0 - P1)
    call ViewPt(P, 'DRAW')
else
    call ViewPt(P1, 'DRAW')
```

`NontrivReject:`

Note that we actually do the interpolation arithmetic only if an endpoint is out. Also, we never need to do an explicit `ViewPt(P0, 'MOVE')` here, because we are guaranteed that this was already done by a previous call (move or draw) if `P0` is visible.

# Homogeneous Clipping

There often seems to be some confusion about how homogeneous coordinates affect a clipper, especially after points are passed through a homogeneous perspective transformation. A paper I co-wrote with Martin Newell might have scared some people,[4] but it's really not that big a deal. This algorithm works just dandy for all but the most perverse of cases. In particular, stuff behind the eye gets clipped properly with no special cases required.

What are the perverse cases that cause problems? (I of course keep

---

4  J. F. Blinn and M. E. Newell, Clipping using homogeneous coordinates, *SIGGRAPH '78 Conference Proceedings* (New York: ACM), pages 245–251.

stumbling onto them.) Well, sometimes some lines will get clipped that should, in fact, be visible. In Figure 13.4a you see the region we are clipping to in homogeneous space, a sort of inverted pyramid. In Figure 13.4b you see the region we should be clipping to, a double pyramid. All points in the bottom pyramid do indeed, when projected to $w = 1$, wind up in the visible region. So what sorts of things reside in the bottom pyramid with negative $w$s? If you start with good honest positive $w$s, the homogeneous perspective transform will not put anything there. The only time you need to worry is when you have negative $w$ values in your original model (not usually necessary) or when the original model has infinite segments (those which connect their endpoints through infinity rather than directly) indicated by a positive $w$ on one end and a negative $w$ on the other. And sometimes not even then. For example, in Chapter 6 we ran into this problem with perspective shadows, but the clipper "bug" worked to our advantage. Some stuff got generated in the bottom pyramid, but we actually wanted it clipped since it just generated the "antishadow."

The easiest solution if you want negative pyramid stuff is to draw your object, multiply the whole $\mathbf{T}_1$ matrix by $-1$, and draw the object again.

# Z Clipping

**Z** clipping is very confusing to a lot of users of graphics systems: things near the viewer keep disappearing. $X$ and $Y$ clipping make sense; you don't expect to see things that are off the screen. But try to explain the near and far clipping planes to an artist, and you are stuck with the question of why you'd ever want to do something like that.

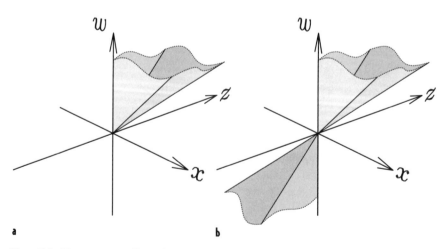

a                                              b

**Figure 13.4**  *Homogeneous clip regions*

Well, Z clipping is sort of optional. The trouble with eliminating it has to do with the homogeneous division. In the pipeline of Figure 13.1, the homogeneous division occurs after the clipping stage. (Contrary to popular belief, with a few reasonable assumptions it *is* possible to clip after doing the homogeneous division. It's just a real algorithmic nuisance. Juicy item for Chapter 18.) What happens if we get $w = 0$ and try to divide? Well, with Z clipping enabled (see Figure 13.4a), there is only one point that can generate $w = 0$, that is (0, 0, 0, 0). It's real hard to get this point out of the clipper. If, on the other hand, you disable Z clipping, you get the region in Figure 13.5. For the most part, this still works. Lines that come towards you in real space project into lines that puncture the sides of the v-shaped trough. The only lines that generate $w = 0$ after clipping are those that pass through the $z$ axis, the valley of the trough. These are lines that pass exactly through the eyepoint. After which you are dead and don't care about divide-by-zero errors. But seriously folks, no matter how unlikely it is to get $w = 0$, you should still test for it before dividing. Having a program die because of a zero divide error is a most unpleasant experience.

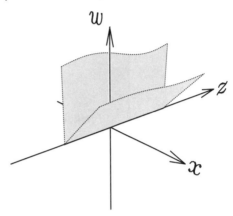

**Figure 13.5**  *Clip region with Z clipping disabled*

# Global Clipping

Of course the best way to speed up clipping is to not do it at all. Our outcode machinery allows us to do this in a very straightforward manner. We just apply trivial accept and reject tests to the convex hull of a whole object. What is a convex hull? Well, imagine blowing up a balloon. Insert your object inside and then let the air out. The resulting shape is the convex hull.

Why is this nice? Well, if all the points of the convex hull are trivially visible, the whole object is trivially visible. And if all the points of the convex hull are trivial rejects, the whole object is a trivial reject.

The actual convex hull is sometimes hard to come by, but you don't really have to use it. Related shapes that I have tried that work just as well are

- Control points for Bézier curves and surfaces
- Corners of bounding volume formed from max/min $(x, y, z)$ of objects (eight points)

■ Max/min $(x, y)$ for 2D objects (four points)—this is good for explicitly modeled text

To make use of this, before you draw an object, you calculate the cumulative logical OR and logical AND of the outcodes of the enclosing points:

```
GlobalClipSetup
    Ocumulate = 0; Acumulate = -1
    for I = 1 to NbrEnclosePoints
        transform enclosing point to clip space
        calculate KODE
        Ocumulate = Ocumulate OR KODE
        Acumulate = Acumulate AND KODE
```

Then, outside the drawing loop, you can do a trivial reject/accept test that looks a whole lot like the test inside the DRAWStuff part of the clipper. Furthermore, if you detect a global trivial accept, you can merge the general $4 \times 4$ matrix $\mathbf{T}_1$ with the viewport transform $\mathbf{T}_2$ and avoid doing two transformations inside the drawing loop.

```
GlobalClipDraw
    if (Acumulate == 0)
        if (Ocumulate == 0)
            T = T₁ · T₂
            Transform points of object by T
            divide by w
            Pass them directly to Device
        else
            Draw object through normal clipper
```

Global clipping is a gamble. Suppose you have an object with 100 points, and the bounding volume has eight points. If you do the global test and there's a trivial accept or reject, you win. If it's a nontrivial case, you have had to do a total of 108 transform, BC, and KODE calculations. Not a bad risk. It is especially effective for Bézier curve primitives since the global clipping stage can be built into the primitive curve drawing routine, making it invisible to the caller of the routine.

# Observations

Part of the goal here was to minimize the amount of floating-point arithmetic. I would hazard a guess that integer bit testing is always faster than floating-point arithmetic. Even a floating-point comparison counts as one unit of floating-point arithmetic, so I've made almost all tests into logical or integer comparisons. The only floating-point operations (besides *BC*s) are in the rarely executed part of the code.

The clipping planes have been purposely made as simple as possible, but this algorithm can clip against *any* set of planes. Just supply the proper expressions for (any number of ) boundary coordinates. The location of the clipping planes is completely encapsulated in the calculation of the *BC* values. The normal clipper and the global clipper just use the *BC*s (whatever they happen to be) to calculate the outcodes and the alphas. My implementation of this clipper has the six simple planes built in, but it can optionally include a couple more general ones for some special purposes.

A lot of the streamlining of this algorithm resulted from profiling tests of various earlier versions. You can theorize and fantasize about where you think the time is going, but actual experimental data are the only reasonable things to base optimization on. I've found that most of execution time is still in the calculations of *BC*s, even after making them as simple as I have done. Why is this? Because that is the only code that is executed *every* time the clipper is called. The trivial accept and reject tests allow us to skip most of the rest. Performance of the algorithm depends mostly on how fast it can execute for trivial accept or reject cases, since that is what happens most of the time.

## What Is Publishable

Now, admittedly I haven't compared this algorithm instruction for instruction with all the "historical" clippers mentioned earlier, but it sure seems a lot simpler to me. This is not meant as an insult to Cyrus, Beck, Liang, Barsky, et al. They didn't build on this algorithm probably because they didn't know about it. After all, it has never been published. And why? *I* never published it before because for the most part it wasn't my idea. And also it didn't seem like a big enough idea to publish.

This raises an interesting question: What is publishable? (I mean in terms of being new or different enough to publish.) This question becomes doubly interesting in light of the current flap about software patents. A lot of good ideas don't get published because nobody knows who invented them—they are just classed as "common knowledge." There are channels for publishing new research results, but there are fewer places to put more minor ideas, or ideas that are simply refinements of standard techniques, or just to archive common knowledge. I have an ideal avenue for describing such things in my series of IEEE articles. I can write anything I want to here because it's not a formal technical paper; all things are not expected to be major research results. They are combinations of the results of my own tinkering with common knowledge that might not be well publicized.

Another source of such ideas is the *Graphics Gems* series.[5] These books are collections of short ideas by a variety of people. To see or publish ideas in the future, check out the *Journal of Graphics Tools*. Information is available at `http://www.acm.org/jgt`

After all, from a historical perspective, if you don't publish it, you may as well not have done it.

---

5   The *Graphics Gems* series was initiated by Andrew Glassner of Microsoft. The publisher is Academic Press in San Diego.

# CHAPTER FOURTEEN

# Pixel Coordinates

J U L Y   1 9 9 1

There are some problems in graphics that I've spent a lot of time trying to figure out even though they seem real simple. I don't know if this is because I'm dumb or because these problems are really profound. I've never seen any of them described anywhere in the literature; maybe the people who write books just haven't come across them.

One set of such problems comes from the use of transformations in the graphics pipeline. No, I'm not going to beleaguer you with yet more ravings about how wonderful homogeneous coordinates are. You already know that. What I am going to do in this and the following chapters is to discuss a few of the odd little quirks of the transformation process that I've discovered over the years and how I learned to deal with them. Some of this may look like I'm making a big deal out of nothing, but it's important to get it right.

More specifically I am going to talk about

1. A detailed examination of what it means to be a pixel.
2. A nifty (nift-like?) way to merge the old concept of the window-to-viewport transformation with clipping space, so that it's easy to clip viewports.
3. What's really going on with the homogeneous perspective transform.

# Overview of the Pipeline

Let's start with a general overview of the classic rendering pipeline. Basically the pipeline transforms points (line endpoints, polygon vertices, patch control points, etc.) from some object's definition space to pixel raster space and, along the way, clips the shapes to the boundaries of some given region of space. The pipeline is first *initialized* by setting up various global parameters (primarily transformations) and then it is *used* by passing points through it. There are two ways to look at the setup process: from the user's *external* point of view and from the pipeline implementor's *internal* point of view. The user specifies the parameters that describe what he/she/it wants. The pipeline implementor figures out how these parameters are stored and used by the pass-through process.

## Coordinate Spaces

First let's look at the user's view. There are various coordinate systems that a point experiences as it journeys to the screen. In the interests of solidarity I'll try to relate my notation to that used by Pixar's Renderman interface, which I will refer to as the politically correct Render*person*. In the following list the name used by Renderperson appears in parentheses. I'll list the coordinate spaces in the order in which an object sees them.

*Definition* (object)—The space in which the original object is defined.

*Universe* (world)—A consistent universe into which all modeled objects are placed.

*Eye* (camera)—Eye at origin looking down the *z* axis.

*Perspective*—Distorted space after the perspective transform has been performed. This one is optional. If there is an orthographic projection, this will be the same as eye space.

*Clip*—A special space chosen to make the clipper's arithmetic simple. It maps the desired visible chunk of perspective space to a fixed region.

*Normalized Device Coordinates, NDC* (screen)—A standardized screen coordinate system that doesn't include explicit pixel dimensions.

*Pixel* (raster)—*X, Y* coordinates (usually integers) in the hardware pixel space. In modern usage, with multiple screen windows, this is the screen real estate we have been allocated by the windowing system.

Now some notes about the transformations between these systems.

*Definition to universe*—This is generally a combination of rotation, translation, and possibly non-uniform scales used to squash primitives to the desired shape and place them in the universe. It is sometimes something more bizarre, like the bend-me, twist-me, hurt-me transforms used in general deformation systems. The ability of a 4 × 4 matrix to do perspective is rarely used in modeling, except in rational polynomial curves and surfaces or local light source shadows. I discussed the latter in Chapter 6.

*Universe to eye*—This is just a translation and pure rotation to place and orient the simulated camera. I talked about this in Chapter 8.

*Eye to perspective*—This is a homogeneous perspective transform, the subject of Chapter 18.

*Perspective to clip to NDC*—This is the subject of Chapter 16, which fills in the blanks from Chapter 13.

*NDC to pixel*—This is the subject of most of this chapter and Chapter 15.

## Internal Operation

Many of the above coordinate systems exist only in our minds. In actual implementation, the transforms from definition to clip space are merged into one transform that we'll call $\mathbf{T}_1$. This is usually a full 4 × 4 homogeneous matrix. The transforms from clip to pixel space are merged into $\mathbf{T}_2$. This usually requires only a scale and offset in $X$ and $Y$.

Once the transforms have been set up, processing an object through the pipe requires four steps:

1. Transform to clipping space via $\mathbf{T}_1$.
2. Clip.
3. Divide by $w$.
4. Transform to pixel space via $\mathbf{T}_2$.

# Exemplary Transformations

The only transformation I will need for the next few chapters is a simple scale and offset in $X$ and $Y$ from some input coordinate system to an output coordinate system.

$$s_x X_{in} + d_x = X_{out}$$
$$s_y Y_{in} + d_y = Y_{out}$$

It is easiest to specify these as exemplary transformations. No, this doesn't mean that they are more admirable than others; it just means that they are specified in terms of two *example* input coordinate values and their associated desired output values. I'll denote this for, say, $X$ as

$$X_{in1} \mapsto X_{out1}$$
$$X_{in2} \mapsto X_{out2}$$

Using the magic of linear transformations, we can derive the scale and offset as

$$s_x = \frac{X_{out2} - X_{out1}}{X_{in2} - X_{in1}}, \quad d_x = X_{out1} - s_x X_{in1}$$

These values are what is actually stored for use during the pass-through stage. For the transforms derived below, I'll just use these equations and show you the results.

# NDC-to-Pixel Transformation

Let's start with what might at first seem the simplest transformation: normalized device coordinates to pixel space. The transform is

$$s_x X_{NDC} + d_x = X_{pixel}$$
$$s_y Y_{NDC} + d_y = Y_{pixel}$$

A user/programmer does all screen design in NDC. There are three nasty realities of the hardware that NDC hides from us:

1. The actual number of pixels in $x$ and $y$.
2. Non-uniform pixel spacing in $x$ and $y$. Distances in NDC space are geometrically uniform.
3. Up versus down for the $Y$ coordinate. The NDC-to-pixel transformation will invert $Y$ if necessary so that $Y$ in NDC points up.

The transformation to pixel space is implicit in the system and is set up during device initialization. It turns out that the obvious way to transform NDC to pixel space is wrong. To show why, I'll have to go through several intermediate stages before I get to the correct way. But without all the false starts, the correct way will seem kind of unmotivated. So don't take any of these stepping-stone transformations too much to heart until I tell you we've arrived at the ultimate one.

First let's specify precisely what I mean by the different coordinate systems.

## Pixel Space

Define the pixel coordinate system according to the following typical scheme. The pixel array is $N_x$ pixels across, numbered from 0 on the left to

$N_x - 1$ on the right. The array is $N_y$ pixels high, numbered from 0 on the top to $N_y - 1$ on the bottom. Now in addition to deriving general formulas, I'm going to use explicit values in examples below. I'll use 512 pixels in $X$ and 480 pixels in $Y$, not so much that they are typical as because these numbers are familiar and you will be able to see what's going on with them.

Sometimes the pixel array doesn't start at (0, 0) but at some offset. I won't specifically deal with this here; it only requires adding the constant $(X, Y)$ offset to the pixel coordinates we calculate. Also sometimes $Y = 0$ at the bottom of the screen instead of at the top. I'll let you figure out the slightly different transform necessary in that case.

Now in addition to pixel counts, the display hardware will imply a physical aspect ratio of this rectangle of pixels that might not necessarily equal $N_y / N_x$. Thus pixels might not be the same distance apart horizontally and vertically. For our numerical example I'll use a standard TV screen, which has an aspect ratio of 3:4 = .75. This number represents the height divided by the width of the region that the display electronics will scan out. For some reason Renderperson describes the aspect ratio as width over height; I'm not sure if there is a standard.

At some level it might not make any difference. I think the aspect ratio-sensing neurons of the general public are getting burned out because so many computer displays are not really adjusted to the proper hardware aspect ratio and are distorted horizontally. In addition, people see so many images on TV that are distorted via Digital Video Effects units that pretty soon they don't even notice it anymore. This is similar to how my flicker sensors have been burned out from my early years of looking at displays that refreshed only about 10 times a second.

## NDC Space

Normalized device coordinates run from –1 to +1 in $X$ and $-a$ to $+a$ in $Y$, where $a$ is the abovementioned physical aspect ratio. NDC thus has a little bit of device dependency. See the left side of Figure 14.1.

The Renderperson approach is perhaps a bit better. It guarantees that the region –1 to +1 is visible in both $X$ and $Y$; the longer dimension then extends to values beyond 1. They would therefore say that TV screen space extends from –1.333 to +1.333 in $X$ and from –1 to +1 in $Y$. I'll stick to my way for now so I don't get confused.

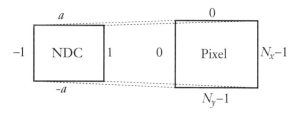

**Figure 14.1** *The naive NDC-to-pixel model*

## The Naive Transform

In Figure 14.1 we see our first attempt at the required transformation. Let's derive the exemplary transformation from this figure. In $X$

$$-1 \mapsto 0$$
$$1 \mapsto N_x - 1$$

This leads to

$$s_x = \frac{N_x - 1}{2}, \quad d_x = \frac{N_x - 1}{2}$$

For our sample pixel range this leads to

$$s_x = 255.5, \quad d_x = 255.5$$

Now we do the same thing for $Y$. Here we incorporate the physical aspect ratio of the screen, $a$, as the vertical bounds for NDC. This implicitly corrects for non-uniform $x$, $y$ pixel spacing.

$$-a \mapsto N_y - 1$$
$$a \mapsto 0$$

so

$$s_y = \frac{N_y - 1}{-2a}, \quad d_y = \frac{N_y - 1}{2}$$

For our sample pixel range this leads to

$$s_y = -319.333, \quad d_y = 239.5$$

Every computer graphics book I've seen (at least every one that describes this explicitly enough to tell) uses this transformation.

## A Crinkle

There's a problem lurking here, though. The scale factor is icky. In the $X$ direction, we are taking two units of NDC space and dividing it up into $N_x$ pixels. We sort of expect the scale factor to be $N_x/2$. What did we do wrong? We forgot that pixels have size. Imagine a row of samples with a Gaussian spot centered at each one, and you realize that the resultant intensity swath sticks out about ½ pixel spacing to the left and right.

This little offset doesn't seem like much, but it can really screw things up for more advanced rendering situations. I did this wrong in my original teapot pictures in my 1976 paper.[1] There, due to memory limitations, I had

---

1  J. Blinn and M. Newell, Texture and reflection in computer generated images, *Communications of the ACM* 19(10):542–547, October 1976.

to make each $512 \times 512$ pixel image from four $256 \times 256$ pixel quadrants. I used a variant of the naive pixel mapping. For the left two quadrants, the $X$ mapping was $-1 \mapsto 0$ and $0 \mapsto 255$, and for the right two quadrants, it was $0 \mapsto 0$ and $1 \mapsto 255$. When the four small pictures were assembled into one large one, you could see the seam. (This was only really noticeable when the digital image was zoomed up—another example of the principle that if you shrink a crummy picture down, it looks good.)

So what's the right way? Looking at the pixels through a microscope, what we *really* want is shown in Figure 14.2. Each small square represents an area that we want to map to the pixel coordinate at its center. For the $X$ coordinates we use

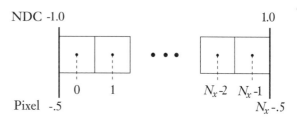

**Figure 14.2** *Microscopic view of pixels at the edge of NDC*

$$-1 \mapsto -.5$$
$$1 \mapsto N_x -.5$$

so

$$s_x = \frac{N_x}{2}, \quad d_x = \frac{N_x - 1}{2}$$

With explicit coordinates we get

$$s_x = 256, \quad d_x = 255.5$$

For the $Y$ coordinate we use

$$-a \mapsto N_y -.5$$
$$a \mapsto -.5$$

so

$$s_y = \frac{-N_y}{2a}, \quad d_y = \frac{N_y - 1}{2}$$

and

$$s_y = -320, \quad d_y = 239.5$$

## Integerizing

When we go from floating-point pixel coordinates to integer pixel coordinates, we need to round to the nearest pixel. This is the same as adding .5 and truncating. We might as well build this into the displacement part of our transformation. This implies an $X$ map of

$$-1 \mapsto 0$$
$$1 \mapsto N_x$$

and a $Y$ map of

$$-a \mapsto N_y$$
$$a \mapsto 0$$

This changes just the displacements to

$$d_x = \frac{N_x}{2} = 256$$

$$d_y = \frac{N_y}{2} = 240$$

This works as long as all the numbers are positive, which they are here.

### The Dangling Edge

Now there's another problem. An NDC $X$ coordinate value of 1.0 will map, after truncation, into $N_x$, which is one pixel beyond the right edge of the screen. There are two ways we can react to this situation.

First, we could disallow the value of +1.0 as a visible coordinate, that is, fix it so the clipper keeps things only in the region $-1 \le X < +1$. But this leads to some unexpected and undesirable results. For example, if you try to frame the screen by lines tracing out what you think are the screen boundaries ($-1$ and $+1$), you won't get to see the line on the right.

Second, we can arrange to keep this one extra NDC value in a way that won't mess us up. Set up the clipper to keep both ends: $-1 \le X \le +1$. We could then test for the pixel coordinate of $N_x$ and explicitly set it back to $N_x - 1$, but this is not what I do. I do what all good computer graphicists do: I cheat. I contract the NDC space by a microscopic amount to fit the extra one value into the allowable pixel range.

In $X$

$$-1 \mapsto 0$$
$$+1 \mapsto N_x - \varepsilon$$

This will make +1 truncate to $N_x - 1$. The scale and displacement are

$$s_x = \frac{N_x - \varepsilon}{2}, \quad d_x = \frac{N_x - \varepsilon}{2}$$

You could use numerical analysis to figure out the optimal value for $\epsilon$, but I just use .001, which is pretty close to the minimum value whose effect still fits in a single precision number.

$$s_x = 255.9995, \quad d_y = 255.9995$$

In $Y$

$$-a \mapsto N_y - \epsilon$$
$$+a \mapsto 0$$

so

$$s_y = \frac{N_y - \epsilon}{-2a}, \quad d_y = \frac{N_y - \epsilon}{2}$$

and

$$s_y = 319.9995, \quad d_y = 239.9995$$

This, then, is the final approved NDC-to-pixel transformation. Write this down.

# What Is Pixel Space Really?

So what have we done here? Considering just the $X$ direction: we've divided the conceptually continuous –1 to +1 range of NDC up into $N_x$ discrete bins, each of which maps to a pixel. There are actually two ways to think about this. We could place the integer pixel coordinate at the center of the pixel and then round each coordinate to the nearest integer. (This was one of our intermediate techniques.) Alternatively we could place the integer pixel coordinate in the cracks between pixels and truncate to the next lowest integer. This is what it looks like we finally wound up with, but it really isn't. What we did is only a convenience to merge the addition of ½ (for rounding) into the transform. The pixel bins are geometrically the same for both techniques; for example, the leftmost pixel bin covers $2/N_x$ amount of distance in NDC, abutting the left edge of the screen.

Simple line drawing algorithms and many early polygon scan conversion algorithms accept line endpoints and polygon vertices as integer pixel coordinates. That's great for quick-look, Bresenham-type line drawing algorithms, plotters, or other output devices that take integer pixel coordinates. But there's more to life than line drawings.

Mulling over some more advanced rendering applications leads to two other requirements of the NDC-to-pixel mapping: subpixel positioning of endpoints/vertices and subsampling of the image for antialiasing purposes. These two enhancements to the transformation interact in strange and mysterious ways. They will be the topic of the next chapter.

# CHAPTER FIFTEEN

# Subpixelic Particles

S E P T E M B E R    1 9 9 1

A n ancient Greek named Democritus first came up with the idea that the world was made of indivisible particles called atoms. (He didn't base this on any physical evidence—it's just that there were so many Greeks coming up with random ideas that one of them was bound to be right.) Of course nowadays we know that atoms can be subdivided into subatomic particles: electrons, protons, etc., and that maybe even protons can themselves be subdivided into quarks.

The ancient computer graphicists thought that images could be subdivided into indivisible parts called pixels. That's in fact what I did in Chapter 14. But there are reasons for subdividing pixels, and so this time I'm going to discus subpixelic particles.

## Review

T o provide some modicum of device independence, graphics systems often describe the screen in terms of what are called normalized device coordinates (NDC) that stretch from –1 on the left to +1 on the right. In the last chapter I proposed that the continuous NDC space should be divided into pixel regions according to the scheme in Figure 15.1. That is, each pixel consists of the rectangular region within $\pm\frac{1}{2}$ of the pixel center, and these pixels fit snugly within the NDC range. Alternatively you could say that NDC is divided up into $N_x$ equal-sized bins with an integer pixel coordinate labeling each bin. This is a bit different from the way it's done in most computer graphics books, which usually align the *centers* of the leftmost and rightmost pixels with the NDC boundaries. Of course, if you

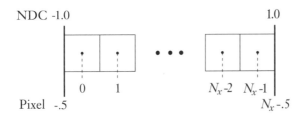

**Figure 15.1** *NDC-to-pixel mapping*

don't do it my way the pixel police will not come and get you, but there are two reasons for doing it my way. First, it gets you into the right mood for doing antialiasing by treating all pixels as finite areas instead of points. Second, it simplifies the coordinates for some higher-level rendering algorithms that divide the screen into smaller regions, each of which is treated as a separate image. In this latter case each region can contain a snugly tiled block of pixels just as the whole screen does, and you are less likely to accidentally wind up with overlapping pixels and visible seams at the region boundaries. To use an overused marketing term, your picture will be "seamless."

Assuming indivisible pixels, the mathematics of the mapping goes as follows. (I will only show the transformation of the $X$ coordinate in most of my examples here; the $Y$ coordinate does something similar.) The mapping rounds to the nearest integer pixel coordinate (by adding $\frac{1}{2}$ and truncating via the floor function) and has a fudge to keep the rightmost NDC value of $+1$ a legal pixel coordinate. The NDC boundaries map according to

$$-1 \mapsto 0$$
$$+1 \mapsto N_x - \varepsilon$$

This implies that the transformation to integer pixel coordinate $I_x$ must be

$$I_x = \text{floor}(s_x X_{NDC} + d_x) \qquad \textbf{(1)}$$

where

$$s_x = d_x = (N_x - \varepsilon)/2$$

# The Problem

This transformation forces all line endpoints or polygon vertices to be centered at the nearest pixel. This introduces some fraction-of-a-pixel distortion in the image, but for quick and dirty display applications this is adequate; aliasing disguises the errors in location. (What's good about aliasing? It makes other errors unnoticeable. What's good about smog? It makes for pretty sunsets.) For higher-quality images we want to be more careful and keep endpoints to subpixel resolution. This gets rid of the subtle positional distortions even if we do no antialiasing, and it also gives us the required information if we do do antialiasing.

# Floating-Point Pixel Coordinates

The easiest way to work with subpixel resolution is to keep in the floating-point domain. The desired transformation from NDC space to pixel space is exemplified by the boundary conditions

$$-1 \mapsto -.5$$
$$+1 \mapsto N_x - .5$$

The transformation from NDC to pixel space is then

$$X_{pixel} = s_x X_{NDC} + d_x \tag{2}$$

where

$$s_x = \frac{N_x}{2}, \quad d_x = \frac{N_x - 1}{2}$$

To illustrate the use of floating-point pixel space, I'll review just the arithmetic aspects of two rendering algorithms here so we can compare them with other versions later. The two I will deal with are an antialiased line renderer and a simple polygon tiler.

## Line Distance Calculation

A simple way to antialias lines is to compute the distance from any given pixel $(I_x, I_y)$ to the line center and plug that into some intensity profile function. The distance is

$$D = \left| a I_x + b I_x + c \right|$$

The coefficients $a$, $b$, $c$ are initialized from the two line endpoints $(x_0, y_0)$ and $(x_1, y_1)$ via

$$d = \sqrt{(y_0 - y_1)^2 + (x_1 - x_0)^2}$$
$$a = \frac{y_0 - y_1}{d}$$
$$b = \frac{x_1 - x_0}{d}$$
$$c = -a \, x_0 - b \, y_0$$

Then in the rendering loop, the value of $D$ is calculated for the relevant pixels via incremental techniques that I won't go into here.

### Polygon Edge Algorithm

Next consider a simple polygon tiler. Each edge is specified in terms of its endpoints, which we'll call (Xbot,Ybot) for the bottom and (Xtop, Ytop) for the top. When an edge is initialized, the tiler must figure out on what integer subrange of scan line coordinates the edge is visible. The edge first becomes visible (assuming we are scanning from bottom to top) on the scan line with the next higher integer coordinate above Ybot:floor(Ybot)+1, called the entering scan line. The edge is last visible on the next lower integer coordinate below Ytop:floor(Ytop), called the exiting scan line. See Figure 15.2. Some authors use the ceiling function to calculate the exiting scan line, but this creates problems for vertices exactly on a scan line. Using the floor function, as I have, works properly in this case. See Figure 15.3. The lower edge is visible through scan line floor(Y), and the upper edge picks up on scan line floor (Y)+1.

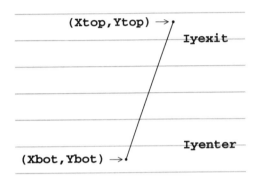

**Figure 15.2**  *Entering and exiting scan lines*

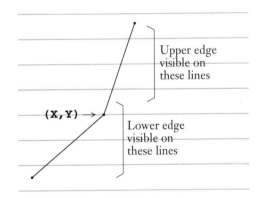

**Figure 15.3**  *Vertex exactly on a scan line*

While an edge is active, the tiler must calculate the *X* intersection of the edge with the current scan line. Each time you progress up a scan line this *X* intersection advances by a constant increment, Dxdy. Further, the initial value of *X* on the entering scan line is not Xbot; it must be advanced by a fraction of Dxdy that represents the distance from Ybot to Iyenter. The initialization for a created edge is as follows. (All variables that start with I are integers; all others are floating point.)

```
Iyenter = floor(Ybot) + 1
Iyexit  = floor(Ytop)
Dxdy    = (Xtop - Xbot) / (Ytop - Ybot)
Fy      = Iyenter - Ybot
X       = Xbot + Fy*Dydx
```

I've left out some details, like data structures for storing X and Dxdy and ensuring that horizontal edges won't kill you. I'm only concerned with the arithmetic here.

During the processing of each scan line, the $X$ intersections of active edges are picked off in pairs and the region between them is colored in. Given two floating-point $X$ edge intersections `Xleft` and `Xright`, we must color in the pixels from `floor(Xleft)+1` to `floor(Xright)`. This ensures that two adjacent polygons don't lay claim to the same pixel if an edge passes exactly through a pixel center.

# Scaled Integer Pixels

Constructing algorithms with floating-point arithmetic is easy, but floating point is really overkill for the resolution we need. Polygon tiling and line generation are inner loops of any rendering algorithm; if possible we'd like to allow them to use integer arithmetic. The solution is to use scaled integers to represent subpixel resolution. There are two scale factors I use: 32 and 65536.

The first factor divides pixel space into $\frac{1}{32}$ pixel-wide bins, which I will call minipixels. This factor allows a typical scaled pixel coordinate to fit into a 16-bit word. Effectively the high 11 bits are the integer part and the low 5 bits are the fraction. This level of minipixel resolution is adequate for storing and retrieving vertex coordinates, especially if antialiasing is going to blur out the pixel.

The larger factor of 65536 gives a lot more resolution but requires a full 32-bit integer. It gives 16 bits to the integer part and 16 bits to the fraction with the binary point in the middle. This allows us to easily extract the integer part with a simple 16-bit load of the high-order half instead of using shifting. I will call these $\frac{1}{65536}$ pixel-width bins micropixels. Micropixel resolution is useful for internal calculations.

One thing to note. You might think that scaled integers would have worse resolution than floating point, but that's really not so. Remember that floating-point values represent bins too, but they only have 24 bits of fractional precision. As long as you know that the range of values is restricted to values within the screen limits, the exponent part of the floating-point number doesn't really contribute much information. For pixel coordinates that range up to about 1023, the integer micropixel representation uses 10 bits for the integer part and 16 bits for the fraction part—a total of 26 significant bits. You can do even better if you scale by a larger factor than 65536, but you lose the easy extraction of the integer part.

In the following discussion we have three different integer coordinate systems to keep track of: pixels, minipixels, and micropixels. To help keep this straight, I will adopt the convention of starting variable names for pixel coordinates with the letter `I` (as I have been doing so far). Floating-point pixel coordinates will still be called Xpixel. Minipixel variable names will start with J or K, and micropixel names will start with L.

## How to Generate Scaled Pixels

Now let's look at how these scalings can be done. There are two different ways to associate the scaled integer bit patterns with pixel coordinate ranges. These can cause subtle problems if they are not understood properly. To keep the arithmetic simple for illustrative purposes, I'll use a minipixel scale factor of 10 and a micropixel scale of 100 in what follows.

The most obvious technique is the standard way to generate scaled integer representations of floating-point quantities: scale by the factor and round to the nearest integer. This comes off as

$$J_x = \text{floor}(10\, X_{pixel} + .5)$$

or, plugging in equation 2, we get

$$J_x = \text{floor}\!\left(\frac{10\, N_x}{2} X_{NDC} + \frac{10\, N_x - 9}{2}\right)$$

The alternative that I actually prefer is the more convenient algorithmic technique of using the existing NDC-to-pixel machinery of equation 1 and simply claiming to have 10 times as many pixels as I really do. When I do this I also specify an extra displacement of –5 to move the zero point of the scaled integers to the center of the leftmost pixel. Almost. Replacing $N_x$ with $10 N_x$ in equation 1 (forgetting about the $\epsilon$ for now) and subtracting 5 leads to

$$K_x = \text{floor}\!\left(\frac{10\, N_x}{2} X_{NDC} + \frac{10\, N_x - 10}{2}\right)$$

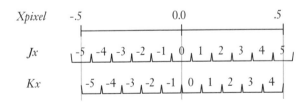

**Figure 15.4** *Two minipixel subdivision techniques*

There is a difference between these two schemes. What does it mean? Well, I've found that scaled integer representations can best be thought of as tokens for some range of real values. The two techniques above generate two different token-to-range mappings offset by $\frac{1}{20}$ of a pixel, as shown in Figure 15.4. Each mapping has the same resolution, the same sized minipixel; they are just positioned differently. Note that if we were to double the scale factor for type J, half of the new minipixel centers would line up with the old ones. If we double the scale factor for type K, none of the new minipixel centers would coincide with the center of an old one;

they go like tick marks on a ruler, ($\frac{1}{4}$, $\frac{3}{4}$) becoming ($\frac{1}{8}$, $\frac{3}{8}$, $\frac{5}{8}$, $\frac{7}{8}$). For type K there is actually no explicit representation for the actual pixel center; a value of –1 represents floating-point pixel range (–0.1, 0.0) and 0 represents (0.0, 0.1). But that's OK; we will deal with this properly later. Incidentally, as an exercise, you can convince yourself that if the scale factor were odd, then the pixel center *will* be the center of one of the minipixels.

We can use either of the above two formulations for minipixels (with care) to represent line endpoints. But when we do calculations within a rendering algorithm—for example, tracking the $X$ intersection of an edge by adding the constant Dxdy for each scan line—we must be more careful. For these situations the more accurate micropixel coordinates are in order. Furthermore, since the micropixel values still are tokens for some (small) range of real values, we would like to arrange it so that normal integer arithmetic on the tokens generates a reasonable approximation to the token for the range of the result. (I talked about this in more detail in my article "Dirty Pixels."[1]) For this reason, micropixels are most conveniently generated using the equation

$$L_x = \mathrm{floor}(100 * X_{pixel} + .5)$$

## Integerizing the Algorithms

Now let's see how our rendering algorithms change if we presume the input line endpoints are given to us in integer minipixel coordinates. The general strategy is to pretend to convert the minipixels back to floating point, plug these expressions into the original algorithm, and do some algebraic simplification. Then convert any values we need for subsequent calculation to micropixels to get to high-precision integer arithmetic.

How do we convert the minipixels back to floating point? An integer token should probably convert to the floating-point value at the center of the range it represents. For type J minipixels this is simply

```
Xpixel = Jx / 10
```

But for type K this is not quite right. A token value of, say, 0 represents the range (0.0, 0.1), so the conversion must be

```
Xpixel = Kx/10.0 + .05
```

I confess: until I realized this, many of my line drawing images were in error by $\frac{1}{20}$ pixel.

If we have occasion to convert K type minipixels to micropixels, the two-step process reduces to

---

1  *IEEE Computer Graphics and Applications*, 9(4):100, July 1989.

$$L_x = (K_x/10.0 + 0.05) * 100.0 + 0.5 = 10\,K_x + 5$$

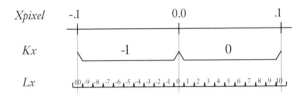

**Figure 15.5** *Relation of minipixels to micropixels*

The addition of .5 (for rounding) has been suppressed, since all other arithmetic is done with integers and the .5 never affects the result. This has the interesting effect of placing micropixel centers in the cracks between minipixel bins, as shown in Figure 15.5.

## Polygon Edge Algorithm

Let's see how the arithmetic looks for the polygon edge initialization. We'll use type K minipixels. First, to find the entering scan line we use

```
Iyenter = floor(Ybot + 1)
        = floor(Kybot/10. + .05 + 1)
```

Since `Kybot` is an integer, the value .05 doesn't ever add enough to matter, so the calculation can be done completely in integers. Note also that, since the K values represent floating-point pixel coordinates like –.15, –.05, +.05, +.15, etc., a vertex can never lie exactly on a scan line.

The remaining calculations convert `Dxdy` and `x` to micropixel coordinates. Note that in the calculation of `Ldxdy`, the scale and offset values for K conversion to floating point cancel out.

```
Iyenter = Kybot/10 + 1
Iyexit  = Kytop/10 + 1
Ldxdy   = (Kxtop-Kxbot)/(Kytop-Kybot)*100+.5
fy      = Iyenter - (Kybot/10. + .05)
Lx      = Kxbot * 10 + 5 + fy * Ldydx
```

During the processing of each scan line, we pick off pairs of edges and then color in the pixel region between them. For x coordinates of `Lxleft` and `Lxright` the desired pixel region is from `High16Bitsof(Lxleft)+1` to `High16Bitsof(Lxright)`.

## Line Distance Calculation

How about the other rendering problem, the line distance calculation? Remember that *a*, *b*, and *c* are all floating-point numbers and are calculated by

$$D = \sqrt{(K_{y0} - K_{y1})^2 + (K_{x1} - K_{x0})^2}$$

$$a = \frac{K_{y0} - K_{y1}}{D}$$

$$b = \frac{K_{x1} - K_{x0}}{D}$$

$$c = -a(K_{x0}/10.0 + 0.05) - b(K_{y0}/10.0 + 0.05)$$

Notice that the calculation of $a$ and $b$ is unchanged, since the scale factor and offsets of the conversion simply cancel out.

# Subsampling

The commonest dodge for doing antialiasing is subsampling. This is another use for subpixel resolution. We simply point sample the image at several locations within the pixel and then apply a downsampling filter to get back the desired number of pixels. Again there are several ways to look at this and several subtle geometric differences between them.

If we are doing non-uniform (stochastic) subsampling, we're probably better off sticking to non-scaled floating-point pixel coordinates (equation 2) and generating the random samples lying $\pm\frac{1}{2}$ (or more) away from the pixel center.

If we are doing uniform subsampling, we will point sample the image at some uniform grid of $f$ subsamples per pixel. The easiest way to do this is to modify the NDC-to-pixel mapping to put the subsamples on to integer coordinates. The tiling algorithm is none the wiser. It just generates an image designed for a higher resolution display than we really have. The downsampling filter then reduces this to the proper number of pixels for the display hardware.

The subsamples can be positioned relative to the pixel centers in the same two ways that we did for minipixels (even though we are keeping to floating-point pixel coordinates for now). This will have an important effect on the downsampling filter.

The two possible transformations are

$$X_{subsamp} = f\, X_{pixel} + \frac{f}{2} \qquad\qquad (3)$$

and

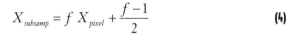

$$X_{subsamp} = f\, X_{pixel} + \frac{f - 1}{2} \qquad\qquad\textbf{(4)}$$

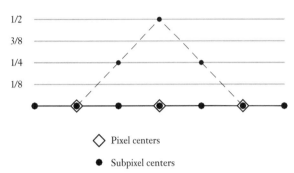

Figure 15.6  *Subsamples centered on pixel*

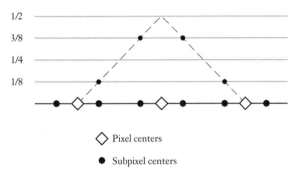

Figure 15.7  *Subsamples snug fit within pixel*

Equation 3 guarantees that a subsample will lie exactly on the $X_{NDC} = -1$ edge; equation 4 fits $f$ subsamples snugly within the range of each pixel.

Depending on whether $f$ is even or odd, the subpixels either will all lie between the original pixel centers, or every $f$ subpixels will align with an original pixel center. This will determine how the downsampling filter aligns with the subpixels. Let's see some explicit examples for $f = 2$. Figure 15.6 uses equation 3. A simple triangle downsampling filter covers three subsamples, so the downsampling weights are $(\frac{1}{4}, \frac{1}{2}, \frac{1}{4})$. Figure 15.7 uses equation 4. The triangle filter straddles four subsamples, so the downsampling weights are $(\frac{1}{8}, \frac{3}{8}, \frac{3}{8}, \frac{1}{8})$.

# Both at Once

If you want to use integer arithmetic in addition to subsampling, the easiest way seems to be to use type K minipixels with snug fit subsamples. The transformation from NDC space to minipixel space can be done in one crack by simply claiming you have $N_x * f * m$ pixels and using equation 1. This makes the minipixels nest nicely between the subsamples. The value of $m$ is the minipixel scale factor; we've used 10 in our examples here. You just have to make sure that $N_x * f * m$ fits within your word size. The integer version of the rendering algorithm needs only slight generalization to point sample at a spacing of $m$ subminipixels (instead of 10), giving the $N_x * f$ samples we need.

# Punchline

B e careful. The simplest darn things can have subtle pitfalls. Whether your micropixels or subpixels are centered on the macropixels or straddle them depends on how you set up your NDC-to-pixel space transformation. It is important to be aware of which situation you are in in order to correctly interpret the numbers.

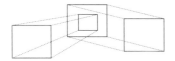

# CHAPTER SIXTEEN

# Grandpa, What Does "Viewport" Mean?

J A N U A R Y    1 9 9 2

Computer graphics has never been much for uniformity in terminology, what with left- or right-handed coordinate systems, row or column vector notation for points, and clockwise or counterclockwise rotation rules and polygon ordering. This is, I guess, the result of different research groups from all over the world approaching similar problems but with their own notational conventions.

One casualty in the war of words is the term *window* and its relation to the term *viewport*. Back in the Old Days (a phrase I find myself using increasingly frequently), there was something called a window-to-viewport transformation that programmers used to specify which parts of a geometrical database should be mapped to what part of the screen. In that scenario, the term *viewport* meant the rectangle on the screen where the picture went, and *window* meant the region of the database coordinate system that should be mapped there. But now there's considerable commercial and political pressure to use the term *window* to mean all those rectangular pieces of screen with their enclosing frames, title bars, and assorted bric-a-brac. Confusion reigns if you are not sure which type of window somebody might be talking about.

This is not all bad. There has always been something creepy about the window-to-viewport transformation, hereupon called w-to-v, that I have just recently resolved in my own mind. So in this chapter I am going to describe how I have extracted the desirable aspects of w-to-v while discarding the disquieting ones.

# The Classic Window-to-Viewport Transform

The original idea here is pretty straightforward. Users specify a rectangular region that they want to display, the window, in their desired coordinate space as $W_l$, $W_r$, $W_b$, $W_t$. Then they pick a rectangular region on the screen, the viewport, where they want to put it, $V_l$, $V_r$, $V_b$, $V_t$. This looks like Figure 16.1. The computer then miraculously calculates and performs the necessary scale and offset to get from one to the other (equation 1):

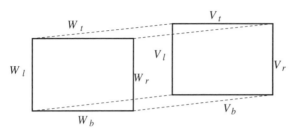

**Figure 16.1**  *The window-to-viewport map*

$$X_{view} = s_x X_{wind} + d_x$$
$$Y_{view} = s_y Y_{wind} + d_y$$

(1)

where the scale and displacement come from the requirement

$$W_l \mapsto V_l$$
$$W_r \mapsto V_r$$
$$W_b \mapsto V_b$$
$$W_t \mapsto V_t$$

This, using the exemplary transformation technique mentioned in Chapter 14, gives us

$$s_x = \frac{V_r - V_l}{W_r - W_l}$$
$$d_x = V_l - s_x W_l$$
$$s_y = \frac{V_t - V_b}{W_t - W_b}$$
$$d_y = V_b - s_y W_b$$

(2)

We expect to precalcuate these scales and offsets during some initialization routine, save them in some static variables, and then use them in drawing routines that transform them via equation 1.

# How Does This Fit In?

How does this relate to the graphics pipeline I have been discussing for the last few chapters? Let's review the stages of coordinate transformations in the pipeline (leaving out clipping for now).

*Definition*—Objects are defined in this system.

*Universe*—They are placed via possibly nested modeling transformations in a consistent universe space.

*Eye*—An eye location and viewing direction are selected and the universe is transformed so that the eye is at the origin and the viewing direction is down the $z$ axis.

*Postperspective*—A perspective distortion is performed that transforms the viewing pyramid to a parallel-sided rectangular parallelepiped ("brick" in the vernacular). I called this *perspective space* in previous chapters. I'm changing the name here for emphasis.

*Normalized device coordinates (NDC)*—The viewable brick is squashed into a region of a device-independent screen coordinate system.

*Pixel*—The NDC is reinterpreted by device-dependent code into the correct hardware pixel coordinates.

According to the original usage of the term *window-to-viewport transformation*, the window would be in definition space and the viewport in pixel space. But this doesn't work very well. First, it's better to specify the viewport in NDC space for device independence. No problem; that doesn't change things conceptually. But the window specification in definition space is usually inconvenient if we are doing complex nested 3D transforms. In fact, we already have a mechanism (full nested $4 \times 4$ homogeneous matrices) to do much more general transformations than the simple scale-and-offset of w-to-v. Furthermore, there is something clumsy about the w-to-v we have so far defined—non-uniform scale factors. If we pick a window and a viewport that don't happen to have the same aspect ratio, that is, if

$$\frac{W_t - W_b}{W_r - W_l} \neq \frac{V_t - V_b}{V_r - V_l}$$

the scale factor will be different in $x$ and $y$. I have rarely found this to be useful, and in fact, it's usually something to be avoided. Though it's possible to force the above two ratios to be equal by fiddling with one or the other of the rectangles, it's a nuisance.

For these reasons I have adopted a modified form of the w-to-v transform as part of the initialization of my image rendering system. The initialization takes a viewport (though the modern term would now be *window*) specified in NDC. In fact, for animations I find it more convenient to describe the viewport in terms of its center ($V_x, V_y$), size ($V_s$), and aspect ratio ($V_a$) and generate the boundaries via

$$V_l = V_x - V_s$$
$$V_r = V_x + V_s$$
$$V_b = V_y - V_s V_a$$
$$V_t = V_y + V_s V_a$$

I then force the viewport to be mapped from a *canonical window* in perspective space with the same aspect ratio, as shown in Figure 16.2. This canonical window always has the boundaries

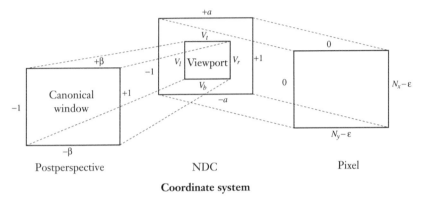

$$W_l = -1$$
$$W_r = +1$$
$$W_b = -\beta$$
$$W_t = +\beta$$

where β is the aspect ratio of the viewport, i.e.,

$$\beta = \frac{V_t - V_b}{V_r - V_l}$$

**Figure 16.2** *The canonical window-to-pixel map*

Plugging these constants into equation 2 gives

$$s_x = \frac{V_r - V_l}{2}$$

$$s_y = \frac{V_t - V_b}{2\beta}$$

but using the definition of β, this degenerates to

$$s_x = s_y = \frac{V_r - V_l}{2}$$

Voila! Equal scale factors in *x* and *y*. Whereupon

$$d_x = \frac{V_r + V_l}{2}$$

$$d_y = \frac{V_b + V_t}{2}$$

I then merge this transformation with the NDC-to-pixel transformation built up in Chapter 14 to form one big fat scale and displacement to go from postperspective coordinates directly to pixel coordinates. This is what I use to initialize the $4 \times 4$ current transformation matrix (CTM) that multiplies all points entered into the graphic system. After this initialization the user can multiply in other transformations as described in Chapter 3. Multiplying in a perspective matrix makes the CTM go from eye space to pixel space. Then multiplying in a pure rotation and a translation makes it go from universe space to pixel space. Further multiplying in some other modeling transformations makes it go from definition space to pixel space. The whole trick is that you start, not with an identity matrix, but with the above scale and offset from the canonical window to the user-selected viewport.

# Clipping

**n** ot quite. We still have to fit clipping into our world view. In Chapter 13 I described how clipping can be real fast if it's done to its own standardized region: $(0, 1)$ in $x$, $y$, and $z$. To accommodate this, we split our newly minted w-to-v transformation into two parts.

First a pause for notation control. We are shortly going to experience a whole lot of scales and displacements between a whole lot of intermediate coordinate systems. I will abbreviate the coordinate systems with the single letters:

P—Pixel space.

N—NDC space. The viewport is defined in this space.

C—Clip space.

W—Postperspective space. (We've already used P and the canonical window is defined in this space, hence W.)

Then the scale and displacement to take $x$ from clip space to NDC space would be denoted

$$S_{xCN}, \quad D_{xCN}$$

and what we've been calling $s_x$ is really $s_{xWN}$, and similarly for $s_y$, $d_x$, and $d_y$.

Now back to our program. Part one of the fragmented w-to-v maps the canonical window to the canonical clipping region. In $x$

$$-1 \mapsto 0, \quad \text{and} \quad +1 \mapsto 1$$

In $y$

$$-\beta \mapsto 0, \quad \text{and} \quad +\beta \mapsto 1$$

The result is

$$S_{xWC} = \frac{1}{2}, \qquad D_{xWC} = \frac{1}{2}$$
$$S_{yWC} = \frac{1}{2\beta}, \qquad D_{yWC} = \frac{1}{2}$$

Part two of the transform maps the clipping region to the viewport. In $x$

$$0 \mapsto V_l, \quad \text{and} \quad 1 \mapsto V_r$$

In $y$

$$0 \mapsto V_b, \quad \text{and} \quad 1 \mapsto V_t$$

The result is

$$S_{xCN} = V_r - V_l, \qquad D_{xCN} = V_l$$
$$S_{yCN} = V_t - V_b, \qquad D_{yCN} = V_b$$

Now, if all is right with the world, the composition of these two should give us back the new-and-improved w-to-v transform we derived above. Let's see . . .

$$s_x = S_{xWC}\, S_{xCN} = \frac{V_r - V_l}{2}$$

$$d_x = D_{xWC}\, S_{xCN} + D_{xCN} = \frac{V_r + V_l}{2}$$

$$s_y = S_{yWC}\, S_{yCN} = \frac{V_t - V_b}{2\beta} = \frac{V_r - V_l}{2}$$

$$d_y = D_{yWC}\, S_{yCN} + D_{yCN} = \frac{V_b + V_t}{2}$$

It works. This means that the insertion of clip space between perspective and NDC spaces has no net effect on the geometry of viewing or where the picture gets mapped.

The WC transform is what is actually used to initialize the CTM. I called it $\mathbf{T}_1$ in Chapter 13. Next we compose the CN part of the transform with the NP (NDC-to-pixel) transform to take us straight from clip space to pixel space. I called this scale and displacement $\mathbf{T}_2$ in Chapter 13 and we apply it after clipping and after the homogeneous division by $w$. See Figure 16.3.

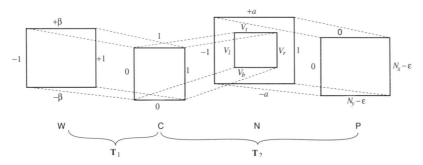

**Figure 16.3** *The window-to-pixel map including clipping*

# Offscreen Viewports

ow what if some bozo—I'm sorry—what if some user tries to initialize a viewport with coordinates that extend outside the allowable NDC range of $(-1, +1)$ in $x$ or $(-a, +a)$ in $y$? What do we do? Well, what would be reasonable to do? If the user moves the viewport past the edge of the screen they would expect to still see the part of the viewport that is still visible with the dangling part clipped off. It so happens that we can use the same clipping machinery we already have lying around to accomplish this. We just do some more elaborate initialization of $\mathbf{T}_1$ and $\mathbf{T}_2$. We'll do this by a four-step process:

1.  Find the intersection of the given viewport rectangle with the available NDC range. This forms the *visible viewport range*, a subset of the given viewport.
2.  Inverse transform the visible viewport range to postperspective space to determine that chunk of the canonical window that the clipper should keep.
3.  Find the transform from that region of the canonical window to the (0, 1) clip region. This is $\mathbf{T}_1$.
4.  Find the transform from the clip region to the visible viewport range. Merge this with the NP transform. This is $\mathbf{T}_2$.

First let's take care of the extreme situation: what if someone shoves the viewport completely off the screen? It might happen; you never can tell. This occurs if

$$V_l \geq 1 \quad \text{or} \quad V_r \leq -1 \quad \text{or} \quad V_b \geq +a \quad \text{or} \quad V_t \leq -a$$

In this case we want to set things up so that *everything* gets clipped off. One way to do this is to just force

$$S_{xWC} = 0, \quad D_{xWC} = -1$$
$$S_{yWC} = 0, \quad D_{yWC} = -1$$

That is, the universe is shrunk to a point that is outside the clipping boundaries. Alternatively you could set a switch inside the clipper, causing it to return immediately upon each call.

But what if the viewport is at least somewhat visible? Look at Figure 16.4. In most cases the visible viewport region has the boundaries

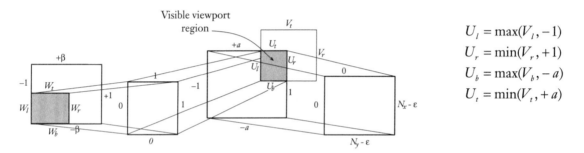

$$U_l = \max(V_l, -1)$$
$$U_r = \min(V_r, +1)$$
$$U_b = \max(V_b, -a)$$
$$U_t = \min(V_t, +a)$$

**Figure 16.4**  *The offscreen viewports*

Now inverse transform these boundaries back to perspective space to get the new window boundaries:

$$W_l = \frac{U_l - d_x}{s_x} = \frac{2U_l - V_r - V_l}{V_r - V_l}$$

$$W_r = \frac{U_r - d_x}{s_x} = \frac{2U_r - V_r - V_l}{V_r - V_l}$$

$$W_b = \frac{U_b - d_y}{s_x} = \frac{2U_b - V_t - V_b}{V_r - V_l}$$

$$W_t = \frac{U_t - d_y}{s_x} = \frac{2U_t - V_t - V_b}{V_r - V_l}$$

The denominators above for $y$ are not typos. Remember that $s_x = s_y$. Note that, as a reality check, if $U_l = V_l$, the above expression for $W_l$ reduces to $-1$, and similarly for the other boundaries.

To get the new $\mathbf{T}_1$ we map, in $x$

$$W_l \mapsto 0, \quad \text{and} \quad W_r \mapsto 1$$

In $y$

$$W_b \mapsto 0, \quad \text{and} \quad W_t \mapsto 1$$

The result is

$$S_{xWC} = 1/(W_r - W_l), \quad D_{xWC} = -W_l/(W_r - W_l)$$
$$S_{yWC} = 1/(W_t - W_b), \quad D_{yWC} = -W_b/(W_t - W_b)$$

If you want you can plug in the W definitions and boil this down to

$$S_{xWC} = \frac{V_r - V_l}{2(U_r - U_l)} \qquad D_{xWC} = \frac{-2U_l + V_r + V_l}{2(U_r - U_l)}$$

$$S_{yWC} = \frac{V_r - V_l}{2(U_t - U_b)} \qquad D_{yWC} = \frac{-2U_b + V_t + V_b}{2(U_t - U_b)}$$

and you never have to calculate W's. *Warning, danger . . . there is a potential for divide by zero.* You'd better check for $U_r = U_l$ and $U_t = U_b$ and avoid having the rug pulled out from under you if they are equal. This can only happen if the requested viewport has an $x$ or $y$ size of zero. In that case, just use the transformation from the previous section.

Finally, part two of the transform maps the clipping region to the visible viewport. In $x$

$$0 \mapsto U_l, \quad \text{and} \quad 1 \mapsto U_r$$

In $y$

$$0 \mapsto U_b, \quad \text{and} \quad 1 \mapsto U_t$$

The result is

$$S_{xCN} = U_r - U_l, \quad D_{xCN} = U_l$$
$$S_{yCN} = U_t - U_b, \quad D_{yCN} = U_b$$

Merge this with the NP transform and you're in business.

# So What?

I've rarely seen any computer graphics books address the problem of non-square screens during initialization of the transforms of the graphics pipeline. The offscreen viewport calculation does this nicely. You just initialize a default viewport to go to $(-1, +1)$ in both $x$ and $y$. If this sticks out beyond the NDC range, e.g., in $y$ for a landscape-oriented display, the proper visible subregion will be automatically extracted with the CTM set up to map that region to the standard clip region. The clipper is none the wiser, but you get a non-distorted picture on the screen. It's taken me a good long time to figure this out, but now I'm finally happy with it.

# CHAPTER SEVENTEEN

# Hyperbolic Interpolation

JULY 1992

It's always a red-letter day when I can figure out a new use for homogeneous coordinates. This time I'll tell about a way to use them to do interpolation of various parameters properly when tiling polygons. The exact definition of "properly" comes from one of those things that homogeneous coordinates is good at—perspective.

## The Existing Machinery

First some notational conventions: I'll write matrices in boldface, vectors in roman type, and vector elements in italics with subscripts. A general homogeneous vector, one whose $w$ component is not 1, will appear with a tilde over the name. A vector of the same name with no tilde represents that homogeneous vector with the $w$ component divided out.

### Coordinate Systems

Let's review some basic operations of the graphics pipeline and define some coordinate systems. In general, the pipeline transforms a coordinate point through a whole chain of coordinate spaces on its way to the screen. I'm going to vastly simplify the process for the purposes of this discussion. There are only two coordinate spaces that we'll really need to deal with here: eye space and pixel space.

We'll start with polygon vertices in eye space, the coordinate space with the eye at the origin looking down the Z axis. This space is significant because it's the last one of the chain where physical distances are meaningful. For example, it's where we must perform all lighting calculations. Let's call a point in this space E. In homogeneous coordinates this is

$$E = \left[ E_x, E_y, E_z, 1 \right]$$

We then do the perspective distortion necessary to get to hardware pixel space in two steps. First we multiply by a $4 \times 4$ matrix consisting of a perspective transformation and a viewport transformation. I'll call this matrix **M**. Since **M** has a perspective component, the $w$ coordinate of the transformed point will not be 1.

$$E\,\mathbf{M} = \tilde{P} = \left[ \tilde{P}_x, \tilde{P}_y, \tilde{P}_z, \tilde{P}_w \right]$$

We will perform clipping in this coordinate system. (This is different from the optimized clipping space I discussed in Chapter 13, but that just changes the coefficients of the clipping planes used. It doesn't change the basic mathematical relationships.)

After clipping, we perform the second operation: we divide out the $w$ component to get coordinates in nonhomogeneous hardware pixel coordinates.

$$\tilde{P} / \tilde{P}_w = P = \left[ P_x, P_y, P_z, 1 \right]$$

I've diagrammed these relations in Figure 17.1. The key thing that we are going to worry about is the manipulation of coordinates either *before* or *after* the homogeneous division.

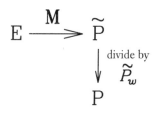

**Figure 17.1** *Transformations between coordinate systems*

## Polygon Tilers

Now let's have a quickie review of the mathematics of a polygon tiler. A 3D polygon tiler begins with a list of the pixel space coordinates of each vertex, $[P_x, P_y, P_z]$. It must then do two things. First, it must identify which pixels lie inside the polygon. Second, it must calculate a $Z$ depth value for each pixel inside the polygon to use in occlusion tests. We are primarily interested in this second calculation.

A tiling algorithm consists of two nested loops, representing two successive reductions in dimensionality. The outer, $Y$, loop tracks the intersection of each edge with a *current scan line*. That is, it interpolates values for $[P_x, P_z]$ between the endpoints of the edge as a function of the pixel coordinate $Y$. The inner, $X$, loop then interpolates the $[P_z]$ value horizontally between pairs of edge intersections.

Let's examine the mathematics of the $Y$ loop more closely. We are given coordinates at two endpoints of an edge; let's call them P′ and P″. The edge intersects scan line $Y$ at a proportional distance between these two points of

$$\alpha = \frac{Y - P'_y}{P''_y - P'_y}$$

$\alpha$ goes from 0 at P′ to 1 at P″. The intersection is then

$$P = P' + \alpha(P'' - P')$$

We step down the screen in equal steps of $Y$, which means we are going to evaluate the above for equal steps in $\alpha$. We typically do this in an incremental manner; we precalculate the change in P for each scan line jump and just add that increment to P each time through the $Y$ loop.

There is an implicit assumption here. The $Y$, $X$ nested interpolation works consistently only if the polygon is well behaved. By that I mean that all the vertices in P space are coplanar. Effectively, the relation of $P_z$ to pixel coordinates is of the form

$$P_z = aX + bY + c$$

## Another Question

But there's another question about why this works. What we actually start with is a flat polygon in *eye* space. We then put it through this weird perspective-distorting transform and expect that mere linear interpolation in pixel space gives us the correct $Z$ value. To show that this is really OK, let's start with a point a distance $\beta$ along an edge in eye space.

$$E = E' + \beta(E'' - E')$$

Transform it by **M** to get $\tilde{P}$:

$$\tilde{P} = E\,\mathbf{M} = E'\,\mathbf{M} + \beta(E''\mathbf{M} - E'\mathbf{M}) = \tilde{P}' + \beta(\tilde{P}'' - \tilde{P}')$$

Divide out the $w$ component to get P:

$$P = \frac{\tilde{P}' + \beta(\tilde{P}'' - \tilde{P}')}{\tilde{P}'_w + \beta(\tilde{P}''_w - \tilde{P}'_w)}$$

Now we want to write this in terms of the endpoints of the edge in pixel space. Each endpoint satisfies

$$P' = \frac{\tilde{P}'}{\tilde{P}'_w}$$

or

$$\tilde{P}' = \tilde{P}'_w \, P'$$

Plug this and a similar expression for $\tilde{P}''$ into the above, do a little algebra, and you get

$$P = P' + \left( \frac{\beta \tilde{P}''_w}{\tilde{P}'_w + \beta(\tilde{P}''_w - \tilde{P}'_w)} \right)(P'' - P')$$

What does this mean? Compare this with linear interpolation in pixel space

$$P = P' + \alpha(P'' - P')$$

It means that a point, say, halfway between E′ and E″ transforms to a point *somewhere* on the line connecting P′ and P″, but *not* necessarily halfway between them. To generalize, equally spaced dots along an edge in eye space transform into dots that are indeed colinear in pixel space; they just aren't equally spaced any more. This means that a flat polygon in eye space transforms into a flat polygon in pixel space, and we can use linear interpolation for the $Z$ values in pixel space.

# Getting Colorful

With the invention of Gouraud shading, polygon tilers began linearly interpolating colors across the polygon in the same way they interpolated $Z$ values. To make the tiler do this, modify the machinery as follows. For each vertex build a larger vector of values that include colors as well as position coordinates. Each vertex looks like

$$\left[ E_x, E_y, E_z, 1, C_{red}, C_{green}, C_{blue} \right]$$

Then feed this down the pipe. The first stage transforms the positional components according to matrix **M**, yielding

$$\left[ \tilde{P}_x, \tilde{P}_y, \tilde{P}_z, \tilde{P}_w, C_{red}, C_{green}, C_{blue} \right]$$

This then goes to the clipper. Any interpolation done here is performed on the color components as well as the positional components. (The perceptive reader might suspect that there is something fishy about the way we are clipping colors. We will deal with this later.)

After clipping, divide the $w$ component out of the positional components:

$$\left[ \frac{\tilde{P}_x}{\tilde{P}_w}, \frac{\tilde{P}_y}{\tilde{P}_w}, \frac{\tilde{P}_z}{\tilde{P}_w}, C_{red}, C_{green}, C_{blue} \right] = \left[ P_x, P_y, P_z, C_{red}, C_{green}, C_{blue} \right]$$

The tiler gets an array of this form for each vertex. It then uses the same machinery to interpolate color values as it uses to interpolate $P_z$ values.

To get consistent results regardless of how the polygon might be rotated, we must have well-behaved color assignments. I use "well-behaved" here in the same sense I did for $P_z$ values. For, say, the red color primary, the vertex color assignments expressed as $[P_x, P_y, C_{red}]$ should be coplanar (with a similar requirement for green and blue values). This makes the color a linear function of the pixel space coordinates; that is, each color primary is expressible in the form

$$C_{red} = aX + bY + c$$

This is, of course, guaranteed if the polygon is a triangle, but it's perfectly possible for polygons with more sides. If the color assignments don't satisfy this constraint then—according to most computer graphics books—you split the polygon into triangles. But, as I explain below, this isn't an adequate solution.

# More Stuff

Why stop at color? Phong shading requires that we interpolate normal vector components between endpoints. No problem. Just treat each component the same way we do color components.

How about some more elaborate shading models? Suppose that we have local light sources and that our lighting model depends on the location of the viewer. For each point on the object, a different vector extends from it to the light source and to the eye. We therefore need to calculate the eye space point, E, corresponding to each pixel inside the polygon.

And then there's texture mapping. We can assign texture coordinates, $[u, v]$, to each vertex and interpolate them at each pixel, then use the interpolated values as input to some texture function.

The naive approach is to just tack on more elements to our array

$$\left[ P_x, P_y, P_z, C_{red}, \ldots, N_x, \ldots, E_x, \ldots, u, v \right]$$

and linearly interpolate them all between polygon vertices. But there's a hidden error here. Doing pure linear interpolation in pixel space for E, $u$, and $v$ is really not correct. To appreciate this fully, let's look at a common example.

# A Problem of Perspective

$\int$ uppose we have a square polygon with parametric coordinates [*u*, *v*] defined at the four corners as [0, 0], [0, 1], [1, 0], [1, 1]. Now let's be really original and map a checkerboard onto the square and view it in perspective. If we simply interpolate the [*u*, *v*] parameters linearly across and down the polygon according to the standard tiling machinery, we would get the checkerboard like Figure 17.2b, with equal vertical spacing of the small squares. This is not right. How can you tell? Use a standard artists' trick: draw a diagonal to the perspectivized square. If the perspective is correct, the corners of the small squares should pass through this line. Try it; I'll wait. . . . Not too good, right? What we really want is for the checkerboard to look like Figure 17.2a. Try drawing the diagonal line now and you'll see that it works.

**Figure 17.2a**   *Correct perspective*

**Figure 17.2b**   *Incorrect perspective*

But this isn't the worst thing that can happen. Try rotating the square a bit. You'd like to see the nice picture in Figure 17.3a. Instead you'll get the weird mess shown in Figure 17.3b. Let's see how this comes about. Figure 17.4a shows the results of *v* interpolation. As the tiler scans out the top half of the polygon, *v* stays a constant 0 on the left edge, and interpolates from 0 to 1 on the right edge. Interpolating across each scan line then gives the constant *v* lines shown. On the bottom part of the polygon, *v* interpolates from 0 to 1 on the left edge and stays a constant 1 on the right edge. Interpolating across each scan line gives the constant *v* lines shown. They are all unpleasantly bent. It's not quite so bad for interpolation of *u* values shown in Figure 17.4b. Here the lines aren't bent, but they still are incorrectly equally spaced.

**Figure 17.3a**   *Correct perspective*

**Figure 17.3b**   *Incorrect perspective*

# Correct Mapping

$L$ et's see how to do this correctly. This turns out to be easier if we change the problem slightly. Let's instead solve the problem of finding eye space coordinates, E, at each pixel. First we'll do this a simple but stupid way. We simply take each interpolated pixel space coordinate $[P_x, P_y, P_z]$ and transform it by the inverse of $\mathbf{M}$ to get back to eye space. This will produce something with a nonunit $w$ component, so we have to divide it out to get back to true eye space.

$$\mathrm{P}\,\mathbf{M}^{-1} = \tilde{\mathrm{E}} = \left[\tilde{E}_x, \tilde{E}_y, \tilde{E}_z, \tilde{E}_w\right]$$

$$\tilde{\mathrm{E}}\big/\tilde{E}_w = \mathrm{E}$$

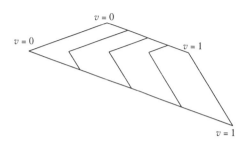

**Figure 17.4a** *Lines of constant v*

# A Faster Way to Be Correct

Doing a full matrix multiplication at each pixel is slow and, fortunately, unnecessary. Look at the above equation again:

$$\tilde{\mathrm{E}} = \mathrm{P}\,\mathbf{M}^{-1}$$

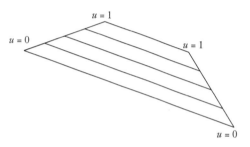

**Figure 17.4b** *Lines of constant u*

Remember that we are calculating the pixel space vector P by linearly interpolating between endpoints in pixel space. Since P is related to $\tilde{\mathrm{E}}$ by a nice linear matrix multiplication, we can effectively "factor" the matrix multiplication out of the loop by linearly interpolating between $\tilde{\mathrm{E}}$ values at its endpoints. We only need to find the $\tilde{\mathrm{E}}$ coordinates at each endpoint of the edge.

In general, for any point $\tilde{\mathrm{E}}$

$$\tilde{\mathrm{E}} = \mathrm{P}\,\mathbf{M}^{-1} = \frac{\tilde{P}}{\tilde{P}_w}\mathbf{M}^{-1} = \frac{E\mathbf{M}}{\tilde{P}_w}\mathbf{M}^{-1}$$

so

$$\tilde{\mathrm{E}} = \frac{\mathrm{E}}{\tilde{P}_w}$$

We can see this diagrammatically in Figure 17.5, an enhanced version of Figure 17.1. Crossing over the dotted line represents a homogeneous division.

What does this mean? To feed our tiler we manufacture an array of values for each polygon vertex as follows:

$$\left[P_x, P_y, P_z, \frac{E_x}{\tilde{P}_w}, \frac{E_y}{\tilde{P}_w}, \frac{E_z}{\tilde{P}_w}, \frac{1}{\tilde{P}_w}\right] = \left[P_x, P_y, P_z, \tilde{E}_x, \tilde{E}_y, \tilde{E}_z\,\tilde{E}_w\right]$$

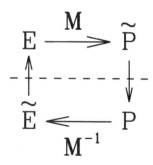

**Figure 17.5** *Division between eye space and pixel space and their linearly related spaces*

The first three elements are the positional coordinates in postperspective pixel space. The last four are values that, when linearly interpolated along edges, give four homogeneous coordinates of the point in eye space. You can use the same interpolation technique used to interpolate the $P_z$ value. We still must divide, on a pixel-by-pixel basis, the interpolated $\tilde{E}_x$, $\tilde{E}_y$, and $\tilde{E}_z$ values by the interpolated $\tilde{E}_w$ value to get the true eye space vector E.

We have basically shown that while we can interpolate $P_z$ linearly since it's of the form

$$P_z = aX + bY + c$$

we should interpolate, say, $E_z$ *hyperbolically* since it is of the form

$$E_z = \frac{aX + bY + c}{dX + eY + f}$$

This hyperbolic interpolation is just the quotient of two linearly interpolated quantities. We might have seen this by the relation between $\alpha$ and $\beta$ under the "Another Question" section earlier.

Again, referring to Figure 17.5, we find that linear interpolation of coordinates below the dotted line implies hyperbolic interpolation for coordinates above the line. And vice versa. Note, however, that while each *component* of E is a hyperbolic function of P, all the points of E are still coplanar.

Now back to texture parameters. In order for them to be well behaved they must be related to eye space coordinates by another nice linear function. We can then calculate them by the same machinery we use to calculate the eye space coordinates. We build a vector of

$$\left[ P_x, P_y, P_z, \frac{u}{\tilde{P}_w}, \frac{v}{\tilde{P}_w}, \frac{1}{\tilde{P}_w} \right]$$

Interpolate the last three values across the polygon just like before. Then, at each pixel, divide the interpolated $u/\tilde{P}_w$ and $u/\tilde{P}_w$ by the interpolated $1/\tilde{P}_w$. It works.

# Clipping

Whenever you see a division in an expression you should immediately be worried by the possibility that the denominator might be 0. What does this mean here? If $\tilde{P}_w = 0$, it means that the point P is at infinity. This will come from a point in eye space that's in the same plane as the eye, that is $E_z = 0$. This is a perfectly reasonable situation and we have to be able to deal with it.

Why didn't we worry about this when we did the homogeneous division of $\tilde{P}$ by $\tilde{P}_w$ to get P? Because these parts of the polygon are removed by the clipping process. Revelation! We want to defer the division by $\tilde{P}_w$ of all our other auxiliary coordinates until *after* clipping. Now all we have to show is that this generates the correct values geometrically.

Clipping happens in postperspective space before the homogeneous division. That is, it happens to $\tilde{P}$ coordinates and is itself a linear interpolation of the points in homogeneous space. Let's say our edge from $\tilde{P}'$ to $\tilde{P}''$ straddles a clip boundary. The clipper calculates a proportional distance $\gamma$ where the edge hits the boundary. The clipped point is then

$$\tilde{P}''' = \tilde{P}' + \gamma(\tilde{P}'' - \tilde{P}')$$

We then divide this interpolated point by its interpolated $w$ component

$$\tilde{P}'''_w = \tilde{P}'_w + \gamma(\tilde{P}''_w - \tilde{P}'_w)$$

to give the endpoint of the edge in pixel space

$$\frac{\tilde{P}'''}{\tilde{P}'''_w} = P''' = \left[P'''_x,\ P'''_y,\ P'''_z,\ 1\right]$$

Now apply this to $\tilde{E}$ interpolation. The $\tilde{E}$ vector corresponding to this clipped P is

$$\tilde{E}''' = P''' \, \mathbf{M}^{-1} = \frac{\tilde{P}''' \, \mathbf{M}^{-1}}{\tilde{P}'''_w} = \frac{(\tilde{P}' + \gamma(\tilde{P}'' - \tilde{P}')) \, \mathbf{M}^{-1}}{\tilde{P}'_w + \gamma(\tilde{P}''_w - \tilde{P}'_w)}$$

$$= \frac{E' + \gamma(E'' - E')}{\tilde{P}'_w + \gamma(\tilde{P}''_w - \tilde{P}'_w)}$$

That is, if we clip the E vector just like we do the $\tilde{P}$ vector and *then* divide it by the clipped $\tilde{P}_w$ value, we will get the correct $\tilde{E}$ vectors to interpolate between in the polygon tiler. We are guaranteed that $\tilde{P}_w \neq 0$ because the clipper is designed to clip away just those types of points. Notice that clipping applies to coordinates above the dotted line of Figure 17.5. The moral: clip first and divide later.

# More about Color

So what about colors, C, and normal vector components, N? So far we have been interpolating them linearly in P space. This sounds OK, but consider the following. Suppose you had a square polygon and your shading calculations gave one color to the two left vertices and another to the two right vertices, a simple gradation of color across the square. You might think that this would be well behaved according to our definition above. But it's not well behaved if the square is viewed in perspective. Look again at Figure 17.4a and pretend that *v* represents color. Ick. *And dividing it into triangles won't help*, since that is effectively what the tiler did for the specific orientation I picked for Figure 17.4a.

Now admittedly real shading situations aren't so violent, because the values of the colors and normal components aren't usually radically different for the various vertices. A lot of renderers don't worry about it for this reason. But it's not too hard to do it right; we interpolate colors hyperbolically. And when you think about it, it really makes the most sense to define color values and normal vector components to be linearly interpolated in preperspective eye space just like texture coordinates. This is a sensible approach because distance measurements still make sense in eye space.

The added bonus is that interpolating colors hyperbolically means that we clip the colors correctly.

# The New Mechanism

So here's the whole story.

1.  Construct an array of values for each vertex of the polygon

$$\left[\tilde{P}_x, \tilde{P}_y, \tilde{P}_z, \tilde{P}_w, E_x, \ldots, N_x, \ldots, u, \ldots, 1\right]$$

    The auxiliary components following $\tilde{P}_w$ can be any values you intend to linearly interpolate in non-perspective-distorted eye space. Note the constant 1 at the end.

2.  Perform the standard clipping process, interpolating *all* values if any clipping is done.

3.  After clipping it's time for the homogeneous division. In the original algorithm we just divided $\tilde{P}$ by $\tilde{P}_w$. Now, the correct thing is to divide the *entire* array by the $\tilde{P}_w$ value, colors and all. This gives

$$\left[\frac{\tilde{P}_x}{\tilde{P}_w}, \frac{\tilde{P}_y}{\tilde{P}_w}, \frac{\tilde{P}_z}{\tilde{P}_w}, 1, \frac{C_{red}}{\tilde{P}_w}, \ldots, \frac{E_x}{\tilde{P}_w}, \ldots, \frac{N_x}{\tilde{P}_w} \ldots, \frac{u}{\tilde{P}_w} \ldots, \frac{1}{\tilde{P}_w}\right]$$

or

$$\left[P_x, P_y, P_z, 1, \tilde{C}_{red}, \ldots, \tilde{E}_x, \ldots, \tilde{N}_x, \ldots, \tilde{u}, \ldots, \tilde{1}\right]$$

This final value, which I have fancifully written as $\tilde{1}$, is the homogeneous coordinate, the $w$ value, for each of the auxiliary vectors we are interpolating. That is,

$$\tilde{1} = \tilde{C}_w = \tilde{E}_w = \tilde{N}_w = \tilde{u}_w$$

4. Interpolate all values linearly down polygon edges and across scan lines internal to the polygon. Remember, the value of $\tilde{1}$ is different at the various vertices, so it too changes across the polygon.
5. At each pixel, divide the auxiliary components ($\tilde{C}$, $\tilde{E}$, $\tilde{N}$, $\tilde{u}$, and $\tilde{v}$) by the final element, $\tilde{1}$, to get the proper perspectively projected value. We are guaranteed that $\tilde{1}$ will never be 0. Why? Because after clipping all $\tilde{P}_w$ values are positive.
6. Calculate the pixel color using these values as input to some shading model.

There is another organizational thing going on here. The clipping and homogeneous division, and even the tiler, do not need to know the meaning of the auxiliary components. They can operate just fine given only the total length of the array. The only code that needs to know the array's interpretation is the code that feeds vertices into the pipe and the code that colors the vertices that come out of it, that is, steps 1 and 6. This means that you can make a system that lets users select which and how many things to interpolate, without needing to change steps 2 through 5.

# Anything Else?

The new way to do interpolation is pretty simple. Within the polygon tiler we have just one more extra value, $\tilde{1}$, to interpolate. But then we must divide this into all our auxiliary variables on a per-pixel basis. Can we get rid of the nasty old division?

If the $\tilde{1}$ values on each endpoint are equal, you could divide it out before interpolating. This will happen if the $Z$ depths are equal at the left and right edges of each scan line. This places certain restrictions on the polygons and their 3D orientation, but in these situations it can obviously speed things up considerably. The rendering engine for the popular Doom game works this way; in fact, it scans out polygons vertically when they are oriented so that vertical scan columns have equal $Z$ depth on top and bottom.

In the more general case, we could approximate the hyperbolic curve we want by some sort of higher-order polynomial approximation. That's the approach taken in Wolberg's book.[1]

The technique I described in this chapter was also independently discovered by Heckbert and Moreton.[2]

---

1   George Wolberg, *Digital Image Warping* (Los Alamitos, Calif.: IEEE Computer Society Press, 1990).

2   Paul S. Heckbert and Henry P. Moreton, Interpolation for polygon texture mapping and shading, in *State of the Art in Computer Graphics*, David Rogers and Rae Earnshaw, editors (New York: Springer-Verlag, 1991).

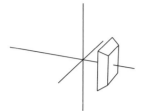

# CHAPTER EIGHTEEN

# The Homogeneous Perspective Transform

M A Y    1 9 9 3

ost of the transformations used in computer graphics are pretty boring: rotations, scales, translations, and even shears. But for pure weirdness you can't top the perspective transformation. Most people don't have an intuitive feel for what this transform does to a shape, so in this chapter, I will try to provide one. This intuition will have practical application in selecting near and far clipping planes to avoid depth resolution problems with many types of rendering algorithms. To understand perspective, we will first have to review some interesting topological properties of the space represented by homogeneous coordinates.

## Homogeneous Coordinate Representation

irst, let's review how homogeneous coordinates work. We represent a 3D point in what I'll call real space, $[X, Y, Z]$, as a four-element vector $[x, y, z, w]$ in homogeneous space. To help distinguish real space from homogeneous space, I'll write real space coordinates in uppercase and homogeneous space coordinates in lowercase. The relation between them is

$$[X, Y, Z] = \left[\frac{x}{w}, \frac{y}{w}, \frac{z}{w}\right]$$

(Notice that many different homogeneous space vectors can represent the same real space point.) Even though we might have points represented as a four vector during some of the processing, we ultimately will need to convert back to real space by dividing out the $w$ component.

Transformations consist of multiplying a point by a 4 × 4 matrix. By manipulating various elements in the matrix, we can rotate, scale, shear, translate, and, our favorite, perform a perspective projection.

# Moebius Space

One of the interesting features of homogeneous coordinates is that they provide a computationally tractable way to represent points that are infinitely far away. For example, consider the point $[1, 0, 0, w]$. This represents the real space point $[1/w, 0, 0]$. If we make the value of $w$ smaller and smaller, the point's $X$ coordinate gets bigger. Ultimately, if $w$ reaches 0, we have a point with an infinitely large $X$ coordinate. The homogeneous formulation, however, is simply $[1, 0, 0, 0]$; these values are perfectly ordinary and easy to deal with inside a computer. All points with $w = 0$ are at infinity and form what is called the *plane at infinity*. Of course we can't convert these vectors back to real space points since we can't divide the coordinates by $w$, but we can still perform geometrical calculations with them if we leave them in the form $[x, y, z, 0]$.

Now let's look at what happens if $w$ becomes negative, say −0.1. The real space analog of $[1, 0, 0, w]$ becomes $[−1, 0, 0, 0]$. In other words the point "wraps around infinity" and comes back in from the negative direction. In this scheme, therefore, it make sense to say that the point at infinity in the positive direction, $[1, 0, 0, 0]$, is the same as the point at infinity in the negative direction, $[−1, 0, 0, 0]$. Points at the top of the universe wrap around to the bottom; points at the right wrap around to the left.

At first this overflow property might tempt you to say that the space formed by homogeneous coordinates is a toroidal universe, like the universe formed by overflow of integer coordinates. But the homogeneous universe is different. Consider Figure 18.1, where I labeled several infinite points in the $XY$ plane along with their negative counterparts. When you tie point A with A′, B with B′, C with C′, etc., you get a twist in the fabric of space when it connects around infinity. The shape formed when you do this with the 2D plane of Figure 18.1 is called a *projective plane*. This, together with the *torus* and the *Klein bottle*, is one of the three topological ways to tie 2D space together. Several pictures illustrating these shapes appear in Steven Barr's

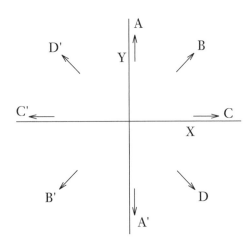

**Figure 18.1** *Points at infinity*

really fun book, *Experiments in Topology*,[1] and in Rich Riesenfeld's article, "Homogeneous Coordinates and Projective Planes in Computer Graphics."[2]

It's important to keep this Moebius twist in mind when we are trying to understand the homogeneous perspective transform since that transform does, indeed, move points through infinity. To best understand how the Moebius twist affects homogeneous shapes in real space, look at Figure 18.2. You should see four triangles. See them? Well, the one in the center is obvious. The other three straddle the plane at infinity, and I've colored them in three different shades of gray. This diagram also illustrates that there are two possible line segments connecting any two points. Look at points A and B. One line segment starts at A and moves to the right to point B and is called an *internal* segment. The other segment starts at B, moves to the right, wraps around infinity, comes in from the left, and terminates at A. This is called an *external* segment. In the homogeneous universe both these segments are equally valid. Finally, note how the Moebius twist along the external segment keeps the proper triangle colors connected.

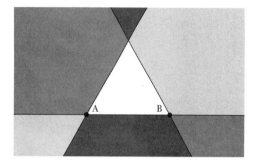

**Figure 18.2** *Four triangles; three of them straddle the plane >*

# Coordinate Systems

There are four coordinate spaces that I'm going to discuss here. Let me give explicit names to each space and to a canonical point in that space.

3D—Real space before the perspective transform, $[X, Y, Z]$.

3DH— Homogeneous space before perspective. We usually form this by appending a $w = 1$ coordinate to the end of each real space vector, so a point is $[X, Y, Z, 1]$. Thus, objects in this space typically lie in the $w = 1$ hyperplane of 4D space.

3DHP—Homogeneous space after perspective. Here objects no longer lie in the $w = 1$ hyperplane and, thus, have the general coordinates $[x_s, y_s, z_s, w_s]$.

3DP—Real space after perspective. This is just the above space with the $w_s$ coordinate divided out. I'll call this *postperspective space*. A point has the coordinates $[X_s, Y_s, Z_s]$.

1   New York: Thomas Y. Crowell, 1964.
2   *IEEE Computer Graphics and Applications* 1(1):50–55, January 1981.

Whenever I draw a diagram in this chapter I will label it with these coordinate system names. The most interesting such diagrams directly compare the shape of an object in 3D space to its distortion into 3DP space. The main purpose of this chapter is to provide an intuitive feel for what that distortion is.

# Simple Perspective

It turns out that the version of the perspective transform that's easiest to understand is not the version typically used in applications. Nevertheless, to help us understand the transform, I'll start with this simple version, and I'll relate it to the more useful form later.

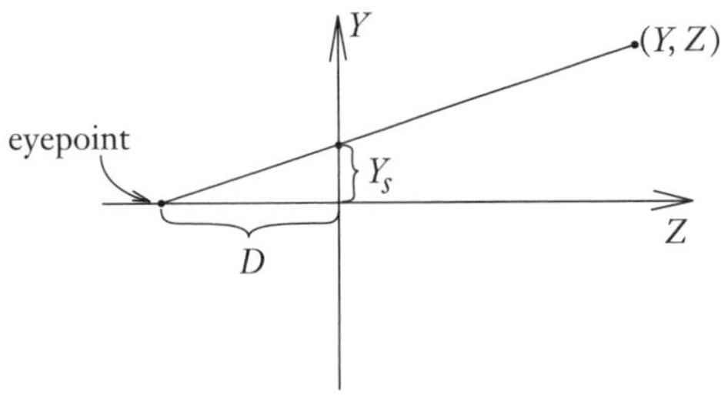

Let's derive the simple perspective transform from the geometry in Figure 18.3, where the eye is a distance $D$ in front of the origin. For an arbitrary point $[X, Y, Z]$ in space, we want to find its perspective projection onto the $XY$ plane, which we will call $[X_s, Y_s]$. Using similar triangles we get

**Figure 18.3** *Perspective geometry*

$$\frac{X_s}{D} = \frac{X}{Z + D}, \quad \frac{Y_s}{D} = \frac{Y}{Z + D}$$

so

$$X_s = \frac{X}{\left(\frac{Z}{D} + 1\right)}, \quad Y_s = \frac{Y}{\left(\frac{Z}{D} + 1\right)}$$

This by itself is not a linear transform. We can, however, piggyback the division onto the homogeneous division by defining

$$X_s = \frac{X}{\left(\frac{Z}{D} + 1\right)} = \frac{x_s}{w_s}$$

$$Y_s = \frac{Y}{\left(\frac{Z}{D} + 1\right)} = \frac{y_s}{w_s}$$

We can define $Z_s$ symmetrically as

$$Z_s = \frac{Z}{\left(\frac{Z}{D} + 1\right)} = \frac{z_s}{w_s}$$

so

$$[x_s, y_s, z_s, w_s] = \left[X, Y, Z, \frac{Z}{D} + 1\right]$$

Now we can express this as a homogeneous matrix multiplication

$$[x_s, y_s, z_s, w_s] = [X, Y, Z, 1] \begin{bmatrix} 1 & 0 & 0 & 0 \\ 0 & 1 & 0 & 0 \\ 0 & 0 & 1 & \frac{1}{D} \\ 0 & 0 & 0 & 1 \end{bmatrix} = [X, Y, Z, 1]\mathbf{P}$$

In the homogeneous notation scheme, any column vector represents a plane. In particular, each column of a transformation matrix represents a plane. The right column of the matrix, $(0, 0, \frac{1}{D}, 1)^t$, represents the plane $Z = -D$. This is the plane containing all the points that the matrix will map to $w = 0$. That is, $Z = -D$ is the plane that gets transformed to the plane at infinity. In general you will combine a perspective matrix with other viewing and modeling transformations, making the right-hand column have four arbitrary values. But whatever its contents, the right-hand column, interpreted as a plane, will be the plane containing the eyepoint and perpendicular to the line of sight.

# What Does It All Mean?

We've designed the matrix to generate the correct values for $X_s$ and $Y_s$. But it's the $Z_s$ values it generates that are interesting. Let's play around with this to see what happens to 3D shapes subjected to this transform.

### Cherchez la Point

Let's start out just looking at what happens to the $Z$ coordinate. It transforms according to the equation

$$Z_s = \frac{Z}{\frac{Z}{D} + 1}$$

A plot of this function appears in Figure 18.4. Note that when $Z$ is infinite, $Z_s = D$. The transformation of certain key points is particularly illuminating; see Table 18.1.

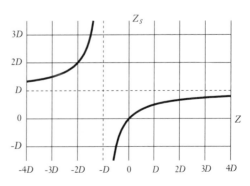

**Figure 18.4** *Postperspective Z versus preperspective Z*

**Table 18.1** *Perspective transformation applied to several interesting points*

| Point transformation | Meaning |
| --- | --- |
| $(X, Y, 0, 1)\,\mathbf{P} = (X, Y, 0, 1)$ | Points in the $z = 0$ plane—the plane of the screen—don't move. |
| $(0, 0, -D, 1)\,\mathbf{P} = (0, 0, -D, 0)$ | The eyepoint moves to infinity. |
| $(0, 0, D, 0)\,\mathbf{P} = (0, 0, D, 1)$ | A point infinitely far forward becomes a local point. |

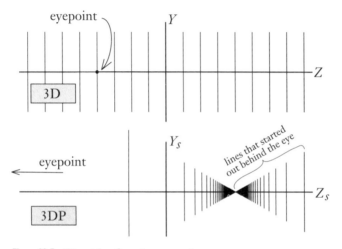

**Figure 18.5** *The picket fence in perspective*

## Picket Fence

Another way to look at this is to see what happens to a bunch of equally spaced parallel lines perpendicular to the line of sight. As shown in Figure 18.5, they transform to parallel lines of different lengths and non-equal spacing.

## Homogeneous Space Interpretation

In homogeneous space, the perspective transform is a simple shear in the $w$ direction. Figure 18.6 shows this process for the $wz$ slice of homogeneous space. Points in 3DH space (with $w = 1$) shear up and down, forming 3DHP space. Then they project back onto $w = 1$ to give 3DP. Note how the eyepoint, the $Z = 0$ point, and the $Z = \infty$ point transform.

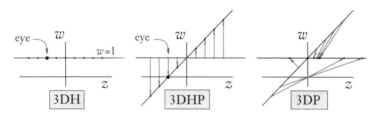

**Figure 18.6** *The homogeneous view of the perspective transform*

Now how about $X$ and $Y$? Look at Figure 18.7. Here I just plotted $x$, $z$, and $w$; the $y$ coordinate operates similarly to $x$. We start with a square seen edge on. Perspective multiplication shears the square in $w$. Dividing out the $w$ distorts the square into a trapezoid.

In Figure 18.8 you see the same thing applied to a cube, turning it into the frustum of a pyramid. Note that this diagram shows the real 3D space transformed to the real 3DP space.

## Region Mapping

The ultimate understanding of this transformation comes from Figure 18.9. Figure 18.9a shows several regions in the $Y$, $Z$ slice of 3D space and 18.9b shows how they get distorted in 3DP space. The $Y$ axis (at $Z = 0$) doesn't move. Region B, stretching from the screen out to infinity, maps to the finite rectangular region B'. The apex of the viewing pyramid (the eyepoint) moves to infinity, so the triangular region A transforms to the infinite triangle A'. Regions H, J, E, and D bend appropriately. The interesting thing is to look at stuff that started out behind the eye: regions C, G, and F. These regions wrap around infinity and come back in front of the old infinite plane. Notice that, reading from the top down, regions G, C, and F map into regions G', C', and F' reading bottom up. This is because of the Moebius property of homogeneous coordinates.

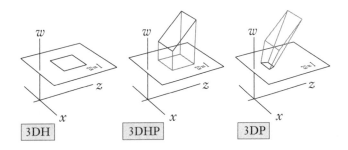

**Figure 18.7** *The homogeneous view of a square's transform*

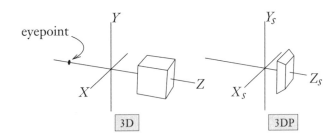

**Figure 18.8** *The perspective transform of a cube*

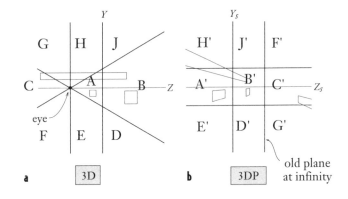

**Figure 18.9** *Which regions map to where*

# A Better Matrix

W hen planning a scene, you generally specify the view in terms of a camera location and viewing direction. You then build up a viewing transformation by translating the camera position to the origin and rotating the viewing direction to point down the $Z$ axis. Then, in order to use the transform we have derived here, you must translate $D$ units backwards in $Z$ to place the eyepoint at $Z = -D$. The following more convenient primitive perspective matrix has this move built in.

$$
\begin{bmatrix}
1 & 0 & 0 & 0 \\
0 & 1 & 0 & 0 \\
0 & 0 & 1 & 0 \\
0 & 0 & -D & 1
\end{bmatrix}
\begin{bmatrix}
1 & 0 & 0 & 0 \\
0 & 1 & 0 & 0 \\
0 & 0 & 1 & \frac{1}{D} \\
0 & 0 & 0 & 1
\end{bmatrix}
=
\begin{bmatrix}
1 & 0 & 0 & 0 \\
0 & 1 & 0 & 0 \\
0 & 0 & 1 & \frac{1}{D} \\
0 & 0 & -D & 0
\end{bmatrix}
$$

The matrix on the right performs eye-at-origin perspective. Note that its rightmost column, $(0, 0, 1/D, 0)^t$, is the plane $z = 0$ that will now transform to the plane at infinity.

It's also convenient to specify the field of view in terms of the angle, *fov*, at the apex of the view pyramid. A screen stretching from +1 to –1 viewed from the distance $D$ has

$$
D = \cot\left(\frac{fov}{2}\right)
$$

The net effect of our new perspective matrix is to map the 3D point $(X, Y, Z)$ to the 3DH point

$$
\left[ D\frac{X}{Z}, D\frac{Y}{Z}, D\frac{Z-D}{Z} \right] = \left[ X_s, Y_s, Z_s \right]
$$

Note that the effect of a change in the field of view on $X_s$ and $Y_s$ is just a simple scaling. In other words, changing the field of view doesn't change the shape of any objects on the screen; it just scales the image uniformly so that more or less of the environment fits within the screen boundaries.

# Depth Information

Many rendering algorithms use the $Z_s$ values that come out of this transformation to do depth comparisons, so it's good to have some idea of the range of values that $Z_s$ can have. Let's see what happens to a few key $Z$ coordinate values under this new transform. $Z$ coordinates that start at infinity map to $Z_s = D$, and $Z$ coordinates that start out at $+D$ map to $Z_s = 0$. Any points that start out closer to the eye than $Z = +D$ map to some negative value of $Z_s$. Depending on how near the eye it is, a point can map to a rather enormous negative $Z_s$ value. The eye itself, of course, maps to minus infinity. Objects very close to the eye may generate a divide error if the quotient of $z_s$ and $w_s$ is too big for a floating-point number. This is a nuisance. How can we avoid it? Typically we use a clipping plane to remove all objects nearer than a certain distance.

But close objects that generate divide errors are not the biggest problem. The biggest problem is distant objects. What happens to the resolution in $Z$ for objects that are far from the eye? Let's look at a numerical example. Suppose the field of view is about 53 degrees, giving a value of $D$ = 2. Suppose that two points on a viewed object are at distances $Z = 500$ and $Z = 501$. The perspective transform moves these to the positions

$$Z_s = 2\frac{500-2}{500} = 1.992$$

and

$$Z_s = 2\frac{501-2}{501} = 1.992016$$

This really starts to push the resolvable limits of single-precision floating-point numbers. And using double precision is the cowardly approach.

We can do everything in single precision if we know the approximate range of $Z$ values (relative to the eye) for objects in our scene. We just scale and translate the postperspective $Z_s$ values to spread more uniformly over the range 0 to 1. The easiest way to specify this scale and translation is in terms of two $Z$ values in preperspective (3D) space. We'll call these $Z_n$ for the near value and $Z_f$ for the far value. We then calculate the scale and transformation that map these values to 0 and 1, respectively, in 3DP space. A scale and translation in $Z$ will only modify the third column of the matrix, so let's solve for the matrix elements that do the desired mapping. A point on the near plane maps to

$$[0,\ 0,\ Z_n,\ 1]\begin{bmatrix} 1 & 0 & 0 & 0 \\ 0 & 1 & 0 & 0 \\ 0 & 0 & A & 1/D \\ 0 & 0 & B & 0 \end{bmatrix} = \left[0,\ 0,\ AZ_n+B,\ \frac{Z_n}{D}\right]$$

We want this to map to $Z_s = 0$, so we must have

$$B = -AZ_n$$

Next, a point on the far plane maps to

$$[0,\ 0,\ Z_f,\ 1]\begin{bmatrix} 1 & 0 & 0 & 0 \\ 0 & 1 & 0 & 0 \\ 0 & 0 & A & 1/D \\ 0 & 0 & -AZ_n & 0 \end{bmatrix} = \left[0,\ 0,\ A(Z_f-Z_n),\ \frac{Z_f}{D}\right]$$

We want this to map to $Z_s = 1$, so its $z$ and $w$ components must be equal. This gives us

$$A = \frac{Z_f}{D(Z_f - Z_n)}$$

The resultant matrix maps $Z_n$ to 0, $Z_f$ to 1, and $Z = \infty$ to $\frac{Z_f}{(Z_f - Z_n)}$.

I showed this same matrix in Chapter 3 but wrote it a bit differently. To get to the form used in that chapter, just multiply the above matrix by the constant factor $D \sin(\frac{fov}{2}) = \cos(\frac{fov}{2})$, giving

$$\begin{bmatrix} c & 0 & 0 & 0 \\ 0 & c & 0 & 0 \\ 0 & 0 & Q & s \\ 0 & 0 & -QZ_n & 0 \end{bmatrix}$$

where

$$s = \sin\left(\frac{fov}{2}\right)$$
$$c = \cos\left(\frac{fov}{2}\right)$$
$$Q = \frac{s}{1 - \frac{Z_n}{Z_f}}$$

There are two practical reasons for this way of specifying the matrix. First, if the user specifies a field of view of 0 degrees, the program will not blow up by attempting to calculate an infinite cotangent. (Admittedly the matrix will be a bit weird though.) Second, if the user wants to use an infinite value for $Z_f$ (a perfectly reasonable thing to do), the expression for $Q$ above reduces nicely to $Q = s$.

Now that we have the handles $Z_n$ and $Z_f$ to play with, let's see how it solves our resolution problem. If we use the fairly loose bounds around our object of $Z_n = 400$ and $Z_f = 600$, the perspective matrix gives us

$$Z_s \frac{3Z - 1200}{Z}$$

You can check that $Z = 400$ maps to $Z_s = 0$ and $Z = 600$ maps to $Z_s = 1$. The $Z$ values of 500 and 501 map respectively into $Z_s$ values of .6 and .6048, which are much more readily distinguishable.

The locations of $Z_n$ and $Z_f$ are usually associated with near and far clipping planes. The problem is that users typically don't want anything clipped off in the near and far directions, so they make $Z_n$ very small and $Z_f$ very large. Making $Z_f$ large, or even infinite, doesn't really cause problems, but making $Z_n$ small does. It basically defeats the purpose of our new formulation, cramming the objects in the scene into a depth range very close to $Z_s = 1$. The depth resolution available to the rendering algorithm is then completely lost. I have seen a lot of people have problems with this. My advice is to place $Z_n$ as far away as you can get away with. In fact, for some projects I have had to animate the value of $Z_n$ to track an object as it flies around on the screen.

# Clipping Implications

In Chapter 13 I wrote about a line clipping algorithm that operated with the perspective transformation we derived here. Now that we have a better understanding of homogeneous perspective, I want to clear up a few statements made in that chapter.

First: near and far clipping are optional. We must still, however, specify a value for $Z_n$ and $Z_f$. After all, *some* value of $Z$ is going to map to $Z_s = 0$ and *some* other value of $Z$ is going to map to $Z_s = 1$. We can't do anything about that. But it's not necessary to *clip* to these planes. You do, however, need to be prepared to detect and avoid overflow for objects that come close to the eye and produce large negative values of $Z_s$, but this is actually rather rare. You might as well do the clipping though. The overhead of clipping at $Z_n$ and $Z_f$ as described in Chapter 13 is pretty negligible.

Second, it is possible to clip properly *after* doing the $w$ division, i.e., in 3DP space rather than in 3DHP space. I don't recommend it, but it's *possible*. The reason it is usually thought *im*possible is as follows. Consider a line that has one endpoint in front of the eye and one endpoint behind the eye, running off the top of the screen, as in one of the long edges of the wide rectangle in Figure 18.9. After the perspective multiplication, the endpoint behind the eye will have a negative value for $w_s$. If you clip in 3DHP space, the endpoint will have $y_s > w_s$ and the line will be clipped properly. When you look at the line you will see it disappear off the top of the screen. Now suppose you did the homogeneous division before clipping. The point behind the eye will have wrapped around infinity and may reappear with $Y$ coordinates on the visible portion of the screen, generating an external line segment. This situation has traditionally been thought to be indistinguishable from an internal segment with both endpoints visible in front of the eye. There is a difference, however. The behind-the-eye point has wrapped around infinity and has a $Z$ coordinate greater than $Z_f / (Z_f - Z_n)$. To determine if a line segment that has two visible endpoints is internal (requiring no clipping) or external (requiring clipping), just test if the $Z$ coordinates of its two endpoints straddle $Z_f / (Z_f - Z_n)$. This is more trouble than it's worth perhaps, but it's possible.

# Key Points to Remember

The perspective transform turns space inside out. Flat polygons might have their outlines distorted, but they remain flat. You can therefore use rendering algorithms in 3DP space that linearly interpolate $Z$ values across polygons. The plane $Z = 0$ (the eye plane) becomes the plane at infinity; the plane at infinity becomes $Z_s = Z_f/(Z_f - Z_n)$. Shapes that start out straddling the eye plane split in two.

From a user's point of view the important message here is to make the value of $Z_n$ as big as possible. This makes it easier for the renderer you are using to do depth comparisons.

# CHAPTER NINETEEN

# Backface Culling Snags

N O V E M B E R     1 9 9 3

I've always liked Platonic solids and I'm especially interested in the geometric relationships between them.
Figure 19.1, a reproduction from Chapter 4, shows, for
example, that a dodecahedron has a cube buried in it. I
want to start out this chapter by using this fact to get an
interesting way of transforming a cube into a dodecahedron. In what follows I'll use the transformation notation
that I developed in Chapter 3.

The cube-to-dodecahedron transformation consists
of erecting a "tent" on the surface of each face of the
cube. The tent appears in Figure 19.2 and has a database
as follows:

```
PNT 1, -1,  1, 0
PNT 2,  1,  1, 0
PNT 3,  1, -1, 0
PNT 4, -1, -1, 0
PNT 5,  0,  .618034, .618034
PNT 6,  0, -.618034, .618034
POLY 1, 2, 5
POLY 2, 3, 6, 5
POLY 3, 4, 6
POLY 4, 1, 5, 6
```

The value .618034 is an approximation to the inverse
of the golden ratio: $\frac{1}{\varphi} = \left(-1 + \sqrt{5}\right)/2$. If the tent has the
dimensions shown, a triangular face of the tent on one

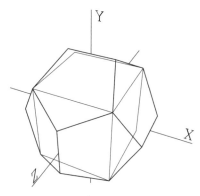

**Figure 19.1** *A cube hidden inside a
dodecahedron*

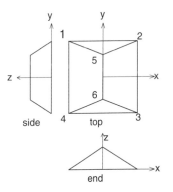

**Figure 19.2** *The tent*

**Figure 19.3** *Cube turning into a dodecahedron*

cube face is coplanar with a trapezoidal face of the tent on an adjacent cube face, and the two together form a pentagon. There are two such pentagons for each of the six cube faces; voila, 12 dodecahedron faces.

I've used this construction to do an animation showing a gradual transformation from the cube to the dodecahedron. I started out by scaling the tent flat in $z$ to form a square. I then translated it out one unit in $z$ to make one face of the cube. Replicating this six times covers each cube face. The database is as follows:

```
DEF CUBEFACE
DRAW TENT, TRAN, 0, 0, 1, SCAL, 1, 1, HEIGHT
----
DEF CUBEDODE
DRAW CUBEFACE,
DRAW CUBEFACE, ROT ,180, 2,
DRAW CUBEFACE, ROT , 90, 2, ROT ,90, 3,
DRAW CUBEFACE, ROT ,-90, 2, ROT ,90, 3,
DRAW CUBEFACE, ROT , 90, 1, ROT ,90, 3,
DRAW CUBEFACE, ROT ,-90, 1, ROT ,90, 3,
----
```

The animation then makes the scale factor HEIGHT grow from 0 to 1 to "inflate" the six tents simultaneously. Some frames from the sequence appear in Figure 19.3.

# Back Culling

At this point, the observant reader will wonder what this has to do with backface culling. Well, this animation uncovers a potential problem in one common implementation of backface culling. This chapter, then, is another in my series on graphics subtleties.

Backface culling, for the uninitiated, is a simple trick used in some polygon-based rendering algorithms to reduce the number of polygons that must be considered. Glossing over some details, the mechanism tests each face to see if it "points toward" the viewer. If it doesn't, you can immediately discard it. If it does point toward the viewer, you add it to the list of polygons to render (by whatever algorithm suits you). This quick culling test can approximately halve the number of polygons that your rendering program needs to deal with.

Let me now discuss some of the details of how I've implemented this in my rendering system.

## Applicability

Backface culling only works in certain cases. The requirements are as follows:

1. The object must be opaque.
2. The object must be completely covered by a "skin" of polygons; there can be no holes to let you see the inside surface.
3. The object must be described consistently in the database with all polygon vertices listed in, for example, clockwise order as seen from the outside of the object.

Now some parts of a database might satisfy these requirements and other parts might not. For this reason I have a command to enable or disable back culling. Specifically this command is BACK CULL (turn on culling) and BACK KEEP (turn off culling).

## Face Testing

How do we turn the phrase "points toward the viewer" into a numerical test? We basically want to calculate a number that is positive, say, for polygons we want to keep and negative for those we want to throw away. There are two ways to do this.

The first way operates in what I call *eye space*. Here the eye is at the origin, looking down the $z$ axis; no perspective has been performed yet. This is the coordinate space where you do lighting calculations and where you already have a normal vector calculated for each face. The test value for a face measures the angle between the normal and a vector to the eye. If the cosine of this angle is positive, the angle is less than 90 degrees and the polygon faces the eye; if the cosine is negative, the angle is greater than 90 degrees and the polygon faces away. You get the cosine by simply taking the dot product between the normal and a vector from any vertex of the polygon to the eye.

The second way operates in *screen space*. This is the space you're in after you do the perspective projection. Here you calculate the area of the polygon on the screen (using only the $x$ and $y$ coordinates). The formula is

$$A = \frac{1}{2} \sum_i (x_{i+1} - x_i)(y_{i+1} + y_i)$$

where the index $i$ is taken modulo the number of vertices in the polygon. (That's a fancy way of saying that the last vertex number wraps back around to the first.) This formula will give a positive number if the points are clockwise and a negative number if the points are counterclockwise. Since you're only interested in the sign, you can skip the factor of $\frac{1}{2}$.

Note that both of these methods are geometrically the same; the difference is the coordinate system they use. Just like the first method, the second method calculates a normal vector and dots it with the vector to the eyepoint. In the latter case the perspective transform has moved the eyepoint to infinity in $z$, so the vector is simply (0, 0, 1). The formula given above is just a calculation of the $z$ component of the normal vector to the polygon in screen space.

### An Old Problem

The next subtlety is one that crops up all the time in computer graphics: the fact that every coin has two sides. The sign test is affected by several binary choices in our modeling and rendering system:

1. Are we using a *right-handed* or *left-handed* coordinate system?
2. Are the polygons in the database defined *clockwise* or *counterclockwise*?
3. Are we keeping polygons whose calculated test value is *plus* or *minus*?

Each choice inverts the sense of whether a polygon is considered front-facing or back-facing. As I've stated before, you can sit and figure out the theoretical answer to all these questions, and you still only have a 50% chance of not making a mistake and keeping all back-facing polygons and throwing away the front-facing ones. I have always used the empirical approach: make a picture, and if the polygons come out wrong, flip the sign of one of the above. The easiest one to flip is item 3.

In fact, since we live in an imperfect world, I've found it convenient to provide for easy debugging of objects, both in terms of global handedness and in terms of consistent clockwiseness of polygons. I've defined the command BACK TEST to throw my renderer into test mode. It then artificially colors all polygons white if they are front-facing and orange if they are back-facing. A few test images in this mode can help find incorrectly ordered polygons.

# Another Problem

But suppose you finally get it right. There's still a situation that can cause problems. If you are modeling a symmetric object like, say, a car body, it is typical to generate a database for only one half and to include it in the whole car with a negative scale factor for one side. This looks like

```
DEF CAR
DRAW CARHALF
DRAW CARHALF, SCAL, -1, 1, 1
----
```

So what's the problem? Well, mirror imaging turns clockwise polygons into counterclockwise polyons. The second half of the car body would have kept the wrong polygons. This leads to a fourth inverting condition:

4.  Is there a negative scale factor in the transformation matrix?

When there is a negative scale factor in effect, you need some way to dynamically flip the sense of item 3 to compensate for it. Now you might think you could do this automatically by just examining the sign of the determinant of the transformation matrix. This, however, doesn't work, and that is the entire crux of this chapter.

Witness our cube-to-dodecahedron animation. When we draw the frames representing the cube, the tents on the cube faces are squashed flat. They have a 0 scale factor, so the transformation matrix has a determinant of 0. Front/backness of polygons is still a well-defined concept though. The test value still produces a non-zero result. We just wouldn't know which sign to keep if we looked only to the determinant of the transformation matrix for guidance.

It gets worse. We could even scale the tent by a negative amount and still expect to get a reasonable picture. The cube faces are simply dished in a bit; see Figure 19.4. Here the matrix has a negative determinant, but the polygon faces actually haven't changed their clockwiseitude. To summarize: sometimes—in perfectly reasonable situations—the transformation matrix is singular or has a negative determinant and we *don't* want to invert the sense of item 3.

**Figure 19.4** *Cube dished in*

"clockwiseitude" HA!

# The Big Fix

There is nothing for it but to force the database designer to include explicit commands to tell when item 3 needs to change. But you don't want the command to simply *set* the sign test to positive or negative. The best way is to have the command *invert* the current setting. You use it as follows:

```
DEF CAR
BACK CULL
DRAW CARHALF
BACK FLIP
DRAW CARHALF, SCAL, -1, 1, 1
BACK FLIP
----
```

The second BACK FLIP command restores the sense of the sign test for subsequent database items. This mechanism has the property that it nests correctly. If you include the car in a symmetric scene that is itself drawn reflected, you would do something like

```
DEF SCENE
BACK CULL
DRAW SCENEHALF
BACK FLIP
DRAW SCENEHALF, SCAL, -1, 1, 1
BACK FLIP
----

DEF SCENEHALF
DRAW CAR, TRAN, 10, 0, 0
----
```

The first time CAR is drawn, the sign test switch is positive. The two car halves are tested with the switch positive and negative, respectively. The second time SCENE calls the CAR routine, it has done a mirror and has flipped the sign test switch negative. The two car halves are tested with the switch negative and positive, respectively.

On the other hand, when drawing the cube-to-dodecahedron animation, you would not put any BACK FLIP commands into the CUBEFACE object. Even though the transformation would have a negative scale factor when the parameter HEIGHT is negative, the polygons will have the same sign test for backfacedness.

# Other Benefits

forcing (or allowing) the user to explicitly flip the sense of item 3 has another benefit. Even though you might carefully design all your objects in the same consistent clockwise vertex order, sooner or later you are going to need to import a database from some bozo who has a world view that's different from yours. (Like maybe they're from a country where they drive on the wrong side of the road.) If a foreign object is consistently backwards in polygon vertex ordering, you can still use it by bracketing it with another pair of BACK FLIP commands.

Finally, I have encountered situations where I *wanted* to keep the backfaces and throw away the front ones. For example, Figure 19.5 (color plates) is from a *Mechanical Universe* episode about angular momentum. It consists of a transparent polygonal spinning top with letters and arrows inside it. Since I wanted to draw the lines and text with a separate program, I used a hybrid rendering approach. First the line drawing program draws the background grid and shadows. Then the polygon renderer draws the back half of the transparent top with back culling deliberately set to keep just the backfaces (Figure 19.5a). Then the line drawing program draws the letters inside the top (Figure 19.5b). Then the polygon program draws the transparent frontfaces with back culling set normally. Finally the line program draws the top layer of arrows and equations (Figure 19.5c). This might at first seem like a very specialized trick, but I have actually used elaborations of it in many cases where I needed to mix the visual styles of several different rendering programs. After all, remember that a *technique* is just a *trick* that you use more than once.

# CHAPTER TWENTY

# Farewell to FORTRAN

MARCH 1994

I recently bought an excellent numerical analysis book called *Numerical Recipes*,[1] largely to read its section on wavelet transforms (which, by the way, is only in the second edition). The book comes in three versions, with example programs in FORTRAN (blue cover), C (red cover), and Pascal (yellow cover). The significance of my purchase comes from the fact that I bought the one with the red cover. Yes, folks, I'm giving up on FORTRAN and moving over, not to C, but to C++.

Now I've found an interesting phenomenon concerning the acceptance of computers and word processors among some of my favorite authors, like Isaac Asimov and Piers Anthony. At first they write about how they don't trust computers and won't use them. Then, when they finally get hooked, they feel compelled to write some rhapsody about how wonderful they are. Well, I'm going to do that here in this chapter. I've programmed in FORTRAN almost all my life but, now that I'm converting to C++, here is my rhapsody.

## Why FORTRAN?

Many of you young'uns out there may wonder why anybody would want to use FORTRAN in the first place. (Not that I have to apologize, of course.) Well, I got into using it for the simple reason that it was the only

---

1 William Press et a.l, *Numerical Recipes in FORTRAN: The Art of Scientific Computing*, 2nd ed. (New York: Cambridge University Press, 1992).

high-level language available on the machines I had at the time. After many years and several hundred thousand lines of code, it takes a great deal of effort to change. Why? Consider the following. What do you do when someone asks you how to spell something? You typically write it down and see if it "looks right." After reading English for many years, you can easily detect misspellings visually. Well, after using a particular programming language long enough, you develop the skill of just looking at code and seeing bugs. This long-established skill is something that you don't give up lightly.

Also, using FORTRAN made me think of myself as something of an antiquarian. Even the convention of spelling its name all in capital letters harkens back to the days when computers didn't even *have* lowercase letters. I felt like one of those music hobbyists that continue to build and play Renaissance instruments like the crumhorn. I was sure that when I retired there would be a place for me in the Computer Museum as the Last Remaining FORTRAN Programmer.

# Why Not C?

My only serious foray into the wilds of the C language was in the summer of 1976, when I was at the New York Institute of Technology. The very first C program I wrote broke the compiler! A fairly simple program generated incorrect object code. I was amazed! I had never heard of such a thing. I never trusted C compilers after that. Admittedly that was a very early version of the C compiler. It even used the now obsolete syntax of =+ instead of += for in-place addition.

Furthermore, C allows, nay encourages, perverted constructs like

```
if (c == getchar()) {...}
```

This nested behavior looks suspiciously like APL.

But the real reason I never switched from FORTRAN to C is that C isn't really enough better than FORTRAN to make the change worth it. A lot of people don't realize that most of the nice "structured programming" constructs in C like `if...then...else` and `struct` variables are also currently present in FORTRAN77 (and I'm not even talking about FORTRAN88 or FORTRAN99 or whatever it winds up being when it finally comes out). It's like the situation with disk drives: as new memory technologies threaten to replace them, they continue to make slow incremental advances and still beat out any other competing technology.

HA! { Aside from minor syntactic sugar, the original C language only has two advantages over FORTRAN: it has pointers and it has recursion. It also has two disadvantages over FORTRAN: it has pointers and it has recursion.

## Pointers

Pointers encourage you to *always* declare things dynamically. This is not always good. Here's an example. In my computer graphics course, I have always let students use whatever language they like, and they usually use C. Now, as one of the assignments I have them use a profiler on their rendering code. Some students reported that their program spent more than 60% of the time in `malloc`, the memory allocation routine. This is one of the seven deadly warning signs that something is wrong.

Contrary to popular belief, you can manipulate pointer-based data structures in standard FORTRAN. You use a static array for the data blocks and use indices into the array as pointers (perhaps better called handles). For example, a linked list of points would look like

```
c Define POINT type
STRUCTURE/POINT/
        INTEGER NEXT   !Index of next point
        REAL X,Y       !Coordinates of point
        END STRUCTURE
c
c Declare 100 points
        RECORD/POINT/ DATA(100)
c
c Initialize chain of free points
        IFREE = 100   !Index of first free point
c Chain points on free chain
        DO I = 1, 100
            DATA(I).NEXT = I - 1
            ENDDO
c
c Initialize empty list LIST
        LIST = 0
c
c Allocate a free block into IP
        IF(IFREE.EQ.0) GOTO ... !Out of space
        IP = IFREE
        IFREE = DATA(IP).NEXT
c
c   Set coordinates
        DATA(IP).X = something
        DATA(IP).Y = something
c
c   Link free block onto LIST list
```

```
          DATA(IP).NEXT = LIST
          LIST = IP
```

The disadvantage, of course, is that you must build in a maximum number of blocks (here it's 100) at compile time. The advantage is it's fast, pointers (handles) are verifiable (they all must be from 1 to 100), and it's fast.

In C++ you can also do pretty much the same as the above. But you are encouraged to do something like

```
// Define point type
   struct point{
       point* next;
       float x, y;
       };


// Initialize empty list
       point* list = 0;

// Allocate a free block
       point* ip = new point;

// Set coordinates
       ip -> x = something;
       ip -> y = something;
// Link free block into list
       ip -> next = list;
       list = ip;
```

You are at the mercy of the system memory allocator. Also now ip is an address, and it can be the address of anywhere in allocatable memory. You can't do a consistency check on it like you could with IP.

*Lots of room for unsafe programming.*

## Recursion

I've always been suspicious of recursion. It seems like the ultimate procrastinator's way of writing code; if you don't feel like working, just subtract one and recurse. The typical textbook example of recursion, calculating factorials, is in fact a really bad example. Nobody in their right mind would actually do it that way. Some things *can* benefit from recursion though, like expression parsing or (perhaps) polygon clipping or (perhaps) ray tracing. The criterion seems to be, if you need a function to call itself from *two or more* different places within itself, it's worth making the function recursive.

The thing that bothers me is that you have less control of recursion depth if you are recursing than if you are explicitly maintaining a stack. If your program recurses too far, the system takes over with a stack overflow instead of your program being able to detect the problem itself and back out gracefully.

# Why C++

C++, on the other hand, *is* sufficiently improved over FORTRAN to make the change worthwhile. In fact I sort of think of myself as a third-world country, leapfrogging technology over wood-burning steam engines and going directly from oxcarts to electric cars.

## Seatbelt and Suspenders

In the book *1984*, George Orwell described the government invention of a language called Newspeak. The idea with this new language was to make it impossible to form any sentences that disagreed with the party line of the state. This is a good analogy to the efforts of computer language designers; the idea is to make it syntactically impossible to compile statements that have bugs. This goal cannot be reached exactly, but C++ gets a lot closer than FORTRAN.

For example, in FORTRAN you can compile a call to a routine with the wrong number or wrong type of parameters. When you try to execute this, your program sinks like a rock. C++ forces you to declare all functions explicitly and encourages you to use the same declaration file (a header file) for both the declaraton and the usage of the function. This makes it almost impossible to call a routine with the wrong number of parameters.

Programs often contain a lot of hidden assumptions about their structure and data. C++ enables you to make many of these assumptions explicit. For example, consider a routine that is just supposed to examine an object but not change it. If you declare this routine `const`, the compiler will flag as errors any statements that store into the object. You can also define objects as `const`, and the compiler will only let you call `const` functions on them. These declarations both help the compiler find errors and serve as useful documentation to a human reader about the intent of a function. C++ officializes a lot of the tricks that you must resort to in dumber languages (I especially like the bit field extraction operators). This makes it possible for the compiler to do many consistency checks, and C++ does so with a vengeance.

This is not always good. Imagine a piano that had a lockout that prevented you from pressing two keys simultaneously if they would create a dissonance. You could just mash around on the keys and anything you did would sound OK. For most early music this might be appropriate, but it

What's a declaration?
Declaration with the
i missing or that
which is declared?
Constant?

would have prevented the invention of some modern music, stuff that the inventors of the piano wouldn't have foreseen, or liked.

## Build Your Own Universe

But the most fun part of C++ is overloading operators. I've been happily creating vector classes and matrix classes and defining addition and (scalar and vector) multiplication operators between them. I've always looked forward to the time when I can write vector algebraic operations simply as

```
Vector3 = Vector1 + alpha*(Vector2 - Vector1);
```

And now I can write matrix multiplication as

```
Vector2 = Vector1 * Matrix1 * Matrix2;
```

Soon I want write a symbolic algebra class that allows you to do arithmetic operations on symbolic expressions. And how about a class that implements interval arithmetic? An object of this class would consist of the upper and lower bound of the interval and the arithmetic operators would calculate the proper resultant intervals. I can't wait. This all shows great promise in simplifying a lot of things, since much of higher mathematics is just the generalization of addition and multiplication to more and more complex objects.

*Oh?*

## Object-Oriented Whatever

I haven't really gotten into C++ virtual functions yet, but I've read enough about object-oriented programming to conclude that a) it is actually a useful concept, and b) it is overhyped (big surprise). Any program that simulates things (which is what almost all programs really do) can benefit from it. In fact, it turns out that I've been simulating virtual functions in FORTRAN for some time now. I just didn't realize it. FORTRAN basically requires that you create an intermediate array of type codes and object pointers. The most obvious example in graphics is a draw routine with several kinds of primitives that you want to draw. It looks like

```
c Define OBJEDT table entry
   STRUCTURE/OBJTBL/
       INTEGER KODE    ! Type code
       INTEGER IHANDL ! Actual handle
                      ! for object of that type
       END STRUCTURE
c
c Declare 100 objects
```

```
    RECORD/OBJTBL/OBJECT(100)
C
    SUBROUTINE DRAW(NAMEOBJ)
       K = OBJECT(NAMEOBJ).KODE
       I = OBJECT(NAMEOBJ).IHANDL
       IF     (K .EQ. 1) CALL DRAW1(I)
       ELSEIF (K .EQ. 2) CALL DRAW2(I)
       ELSEIF (K .EQ. 3) CALL DRAW3(I)
       ENDIF
       END
```

It remains to be seen whether the nontrivial amount of overhead that C++ imposes to automatically do this rigamarole is worth it.

# C++ Has Its Problems

Of course C++ isn't perfect. I've heard object experts bemoan its deficiencies in the subtleties objectness, but I'm not yet sophisticated enough to fully appreciate them. Here are some other odd quirks that I've run across, though.

## Initialization

A big thing in C++ is the attempt to make user-defined types have all the manipulability of the base types like `int` and `float`. There are some cracks in the armor, however. Take the concept of initialization. First the good news. C++ encourages you to declare variables and initialize them in one statement, as

```
int i = 1;
```

This is nice because it means you don't have to declare variables until just before you use them. Instead of having all your declarations at the beginning of the program, you have them spread out and localized to where they are used. I like this because it enhances local understanding of the code. If you are reading it, you don't have to go constantly flipping back and forth between the code and the definition section at the beginning. It also encourages you not to have uninitialized variables hanging about, just waiting to trip you up before you store something in them. But . . . if you want to define and initialize a user-defined type, the syntax looks different. Here's a hypothetical `vector` class.

```
vector v(0.,0.);
```

Instead of using the equal sign, you put the initial values in parentheses after the variable name. This is because you are actually triggering a call to a constructor function, and the parenthesized list is the parameters to that function. The equivalent for an `int` won't work:

```
int i(1);    // syntax error
```

This difference is admittedly not of cosmic importance, but it does point out that C++ is a bit of a patchwork. You can make the two look more the same by doing something like

```
int     i = int(1);
vector v = vector(0.,0.);
```

This explicitly calls the constructor for the vector and just does a type coercion for the integer. In fact, it generates the identical code (on the compiler I use), but it's perhaps a bit of overkill.

## Pointers

When you declare a variable to be a pointer (that is, the address of something) the syntax is

```
int *ptri;
```

*I need to fix this for myself with some preprocessor definitions.*

This seems a bit weird to me. A pointer-to-integer is actually a type in its own right. The above syntax makes it look like the pointer attribute is part of the variable name. Well, it so happens that you can also declare the above in a way I find more sensible:

```
int* ptri;
```

When you use a pointer the syntax is

```
*ptri=5;
```

*Nota bene as Shelton would say.*

So sometimes * means "contents of" and sometimes it means "address of." Now when you pass a pointer to a subroutine, the syntax is

```
func(&i);
```

Wouldn't it have been better for the declaration to use something like

```
&int ptri;
```

to declare `ptri` as the address of an integer? Well, it's too late now. The use of `&` in declarations has been taken over for things called references.

## Exploding Types

Another pitfall I've found in C++ is the explosion of the number of user-defined types (i.e., classes) you tend to generate. You tend to want to make a new type for everything. So far I have defined classes for

- Strings
- 2D vectors and matrices
- 3D vectors and matrices
- 2D homogeneous points, lines, and matrices
- 3D homogeneous points, lines, and matrices
- Rectangular screen regions
- Pixel values (red, green, blue, alpha) in 8 bit, 16 bit, and floating point
- Colors in color spaces RGB, VHS, LUV, CIE, and XYZ
- Headers and footers for several image file formats
- Polygon vertices with 2D integer point coordinates and 16-bit color
- Polygon vertices with 3D point coordinates and normal vector
- Polygon vertices with 3D point coordinates and floating-point color
- Surface properties of a substance
- Lighting environments

and I've only just gotten started.

There is a design philosophy in C++ that you put the intelligence of the program in the definitions (classes), not in the body of program. Then you just have to make a few calls to implement something very powerful. The problem is that a naive reader of the program has to wade through lots of definitions to understand a simple statement.

# The Real Benefit of C++

All in all I would use the word *serviceable* to describe C++. It has quirks, but its advantages outweigh the problems. But when it comes down to it, the syntax and expressive power of a language are not the whole story. Equally important is the development environment that surrounds the language and universality of support. C++ wins here too.

## Fun, Fun, Fun till My Daddy Took the Compiler Away

There are a wide variety of compilers and development environments for C++ available on most every platform you can think of. This is important to me for the following reason. Some of the most interesting programs I've ever written used event-driven programming, drag-and-drop, all the current buzzwords. They were written back in the 60s in PDP-9 assembly language. They'll never run again. Since then I've become very sensitive to writing code in languages and on computers that will disappear. I have every confidence that at any time in the foreseeable future I will be able to run any programs I write in C++.

### I'm Like Everybody Else

I also feel like I'm more in the mainstream of programming now. Most of the programming books I've read recently have their examples in C++. There are even fan magazines for C++. Or maybe it just seems that way since I'm committed to C++ now. After all, there's a basic psychological principle that when you buy X, you suddenly find yourself finding evidence why X is the best thing to have.

### The Real Reason

I'm convinced that the popularity of audio compact discs was enhanced by the fact that it gave us the opportunity to buy all our favorite albums all over again. C++ is allowing me to write all my favorite programs all over again. And what do you optimize for in life but fun?

# Index

## Related Titles from Morgan Kaufmann

*Principles of Digital Image Synthesis*

**Andrew S. Glassner**

A comprehensive presentation of the three core fields of study that constitute digital image synthesis: the human visual system, digital signal processing, and the interaction of matter and light. Assuming no more than a basic background in calculus, Glassner demonstrates how these disciplines are elegantly orchestrated into modern rendering techniques such as radiosity and ray tracing.

1995; 1600 pages; two-volume set; cloth; 1-55860-276-3

*Interactive Curves and Surfaces:*
*A Multimedia Tutorial on CAGD*

**Alyn Rockwood and Peter Chambers**

This interactive software-book tutorial teaches a strong foundation of computer-aided geometric design (CAGD) concepts and discusses the growing number of applications in such areas as geological modeling, molecular modeling, commercial advertising, and animation. Using interactive examples and animations to illustrate the mathematical concepts, this hands-on multimedia tutorial enables users without a mathematical background to quickly gain intuition about CAGD.

1996; 300 pages; book/disk package; 1-55860-405-7

*Wavelets for Computer Graphics:*
*Theory and Applications*

**Eric J. Stollnitz, Tony D. DeRose, and David H. Salesin**

Wavelets are rapidly becoming a core technique in computer graphics, with applications for image editing and compression, automatic level-of-detail control for editing and rendering curves and surfaces, surface reconstruction from contours, and physical simulation for global illumination and animation. This distinctly accessible introduction to wavelets provides computer graphics professionals and researchers with the mathematical foundations necessary for understanding and applying this new and powerful tool.     1996; 250 pages; cloth; 1-55860-375-1

*Radiosity and Global Illumination*

**François X. Sillion and Claude Puech**

An essential book devoted exclusively to the radiosity method and global illumination algorithms. The technical and algorithmic level of the book makes it useful for researchers, students, and graphics programmers with some prior knowledge of computer graphics or simulation techniques.     1994; 251 pages; cloth; 1-55860-277-1

Barnes & Noble
Princeton, NJ
Mon 16 Feb 1998

$40.75 + 2.45 tax